Democracy and Governance Review:

Mandela's Legacy 1994-1999

Democracy and Governance Review:

Mandela's Legacy 1994-1999

Editors

Yvonne G. Muthien

Meshack M. Khosa

Bernard M. Magubane

Human Sciences Research Council

Pretoria

2000

ISBN 0-7969-1970-4

Democracy and Governance Review: Mandela's Legacy 1994-1999
Editors: Yvonne G. Muthien, Meshack M. Khosa, Bernard M. Magubane.

Democracy – South Africa
Governance – South Africa
Political transformation – South Africa

Design and layout: Berta Wheeler, Annemarie Booyens
Cover design: Nico Potgieter

Printed and published in South Africa by Shereno Printers.

Contents

Chapter

List of Tables

List of Figures

Page

List of Contributors

Doreen Atkinson holds a Ph.D. in political science. She has four years' experience as a lecturer in the subject, at Rhodes University and the University of Stellenbosch. After working as a researcher at the Centre for Policy Studies in Johannesburg, she relocated to Philippolis in the Free State, where she works as a development consultant. Dr Atkinson is a member of two research networks, namely McIntosh Xaba and Associates (based in Durban), and Khanya — Managing Rural Change (based in Bloemfontein). Her areas of interest are local government, rural development, governmental institutional systems, intergovernmental relations, and civil society. She is co-editor of two books: *The Small Miracle: South Africa's Constitutional Negotiations*, and *From a Tier to a Sphere: Local Government in the New South African Constitutional Order*.

Gregory Houston is a research specialist at the Human Sciences Research Council (HSRC). He has a Ph.D. in political science and is the author of the book, *The National Liberation Struggle: A Case Study of the United Democratic Front, 1983-1987*. He is currently working on a book on public participation in the National Economic Development and Labour Council, the legislative processes of provincial legislatures, the budgetary formulation process of the national Department of Finance, and the Integrated Development Planning process of the Pretoria City Council. Dr Houston previously lectured in the Political Studies Department of the University of Transkei. His research interests include theoretical and empirical studies of the South African state, the process of democratic consolidation in South Africa, issues of identity and race, and public participation in political processes. He has written several book chapters, journal articles and research reports on these topics.

Meshack Khosa who holds an MA from Wits and a D.Phil from Oxford University in England, is a leading social scientist, research expert and strategist with international experience. Skilled in theoretical, social science and policy research, he has published in national and international scholarly and popular journals. Dr Khosa has written over forty articles on transport, the taxi industry, regional planning, industrial forestry, infrastructure, social transformation, transformation of the higher education sector, and land reform in South Africa. He has also been co-editor of *An RDP Policy Audit, Regionalism in the New South Africa* and *Democracy and Governance Review,* and editor of *Infrastructure Mandate for Change 1994-1999* and *Empowerment through Service Delivery*. Dr Khosa is also a co-drafter of the White Paper, *Public Works towards the 21ˢᵗ Century*. Dr Khosa was appointed member of the Strategic Team of the Presidential Review Commission in 1996/97. A member of the Institute for British Geographers, the Society for South African Geographers, and the South African Sociological Association, he previously worked at the University of Natal and the University of Cambridge. Between 1996 and 1998 Dr Khosa was director of the Centre for African Research and Transformation (CART) in Durban. Dr Khosa was appointed research director of the Group: Democracy and Governance of the Human Sciences Research Council in April 1998, and has been acting as executive director since March 2000. He is also an honorary research fellow in Geography at Wits University.

Ian Liebenberg is the director of All Africa Consultants and a senior research fellow at the Unit for African Studies at the University of Pretoria (UP), South Africa. He is also a project leader on the Social Identities Programme of the Human Sciences Research Council of South Africa. He has published in academic and popular journals inside and outside South Africa. His work includes six edited and co-edited works, one book and more than one hundred articles. He has delivered several papers at national and international conferences — amongst others in Portugal, Belgium, Zimbabwe, Namibia, The Netherlands and Russia. His most recent publication is *Consolidation of Democracy in Africa — A View from the South*. He has acted as advisor and/or consultant to various NGOs and government departments and in this capacity contributed to and/or authored several reports. His current research interests are civil-military relations in young democracies, public participation and public sector transformation.

Bernard Magubane holds an M.A. (University of Natal), and an M.A. and Ph.D. (University of California in Los Angeles). Prof. Magubane taught at the universities of Zambia, California and Connecticut. A professor emeritus, he is the author of five books: *The Political Economy of Race and Class in South Africa; Ties that Bind: African American Consciousness of Africa; From Soweto to Uitenhage: Essays on the Impending African Revolution; The Making of a Racist State: British Imperialism and the Union of South Africa 1870-1910;* and *Toward a Radical African Sociology: Collected Essays.* He is currently engaged at the Human Sciences Research Council, where he is working on a book on race and the construction of the dispensable Other.

Eddy Maloka is the executive director of the Africa Institute of South Africa. He holds a doctorate in South African history, specialising in Lesotho's history and the history of the liberation struggles in Southern Africa. Dr Maloka writes widely on development issues on the African continent. Prior to his appointment at the Africa Institute of South Africa, he was a special advisor to the former Gauteng premier, Dr Motshekga.

Yvonne Muthien joined the Human Sciences Research Council in 1997 as executive director of the Group: Democracy and Governance, responsible for research on democratic consolidation, governance, public policy, population and development, and public opinion. Dr Muthien served in the Commission on the Demarcation/Delimitation of States/Provinces/Regions in South Africa until 1993, and was appointed a commissioner in the Public Service Commission (1994-1997) by President Mandela. She was also a member of governmental delegations to Malaysia, Germany, the United States and Canada. Currently she serves on the Presidential Advisory Council on National Orders. She obtained a D.Phil. in sociology and politics from Oxford University in 1989 and was associate professor in sociology at the University of Natal (1994) and honorary professor in sociology at the University of Pretoria (1996-1999). She has published widely, inter alia on regionalism in the new South Africa and on state and resistance. Her research interests also include civil service reform, affirmative action, gender equity, regional political economy and state formation.

Marlene Roefs is a Ph.D. student in social psychology, Free University, Amsterdam. Affiliated to the Department of Political Studies, University of the Witwatersrand, she is also a research associate at the Human Sciences Research Council. Her research interests include public perceptions of and reactions to local government; intergroup relations; civil society participation in governance and political activities; behaviour change; crime; and social psychological aspects of HIV/AIDS. Her thesis deals with civil organisations in South Africa (1995-2000). Roefs has published several articles in international journals.

Thabo Rapoo is currently a senior researcher and policy analyst at the Centre for Policy Studies in Johannesburg. Most of his research focuses on comparative federalism, decentralisation, intergovernmental relations and provincial governance in South Africa. He holds a master's degree in social sciences from the University of Glasgow, and a master's degree in sociology from the University of the Witwatersrand.

Stephen Rule has been managing the Public Opinion Analysis Programme of the Human Sciences Research Council (HSRC) since March 1999. Dr Rule has analysed nationally representative sample surveys in South Africa, Lesotho and Namibia. He also participated in an evaluation of the June 1999 election in South Africa and investigated the social impact of gambling in this country during 2000. His research interests are political and electoral geography as well as urban population movements and dynamics. In 1997 he served on a sub-committee for the White Paper on Local Government that focused on elections and in 1998 he monitored and analysed the elections in Lesotho and Swaziland. Before joining the HSRC he lectured for ten years at Vista University (Soweto) on urban and political geography, and for three years thereafter he managed research at the Community Agency for Social Enquiry (C A S E) on low-cost housing upgrading, land reform, the implementation of population policy, the distribution of copies of the new Constitution and the relationship between poverty and religion. He has presented and published papers, chapters and reports both locally and internationally. He obtained a Ph.D. in political geography from the University of the Witwatersrand in 1996.

Abebe Zegeye is currently professor of sociology at the University of South Africa. His former academic engagements included chief research specialist at the Human Sciences Research Council; senior research associate of the Centre for the Study of African Economies, University of Oxford; visiting professor at the University of California, Santa Barbara; director of the Centre for Modern African Studies, University of Warwick; director of the Oxford Centre for African Studies; and research fellow of the History Workshop Centre for Social History, University of Oxford. He has authored the books, *Dilemmas of Survival: Social and Environmental Degradation in the Horn of Africa; Law of Return: Ethiopian Jews in Israel,* and *Revolution, and Social Change in Ethiopia.* He has also co-edited *After Apartheid (vol. I)* with David Goldberg, *After Apartheid (vol. II)* with Robert Krige, *Human Rights and Democracy in the Horn of Africa* with Pat Lauderdale, *Ethiopia in Change: Peasantry, Nationalism and Democracy* with Siegreid Pausewang, and *Repression and Resistance in South Africa* with Robin Cohen and Yvonne Muthien. Prof. Zegeye's other publications include journal articles and book chapters, amongst others *Pathway to Democracy? The Case of the South African Truth and Reconciliation Process; State Disintegration and Human Rights in Africa,* and *North, West and the Horn of Africa.* His research interests include the black diaspora, black philosophy, political sociology, rural issues in contemporary Africa, revolution and social change in Africa, environmental issues and human rights in developing countries, race and class in capitalist societies, and nationalism and social identities in the 20th century.

Democracy and Governance Review

Acknowledgements and Preface

This book traces the dramatic transition from apartheid to democracy, and the establishment of a democratic system of governance in South Africa between 1994 and 1999. The extraordinary political and social changes during this period can be contextualised against the large-scale social transformation in Eastern Europe in the 1990s, and Latin America in the 1980s. The book reflects on the difficulties of this profound social transition and examines the institutional forms and capacities that underpin the new democratic order.

The key themes of this volume are:

- the creation of the new state, public accountability, state transformation and bureaucratic reform
- provincial and local government
- public participation in democratic institutions
- party-political support, shifting patterns of support and election outcomes
- shifting cultural and identity patterns

The book dates back to 1998 when the Group: Democracy and Governance of the Human Sciences Research Council identified a need to critically appraise South Africa's transformation and the consolidation of her democracy. We invited scholars from other institutions to join us in writing chapters for this book but, in the interest of vibrant discourse, did not try to harmonise the debates in the chapters. In many ways the Group Democracy and Governance provided us with an extraordinary team of dedicated and committed professionals and democrats who inspired us all to great heights and provided a warm and vibrant intellectual environment.

Several of the chapters were first presented as papers at local and international conferences and workshops in South Africa, France, Namibia, Botswana, Germany, the United States of America and the United Kingdom. The reviewers of the chapters provided us with valuable feedback, which enabled the authors to refine their work.

The book showcases the intellectual prowess of some of South Africa's established and emerging researchers and scholars. The book establishes a sound benchmark for studies on democratic consolidation and governance worldwide.

The target audience are students and academics of all social sciences, African studies and social studies departments at local and overseas academic institutions and research institutes; embassies, too, will find this a useful reference guide.

Apart from providing new insights on the political economy of South Africa's transition, *Democracy and Governance Review* also adds to the international comparative literature on transitions to democracy in Eastern Europe and Latin America.

The editors would like to thank the academics, researchers, activists and policy makers in South Africa who generously shared information and insights towards producing this book. Special appreciation is also due to all contributors to this book for their thought-provoking and insightful chapters. Special thanks to Ina Stahmer, Martie Boesenberg, Berta Wheeler, Annemarie Booyens, Elsa Kruger, Bashni Harry, Anneke Jordaan and Marise Swardt, for their sterling editorial and technical assistance.

This book is dedicated to O.R. Tambo who fought tirelessly in the struggle for democracy but moreover had the vision to prepare for governance. Under his leadership the liberation movements shifted into peaceful negotiations. His dedication inspired many to build a new system of democratic governance. This book is dedicated to his memory and his legacy.

Yvonne Muthien, Meshack Khosa and Bernard Magubane
Pretoria, South Africa
December 2000

Acronyms

ACDP	African Christian Democratic Party
ANC	African National Congress
ANCYL	African National Congress Youth League
AVF	Afrikaner Volksfront
AWB	Afrikaner Weerstandsbeweging
AZAPO	Azanian Peoples' Organisation
BATAT	Broadening Access to Agriculture Trust
BCM	Black Consciousness Movement
BDP	Botswana Democratic Party
BEE	Black Economic Empowerment
CAP	Constitutional Assembly Project
CAPAM	Commonwealth Association of Public Administrators and Managers
CCM	Chama cha Mapinduzi
CDFs	Community Development Forums
CEO	Chief Executive Officer
CGE	Commission for Gender Equality
COSATU	Congress of South African Trade Unions
CP	Conservative Party
CUF	Civic United Front
DA	Democratic Alliance
DCD	Department of Constitutional Development
DCs	District Councils
DDCCs	District Development Co-ordinating Committees
DHS	District Health System
DLGH	Department of Local Government and Housing
DoH	Department of Health
DP	Democratic Party
DPLG	Department of Provincial and Local Government
DTA	Democratic Turnhalle Alliance
DWAF	Department of Water Affairs and Forestry

EAs	Enumerator areas
FF	Freedom Front
FFC	Finance and Fiscal Commission
FRELOGA	Free State Local Government Association
GEAR	Growth, Employment and Redistribution
GNU	Government of National Unity
HDI	Human Development Index
HNP	Herstigte Nasionale Party
HRC	Human Rights Commission
HSRC	Human Sciences Research Council
IBA	Independent Broadcasting Authority
ICU	Industrial and Commercial Union
IDASA	Institute for Democracy in South Africa
IDC	Industrial Development Corporation
IDEA	Institute for Democracy and Electoral Assistance
IDP	Infrastructure development plan
IEC	Independent Electoral Commission
IFP	Inkatha Freedom Party
IGGs	Intergovernmental grants
IMF	International Monetary Fund
ISD	Institutional and Social Development
KID	Khululekani Institute for Democracy
KZN	KwaZulu-Natal
LDFs	Local Development Forums
LDOs	Local Development Objectives
LGTA	Local Government Transitional Act
LQ	Location Quotient
LSM	Living standard measure
MDM	Mass Democratic Movement
MECs	Members of the Executive Council
MF	Minority Front
MINMECs	Minister Members of the Executive Council
MK	Umkhonto we Sizwe (Spear of the Nation)
MMD	Movement for Multiparty Democracy

MPLA	Movimento Popular de Libertacao de Angola
MPLs	Members of Provincial Legislature
MPNP	Multiparty Negotiating Party
MTEF	Medium-Term Expenditure Framework
NCCR	National Convention for Constitutional Reform
NCOP	National Council of Provinces
NEDLAC	National Economic Development and Labour Council
NGK	Nederduitse Gereformeerde Kerk
NIC	National Indian Congress
NNP	New National Party
NOCLOGA	Northern Cape Local Government Association
NUSAS	National Union of South African Students
NWC	National Women's Coalition
NYC	National Youth Commission
PAC	Pan Africanist Congress/Pan-Africanist Congress of Azania
PAGAD	People Against Gangterism and Drugs
PanSALB	Pan South African Language Board
PPP	Petitions and Public Participation
PPPO	Petitions and Public Participation Office
PRA	Population Registration Act
PRC	Presidential Review Commission
PSC	Public Service Commission
RDP	Reconstruction and Development Programme
RENAMO	Resistencia Nacional Mozambicana
RSA	Republic of South Africa
RSCs	Regional Services Councils
SACP	South African Communist Party
SAIRR	South African Institute of Race Relations
SALA	Swedish Association of Local Authorities
SALGA	South African Local Government Association
SANCO	South African National Civic Organisation
SANDF	South African National Defence Force

SANNC	South African Native National Congress
SETA	Sectoral Education and Training Authority
SIDA	Swedish International Development Agency
SMMEs	Small, medium and micro-enterprises
SWAPO	South West Africa People's Organisation
TIC	Transvaal Indian Congress
TLCs	Transitional Local Councils
TRC	Truth and Reconciliation Commission
UCDM	United Christian Democratic Movement
UDF	United Democratic Front
UDM	United Democratic Movement
UN	United Nations
UNIP	United National Independence Party
WPNEPPS	White Paper on a New Employment Policy for the Public Service
WPTPS	White Paper on the Transformation of the Public Service
WSAs	Water Services Authorities
ZANU	Zimbabwe African National Union
ZAPU	Zimbabwe African People's Union
ZCC	Zionist Christian Church

Chapter 1

Consolidating Democracy and Governance in South Africa

Yvonne Muthien, Meshack Khosa and Bernard Magubane

Introduction

Over the past 25 years, authoritarian regimes of various sorts have crumbled worldwide to give way to liberal constitutional democracies. However, regular free and fair elections through which political parties can exercise legitimate authority and citizens obtain protection by the rule of law are a prerequisite for the consolidation of the new democracies. In turn, participation in regular free and fair elections requires a robust civil society that is keen to protect individual freedoms and equality before the law as well as preserve a plurality of interests and rich associational life (Budge & McKay, 1994; Dahl, 1998; Linz & Stepan, 1996; Rebehn, 1999).

The 1994 election in South Africa ushered in a new democracy, delivering not only a universal right to vote but also formal equality before the law, avenues for citizen participation in governance and statutory institutions buttressing democracy. The second democratic election in 1999 took place amidst large-scale societal transformation and reform and presented the first major opportunity to measure the extent of the consolidation of democracy and governance in South Africa. The first year of the second democratic government also provides us with an opportunity to compare and examine policy and delivery shifts between the Mandela and Mbeki eras (Johnson & Schlemmer, 1996; Southall, 1999).

Pillars of Democracy

The sustainability of democratic systems cannot be taken for granted. Robert Dahl points out that the number of democracies increased from 21 in 1950 to 51 in 1996, and that 30 countries achieved democratic status between 1993 and 1996. However, between 1900 and 1985, non-democratic regimes replaced democratic regimes 52 times (Dahl, 1998; Benhabib, 1996).

The fledgling democracy of South Africa has delivered the franchise to the disenfranchised majority. It also put in place the following key pillars of democratic consolidation:

- A functioning multi-party parliamentary system with election processes that are considered to be procedural and substantially free and fair.
- A strong sense of constitutionalism and the rule of law, supported by various institutions buttressing democracy, including the Constitutional Court, the Human Rights Commission, the Commission for Gender Equality, the Office of the Auditor-General, the Public Service Commission, and the Public Protector.
- Mechanisms of accountability, such as the Access to Information Act, which enshrine the right to public information, force government to be transparent and expose acts of corruption among public officials. The Constitution moreover enshrines the values of good governance and sound administration in public affairs.
- A professional civil service functioning on the basis of constitutional values, including impartiality, dedicated service delivery and fiscal accountability.
- Mechanisms for citizen participation in government, including public hearings of parliamentary committees and public participation in policy making.
- An integrated and highly developed economic infrastructure with considerable potential for economic prosperity.

Civil Society and Democracy

A robust civil society is a clear indicator of a strong democracy (McDonough, Shin & Moisés, 1998). Debates over the last decade have created polar, at times antagonistic, relations between the state and civil society. Emanating from the neo-Gramscian literature of the 1980s, the state was perceived as a "hegemony protected by the armour of coercion", whereas civil society was perceived as the bearer of democratisation and the agent of setting limits on state power. Hence a robust civil society came to constitute an essential pillar of a mature liberal democracy. More-over, civil society organisations have come to be viewed as the representa-tives of diverse and sectoral interest groups, widening access to and public participation in public institutions and processes (Muthien & Olivier, 1999; Markoff, 1997; Sagasti et al., 1997; Liebenberg, 1997).

Current debates stress the importance of robust institutions of civil society in generating good governance and economic growth. The social constructionist view asks not only about the nature of the state but also about class, development and societal context, as well as the fabric of civic culture and state-civil society relations (Putman, 1993; Evans, 1995; Tendler, 1997; Samatar, 1999).

The nexus of state-civil society relations can be graphically demon-strated as follows:

Citizens

mobilising, advocacy, resource distribution, participation

Civil society institutions

advocacy, policy dialogue, consultation

State

policy accountability, democratic development

The election to power of South Africa's first democratic government in 1994 had significant implications for not only state-civil society relations, but also for civil society itself. Informed by the social movement literature, the expectation was that civil society would enter a period of demobilisation after the institution of democracy and that the high levels of political mobilisation that characterised much of the 1980s and early 1990s would dissipate.

The Democracy and Governance Research Programme on Social Movements of the Human Sciences Research Council (HSRC) conducted a number of annual surveys since March 1994, in order to trace trends in organisational involvement. The five surveys to date were conducted at the same time of the year among a countrywide sample of about 2 200 respondents (Muthien & Olivier, 1999). Membership (i.e. *active membership* and/or holding an *office-bearer* position) of a range of organisations, including political parties, civic associations, trade unions, women's organisations and stokvels (stokvels are savings clubs where members rotate access to the money among its members on say a monthly basis) was examined (White, 1998; Muthien & Olivier, 1999). A number of trends were evident.

Membership of political parties decreased significantly since the run-up to the 1994 founding election. At the time about one-fifth of the respondents were active members of a political party. This proportion decreased to one-tenth by March 1998. The most active political party membership was found among African respondents (24%), followed by whites (17%) and then coloureds and Indians (about 5% each). The downward trend in active party membership since then clearly suggests overall disengagement from active political involvement. This was most evident among the whites where active membership decreased from 17% in 1994 to 4% in 1998, which can be explained by the loss of political power and the lack of a viable opposition. Active membership among African respondents decreased from its high 24% in 1994 to 13% in 1998.

The new government inevitably drew the leadership of civil society organisations into its ranks. Despite this depletion, though, there was an increase in participation in women's organisations, youth organisations and civic organisations. Stokvels/savings societies showed a significant increase in participation, which points to the emergence of an entrepreneurial spirit in black communities. Membership in those organisations most active during the struggle for democracy, i.e. trade unions and civic organisations, remained fairly constant between 1994 and 1998. The results clearly suggest that there has not been a decline in civil society participation since 1994, but that involvement has come to be channelled differently.

The results of analyses of the extent to which supporters of political parties, trade unions and civic organisations were prepared to engage in protest activities to advance their concerns are revealing. First, the supporters of political parties and trade unions were less prepared to engage in protest activities than supporters of, for example, civic organisations. Second, active members of these three organisations were much more prepared to engage in protest activities than active members of other organisations (Roefs, Klandermans & Olivier, 1998). Overall, organisational involvement seems to have become an important factor in mobilising people to protest against pressing social problems.

Another important indicator of democratic consolidation is the measure of trust in civil society institutions (see Chapter 4). The results of HSRC surveys reveal that trust in civil society institutions, including churches, the media, business and civic associations, was generally high. Trade unions and political parties fared less well, as did the courts and police; the defence force fared slightly better. Trust in the Independent Electoral Commission to deliver free and fair elections was quite high in the run-up to the 1999 election.

Transforming State and Society

Given the legacy of repression and discrimination, systematic destruction of black family life and social capital, and the distorted nature of service delivery and societal structures under colonialism and apartheid, the democratic state faced a formidable challenge to not only establish new democratic forms of governance, but fundamentally transform society. The centrality of the role of the state in social transformation was articulated by the then Deputy President, Thabo Mbeki, in his address to the ANC Youth League Congress in 1996:

> We consider the attainment of political democracy as a precondition for the continuing struggle aimed at the achievement of full social [and] economic emancipation for all the people. Commendable progress is already being made in putting building blocks aimed at ensuring the democratisation of the political order, the deracialisation and rebuilding of the economy, the public service, security organs of state, social services and cultural institutions. The success of our policy of reconciliation, national unity and nation-building also depends on the progress we make in addressing the political and socio-economic divisions in the conditions of life of the people.

A key feature of this transformative agenda is the delivery of substantive political and economic democracy (Khosa, 2000). This agenda was captured in the Reconstruction and Development Programme (RDP), aimed at not only transforming or democratising state and society, but also on substantially improving the material well-being of the majority of the population. This programme would entail large-scale infrastructural investment and development, community-based public works job creation, the expansion of social security investment and expenditure, and improved service delivery to the poor. The programme would however lead to public debt escalation amidst a drive to reduce the size of the civil service. In addition, the RDP Office, created as a "super ministry" in the President's Office, did not realise the aim of policy implementation. Hence the RDP Office was abolished and a new policy framework premised on neo-liberal economic assumptions was operationalised (Bond & Khosa, 1999).

The new macro-economic policy framework, the Growth, Employment and Redistribution (GEAR) policy, emphasises the redistributive thrust of the reprioritisation of government expenditure and the role of social and sectoral policies in meeting basic needs, improving services available to the poor, and building social infrastructure. It stresses that growth needs to be translated into redistribution of incomes and opportunities through appropriate social development policies and programmes, and deliberate promotion of employment creation. GEAR envisages increased state expenditure on infrastructure as an enhancer of growth. Privatisation is seen as a means of reducing debt. At the same time, the government must play a central redistributive role through land reform and the provision of basic social services.

Instituting a New Culture of Governance

The new "paradigm" of governance in international literature underscores the challenge facing the new democratic government of South Africa: Traditional notions of state administration and reform have to be replaced with governance that makes provision for the following:

- multi-agency networks and partnerships,
- interdependence between centres and networks of power,
- the emergence of self-governing networks or clusters,
- the development of new governmental cultures and procedures, and
- public-private sector co-operation and partnerships (Stoker, 1998).

The re-establishment of the rule of law and a culture of constitutionalism in South Africa provided the parameters for a change in organisational culture and behaviour in public administration in South Africa. The new Constitution demands transparency, public accountability and impartiality in service delivery. It has also created new avenues for citizen participation and public scrutiny of the way the country is being governed. The increasing recognition of the interdependence between state and civil society and the establishment of an independent civil society in the new "paradigm" of governance is aptly captured by Dahrendorf (cited in CAPAM, 1995, p. 21):

> [I]nstitutions which are autonomous in that they are not State-run, are not subject to the whims of kings and tyrants, but are sustained by citizens endowed with rights and the wherewithal to make use of them.

Governance in Transition

The 1990s produced widespread political and economic transitions across continents, which augured in an era of bold experimentation and innovation in public sector reform. A new "paradigm", namely that of "government in transition", was introduced in the Commonwealth. Global political changes and socio-economic pressures posed similar challenges to developing and developed countries.

The South African experiment provided a new benchmark for studies of governance in transition. The historic settlement and compromise reached at the multi-party negotiations not only pulled back the country from the brink of civil war, but produced innovative forms of power sharing and limits to majoritarian rule. These compromises included:

- the formation of a Government of National Unity in 1994, which enabled co-responsibility for governance between minority and majority parties,
- a "sunset clause", which provided continuity and stability through job security for the "old guard",
- proportional representation, which provided for better representation of "minority parties",
- the introduction of a new system of co-operative governance between the national, provincial and local tiers of government, and
- an extensive array of institutions for checking on the arbitrary use of political authority.

New Policy Agenda

An important feature of transformation during the first term of office of the democratic state was the democratisation of public policy making. The new political environment introduced a variety of new processes and practices that differed radically from those that marked policy making during the apartheid era. In particular, the previously semi-secretive, technocratic, authoritarian mode of policy making was replaced by a more public and accountable policy making.

Perhaps the most significant example of this new political culture was the Constitutional Assembly Project (CAP), which aimed to draw civil society into constitution writing. Underlying the CAP was the culture of popular participation and public consultation that characterised the Mass Democratic Movement (MDM). The CAP empowered institutions and community organisations outside of the state to participate in decision making. The aim of the CAP was to make constitution writing as inclusive as possible. This was done in a number of ways.

Six theme committees were set up by the Constitutional Assembly to collate and consider submissions from a wide variety of stakeholders, including organs of civil society, ordinary individuals, political parties and all those who had an interest in contributing to the new Constitution. Popular participation in constitution writing was made possible by encouraging the citizenry to make submissions in their own languages, resulting in some 2,5 million written submissions. These were supplemented by thousands of public meetings in almost every town and village to give people an opportunity to express their views on what should be included in the new Constitution. People were encouraged to attend these meetings through advertisements on television and radio. Popular awareness of the issues involved was further raised by the distribution of a regular newspaper, *Constitutional Talk*, a television talk show by the same name, and numerous radio programmes dealing with the constitution-making process.

This new policy-making approach created opportunities for a greater and more active role by civil society in governance. It also provided the drive for the transformation of state-civil society relations. The creation of the new democratic state, which was more inclusive and more responsive to the needs of the previously excluded majority, required a fundamental overhaul of all policy and implementation frameworks for service delivery. The African National Congress (ANC) also took office armed with a basket of new policy initiatives, contained in the RDP, which in itself was developed through constituency inputs and consultation. Hence policy making in the new government became open to mass public input, thus introducing participatory democracy, accountability and transparency. For instance, government ministries held conferences and workshops to include a wide variety of stakeholders in discussions on specific policy issues. In addition, they invited and considered written submissions to Green and White Papers, held public hearings and encouraged the public to interact with parliamentary committees.

Public Accountability

A central feature of the new culture of governance consists of an array of constitutional checks on public authority. Public accountability forms the foundation of good governance and sound public administration. James Madison (cited in Schwella, 1991) captured the rationale for democratic accountability:

> If men were angels, no government would be necessary. If angels were to govern men, neither external nor internal controls on government would be necessary. In framing a government, which is to be administered by men over men, the great difficulty lies in this: you must first enable the government to control the governed; and in the next place oblige it to control itself.

Accountability is embedded in the system of liberal democracy, premised on the election of public representatives, the separation of the legislative, executive and judiciary powers, the upholding of the rule of law through an independent judiciary and a prevailing system of constitutionalism. Moreover, accountability is exercised through a complex system of institutional checks and balances that limit political authority. The sustainability of democracies can in part be tested against the strength of their institutions of accountability.

In a system of parliamentary democracy, the legislature constitutes the supreme authority, as its members are the elected representatives of "the people". The executive derives its authority from the legislature and is accountable to the legislature for its actions. As the law-making authority, the legislature assumes the role of final arbiter of government policy and has the task of balancing the diverse interests of the broader society. The effectiveness of the legislature to hold government accountable depends

on the quality of the elected representatives in terms of professional expertise and direct accountability to constituencies. Specialised committees,
e.g. select committees on public accounts and finance, the holding of open
public hearings and allowing the public to attend the proceedings of parliamentary committees, as well as the provision of research support, enhance
the capacity of the legislature to scrutinise government accountability.

The South African Constitution has enshrined an elaborate array of
institutions that support constitutional democracy through monitoring
political and administrative authority. These include the Public Protector,
the Auditor-General, the Public Service Commission, the Human Rights
Commission, the Commission for Gender Equality, the Independent Electoral Commission and the Commission for the Promotion and Protection
of the Rights of Cultural, Religious and Linguistic Communities. Moreover, the independence and impartiality of these institutions are enshrined
with an injunction to be impartial and "perform their functions without
fear, favour or prejudice". Furthermore, "other organs of state…must
assist and protect these institutions to ensure the independence, impartiality, dignity and effectiveness of these institutions", and "no person or
organ of state may interfere with the functioning of these institutions"
(Constitution, 1996). These are indeed a powerful set of protections and
quite necessary given South Africa's history of human rights violations
and the rule of law by an oppressive state machine.

Democracy and Governance: Quo Vadis?

The aim of this book is to provide critical appraisals of the evolving pillars
of democracy and governance in South Africa since 1994. These
appraisals focus on:

- the historical evolution of race and democracy,

- the imperatives of state formation,

- the new culture of governance, including democratic accountability
  and reform, and public perceptions of governance,

- progress with provincial and local governance,

- public participation in democratic institutions including the legislature,
- changing patterns of identity formation and the protection of diversity, as well as
- changing profiles of political party support and the emerging electoral geography in South Africa.

Chapter 2 examines the historical roots of the racial order and their implications for democracy in post-apartheid South Africa. Professor Bernard Magubane traces racial prejudice to the colonial order and the construction of an oppressive and exploitative state founded on cheap labour, disenfranchisement and the systematic destruction of black family life and social capital in South Africa before 1994. However, the "miracle" of the subsequent creation of an inclusive democratic order premised on the protection of human rights and the restoration of the human dignity of the individual poses a challenge—to decode the complexities and reverse the deeply entrenched patterns of domination and subordination.

In Chapter 3, Gregory Houston and Yvonne Muthien examine the evolution of the state in South Africa (the pre-colonial order (before 1652), the colonial order (1652-1909), the segregationist order (1910-1947), the apartheid order (1948-1993) and the new democratic order (1994-)). Against this background they examine the twin imperatives of the new state, that is, the programme to transform both state and society and the agenda to establish a developmental state.

Chapter 4 examines the democratisation of the state itself. In this chapter Yvonne Muthien outlines the key challenges of establishing public accountability through the creation of multiple institutions that "buttress democracy" and limit political authority. The chapter includes an assessment of the capacity of the legislature to hold the executive accountable and the ability of statutory bodies to place limits on the arbitrary exercise of political power. The chapter illustrates the democratisation of the state by means of a case study of the transformation of the Public Service Commission in the Mandela era.

Thabo Rapoo examines—in Chapter 5—the establishment of a new system of provincial governance in South Africa, including the institutional forms created to give expression to the devolution of power to different tiers of government and the establishment of new forms of intergovernmental relations through a system of co-operative governance.

Chapter 6 presents an overview by Eddy Maloka of the establishment of the new Gauteng Provincial Legislature. It offers an insider view with sober reflections on the institutional and political complexities of establishing a second tier government.

Doreen Atkinson provides—in Chapter 7—a critical assessment of local government in intergovernmental relations, focusing on the case of the Northern Cape. The Northern Cape province is one of the new jurisdictions created by the 1993 Interim Constitution. Atkinson concludes that local government in the Northern Cape has survived a difficult time and may face problems in sustaining effective local governance.

In Chapter 8, Abebe Zegeye, Ian Liebenberg and Gregory Houston pose insightful propositions in examining social identity patterns during the period of nation building. They also analyse various trends in identity formation in post-apartheid South Africa.

Chapter 9 presents an examination by Meshack Khosa of the difficulties and challenges of protecting diversity in a heterogeneous society with a legacy of polarisation, often characterised by violent conflict. This chapter contains an overview and analysis of debates leading up to the second national Consultative Conference (1999) on the Commission for the Promotion and Protection of the Rights of Cultural, Religious and Linguistic Communities.

The culture of governance and legitimacy is critically appraised by Meshack Khosa in Chapter 10. The chapter focuses on public perceptions of government performance at national, provincial and local levels by race, province and income. Trust in national, provincial and local government and in civil society institutions is also assessed according to race, province and income. The chapter reveals the shifting patterns of public support for the way in which South Africa was governed from 1994 up to the run-up to the 1999 election.

In Chapter 11, Marlene Roefs and Ian Liebenberg present their preliminary findings on public participation in governance in South Africa. They conclude that communities need to be involved from the beginning to the end in all programmes aimed at public participation, and that communities should not merely act as rubber stamps for law making and governance.

In Chapter 12, Stephen Rule explores the extent to which party support profiles continue to reflect traditional historical cleavages, using the results of a national survey of public opinion conducted during November 1999. Responses to three of the survey questions are analysed to determine feelings of closeness to each political party, intention to vote for that party and reasons for voting for that party in the June 1999 election.

Chapter 13 offers an examination by Stephen Rule of the regional differences in public opinion about government priorities and economic performance during the months prior to the 1999 election. The chapter highlights the regional differentiation in levels of voter trust in and satisfaction with the national government and the resultant variations in support given to the ANC in the election.

Finally, in Chapter 14, the editors assess the progress and problems with consolidating democracy and establishing new forms of governance in South Africa. The chapter revisits a number of critical issues outlined in the introductory chapter, rather than presenting a comprehensive score card of achievements and failures.

Overall, this publication is an attempt to draw together recent research and appraisals of aspects of South Africa's transition, notably an examination of the establishment of new forms of democracy and governance in post-apartheid South Africa, including state formation, public accountability, deracialisation of the state, co-operative governance, shifting social identities and diversity, and the electoral geography and political outcomes. The book does not claim to be exhaustive in respect of the issues it covers. It is, however, a showcase of some of South Africa's new talent of young and emerging researchers, many of whom write from an experiential insider/participant perspective on the processes and institutions that they analyse.

References

Benhabib, S. (1996), *Democracy and Difference: Contesting the Boundaries of the Political*, Princeton, Princeton University Press.

Bond, P. & Khosa, M. (1999), *An RDP Policy Audit*, Pretoria, HSRC Publishers.

Budge, I. & McKay, D. (1994), *Developing Democracy*, London, Sage.

Dahl, R. (1998), *On Democracy*, New Haven, Yale University Press.

Dahrendorf, R. (1995), cited in CAPAM, *Government in Transition*, Toronto.

Evans, P. (1995), *Embedded Autonomy: States & Industrial Transformation*, Princeton, Princeton University Press.

Johnson, R. & Schlemmer L.A. (1996), *Leveling Democracy in South Africa: The First Open Election, April 1999*, New Haven, Yale University Press.

Khosa, M.M. (ed.) (2000), *Empowerment Through Service Delivery*, Pretoria, HSRC Publishers.

Liebenberg, I. (1997), "Consolidation of Democracy in Africa: Inhibitors on Civil Society", *African Security Review*, vol. 6, no. 4.

Linz, J. & Stepan, A. (1996), "Toward Consolidated Democracies", *Journal of Democracy*, vol. 2, no. 7, April.

Markoff, T. (1997), "Really Existing Democracy: Learning from Latin America in the Late 1990s", *New Left Review*, no. 223, May/June.

McDonough, P., Shin, D.C. & Moisés, J.A. (1998), "Democratisation and Participation: Comparing Spain, Brazil and Korea", *The Journal of Politics*, vol. 60, no. 4, pp. 919-953.

Muthien, Y. & Olivier, J. (1999), "The State and Civil Society: Implications for Democracy in South Africa", *SA Review*, no. 8, Johannesburg, Ravan Press.

Putnam, R. (1993), *Making Democracy: Civic Traditions in Modern Italy*, Princeton, Princeton University Press.

Rebehn, M. (1999), *Learning to Trust Democracy,* ABI, Freiburg.

Roefs, M., Klandermans, B. & Olivier, J. (1998), *Demobilization of the Movement: Transition from Authoritarian Rule to Democracy*, Paper presented at the Workshop on Social Movements in South Africa, November, Pretoria, HSRC.

Sagasti, F. et al. (1997), "Democratization, Modernization, and Legitimization: The Case of Peru", *UNISA Latin America Report*, vol. 13, no. 1, Jan-June.

Samatar, A. (1999), *An African Miracle: State and Class Leadership and Colonial Legacy in Botswana Development*, Portsmouth, Heinemann.

Schwella, E. (1991), "Selected Aspects of Democratic Accountability in South African Public Administration", *Perspectives*, vol. 1, no. 1.

Southall, R. (1999), "The 1999 Elections: Consolidating Democracy or Foreshadowing Decline?", *Indicator*, vol. 16, no. 1.

Stoker, G. (1998), "Governance as Theory: Five Propositions", *International Social Science Journal*, Special Edition on Governance, no. 155, March.

Tendler, J. (1997), *Good Government in the Tropics*, Baltimore, John Hopkins University Press,

Weingast, B. (1997), "The Political Foundations of Democracy and the Rule of Law", *American Political Science Review*, vol. 91, no. 2, June.

White, C. (1998), "Democratic Societies? Voluntary Association and Democratic Culture in a South African Township", *Transformation*, vol. 36, pp. 1-36.

Chapter 2

Race and Democratisation in South Africa: Some Reflections

Bernard Magubane

Introduction

On 28 April 1994, about 20 million South Africans from all walks of life went to the polls to elect the first truly democratic government in the history of South Africa. The result was a stunning victory for the African National Congress (ANC) and its allies, the South African Communist Party (SACP) and the Congress of South African Trade Unions (COSATU). The Government of National Unity (GNU) that replaced the apartheid regime after the election brought to an end 86 years of white supremacist rule and the protracted armed conflict between the apartheid regime and the liberationist movements. However, decades of abuse and want have left wounds whose healing is a daunting challenge. An understanding of what happened before 1994 in South Africa will help to devise strategies to meet this challenge in the short and the long term.

The Period 1910-1990

The Union of South Africa came into existence in 1910. A new dominion of Britain, it was the result of reconciliation between Boer and Brit after the Anglo-Boer War (1899-1902) and a step towards greater independence from Britain. However, the Act of Union of 1909, which was the foundation of the new dominion, excluded Africans in the Union of South Africa from political participation in their land of birth. Their opposition to this exclusion led to the formation of the ANC in 1912. In due course, the more dependent the white ruling class became on African sweat and skills for its prosperity, the more jealous it became of its monopoly over economic and political privileges, and the more finely it sharpened those instruments to suppress black opposition to its hegemony (Slovo, 1976, p. 108).

The Sharpeville massacre of defenceless protesters in March 1960 finally convinced the ANC and its allies that the days of "non-violent" resistance and extra-legal methods were over. The resultant internal revolt was reinforced by worldwide condemnation of white minority rule, spearheaded by the newly independent African states and their compatriots in the Non-Aligned Movement.

In March 1961, the then prime minister, H.F. Verwoerd, called a referendum to let white voters indicate whether South Africa should become a republic or remain a British dominion. The ANC saw this as further entrenchment of arbitrary Afrikaner rule. Therefore it called a national convention in which representatives of all the people of South Africa could make their wishes known. If the regime failed to heed its call for representative government, the ANC would call for a general strike to coincide with the declaration of the Republic of South Africa scheduled for 31 May 1961.

Black opposition to the state was severe. In response, the apartheid regime declared a state of emergency. On 16 December 1961, Umkhonto we Sizwe (Spear of the Nation) started bombing government installations and declared:

> The people's patience is not endless. The time comes in the life
> of any nation when there remain only two choices—submit or
> fight. That time has now come for South Africa.

This development, even though dismissed at the time as a pinprick, proved once again that the past is never past, but active in the present. Indeed, the evolving anti-colonial struggle in southern Africa was a reversal of colonialist expansion—the so-called *Kaffir* wars of the early nineteenth century repeated themselves, but this time around the momentum was from north to south and not from south to north.

In Guinea-Bissau the signal event was the bloody repression, in which fifty workers were killed and many injured. In

Mozambique it was the 1960 Muenda massacre of 600 at a peaceful meeting. In Angola it was the killing of thirty and wounding of 200 at a meeting in Calete to protest the arrest of MPLA leader Agostino Neto, combined with the brutal repression of the Maria uprising led by a militant Christian sect. In Zimbabwe a series of preparations for armed struggle were prompted by the settlers' successful Unilateral Declaration of Independence, which shattered any remaining illusion that Britain might act against the interest of its kith and kin to enforce majority rule. In Namibia, the turn to armed resistance occurred immediately after the abortive 1966 judgement of the International Court of Justice, when the process of international and legal pressure had been tested to its limits and found wanting. (Slovo, 1976, pp. 183-184.)

Southern Africa in the 1960s was not only a sphere of European interest; it was also a promising sphere of interest for the new American empire. Here was produced one-fifth of the world's copper and tin, nearly one-fourth of its manganese, more than half of its gold, four-fifths of its cobalt and almost all of its industrial diamonds. More than half of the world's known supply of uranium lay in the Congo, Namibia and South Africa. The *Chicago Tribune* commented at the time:

> The public investment of United States money in Africa runs into more than half-billion dollars, and private investment may even be as much or more. Imperialism would be a nasty word to describe our expanding interests in Africa but the list of American projects to develop the vast military resources of this continent suggest that the nineteenth century imperialism of England, France, Belgium, and Portugal is a child's play. (*The Nation,* 26 December 1953, p. 557.)

> "However we may feel ideologically", the editorial continued, "we are politically and financially increasingly committed to the Empire—either our allies or our own in competition with theirs. How much of our billions in foreign aid to France, Britain, and

Belgium has gone to strengthen the machinery of colonialism?...Whether we give or invest, we invite responsibility.
And in view of some of our allies at least, we are at last learning
to discharge that responsibility in a proper fashion." The
editorial also noted the behaviour of the United States
representative on the Trusteeship Council, who it said showed
United States support for South Africa.

Thus at a time when the protection of the Western World's
vested interests in Africa south of the Sahara has become
seemingly a matter of life or death the winds of revolution are
sweeping across the continent. If the white man has ever before
been so keenly aware of the value of Africa's resources, the
black man has never before been so keenly aware of the values
of freedom...The United States is in Africa to stay, just as it is
in Europe. (*The Nation*, 26 December 1953, p. 557.)

After 1964, when Nelson Mandela and his compatriots were sentenced to
life imprisonment, white supremacy, with the help of the United States and
its allies, appeared triumphant. Nevertheless, the spirit of resistance of the
peoples of southern Africa was not broken. In 1975 the people of
Mozambique and Angola became independent. In 1976 the situation in
South Africa changed dramatically. The Soweto student revolt broke up
the logjam, whereafter black resistance took a menacing turn. To fortify
itself, the apartheid regime formulated what it called a "total strategy"—
unparalleled repression of the liberationists and "reform" of apartheid. The
latter included "granting" independence to the African reserves (then
called "bantustans") of the Transkei, Ciskei, Boputhatswana and Venda.
The regime also "reformed" the laws governing African labour, and gave
the so-called coloureds and Indians a share in the constitutional
dispensation by means of the so-called tricameral constitution of 1983.
However, whites maintained firm control.

The independence of Mozambique and Angola in 1975 and
Zimbabwe in 1980 was the writing on the wall for the white minority
regime in South Africa. The intensification of the popular struggle in

South Africa and the defeat of South Africa's expeditionary forces in Angola did immeasurable harm to the prestige of the white minority regime. The shock of the military defeat was compounded by the fact that it was with the help of socialist Cuba that the MPLA movement achieved victory over the South African forces in Angola. This situation together with the split in Afrikanerdom between the so-called enlightened faction (*verligtes*) and the hidebound faction (*verkramptes*) caused the white bourgeoisie to take a deep look at what it stood to lose if the extreme elements in Afrikaner ranks triumphed.

The struggle within the country was boosted by the formation of the United Democratic Front in 1983 and COSATU in 1985. The struggle was gathering momentum: students, workers and peasants were striking out against the apartheid regime in all directions. These developments accelerated the disintegration of the apartheid regime. In the summer of 1985, *The London Economist,* in a special issue on South Africa, described the situation that faced P.W. Botha as a "degenerative collapse".

Interest groups with a lot to lose from the escalating conflict began to make tentative approaches to the ANC. In 1985, representatives of South Africa's major capitalist institutions made a pilgrimage to Lusaka to open talks with the ANC. These included representatives of the Premier Group, Barclays Bank, Sanlam and Barlow Rand. The leader of this delegation was Gavin Relly, chairperson of Anglo-American Corporation.

The impending defeat of the apartheid regime in the 1980s elicited fear in the Reagan and Thatcher administrations. Both stood for a capitalist white-ruled southern Africa in contrast to the "chaos" and "disintegration" in the black-ruled "socialist" states north of the Zambezi. However awful the oppressive system of apartheid was, any revolutionary alternative had to be worse in their view. Southern Africa, following the collapse of Portuguese colonial rule in Angola and Mozambique, became the battle-ground of the Cold War as never before.

Throughout the 1960s and 1970s the United States and Britain used their veto right in the United Nations to ensure that the white minority regime was protected from international sanctions. In addition, the United States vetoed (with Britain abstaining) a resolution to condemn South

Africa for its brutal invasion of Angola in August 1981. In May 1986 both the United States and Britain used their veto after Pretoria attacked Botswana, Zambia and Zimbabwe, killing innocent civilians. The following month Britain and the United States vetoed another resolution condemning South Africa for further attacks on Angola. Indeed, between 1980 and 1988 the Western powers vetoed twelve United Nations Security Council resolutions condemning apartheid South Africa—the United States vetoed all twelve, Britain vetoed eleven and France vetoed four. Six of the twelve vetoes related to South Africa's illegal occupation of Namibia, and four related to South Africa's aggression in the Front Line States.

In 1986, following the declaration of the second state of emergency by P.W. Botha, public indignation and pressure in the United States and Britain increased for the imposition of sanctions against South Africa. Reagan and Thatcher tried to establish a moral equivalence between apartheid and sanctions. For instance, Reagan criticised apartheid as morally wrong and politically unacceptable but in the same breath agreed with Mrs Thatcher that punitive sanctions were also immoral and repugnant. Pretoria, he said, was not obliged to negotiate with terrorists of the ANC, but Mandela should be released to participate in the political process. The strongest allies of blacks, Reagan insisted, were the Western businessmen who brought in their own ideas of social justice: "Capitalism is the natural enemy to such feudal institutions as apartheid" (Simpson, 1987, p. 14).

The years of the Reagan and Thatcher administrations will be noted above everything else for the green light they gave the apartheid regime to destroy the economies of the Front Line States. South Africa, the United States, Britain and other Western powers never accepted the regimes that assumed power in Angola, Mozambique and Zimbabwe. Nor did they look favourably on the Southern African Development Co-ordination Conference (SADCC). In order to neutralise Angola, Mozambique and Zimbabwe, the Pretoria regime adopted a three-pronged strategy. First, with the strategic support of the United States and Britain, the regime did everything to prevent SWAPO from assuming power in Namibia. Second, the regime tried to prevent the ANC and SWAPO from obtaining bases in

Angola and Mozambique. Third, Pretoria attempted to suffocate the embryonic nine-nation SADCC.

When the Reagan administration assumed power in 1980, a fourth dimension was added—South Africa worked towards replacing the MPLA with the UNITA bandits in Angola, and FRELIMO with the RENAMO bandits in Mozambique, or at least have both bandit organisations included in coalition governments. From 1981 the South African forces occupied and pillaged the southern part of Angola while RENAMO wreaked havoc on the economy of Mozambique. However, under the guise of "constructive engagement" the apartheid regime obtained freedom from the threat of sanctions with the help of its imperialist allies.

Mandela's Release in 1990

> If we really want to lose everything, then we must hang on to everything now. Donald Masson (retired president of the Afri-kaanse Handelsinstituut, an Afrikaner commercial institution), June 1986, quoted by Simpson, 1987, p. 11.

On 2 February 1990, President F.W. de Klerk, who had replaced P.W. Botha, announced that on 11 February Nelson Mandela would be released from his life-term prison sentence and that the ANC, the PAC, the SACP and other liberationist organisations would be unbanned. He also expressed the hope that a new constitutional settlement including all the people of South Africa would be negotiated. With that announcement the history of South Africa turned full circle. At Groote Schuur (a house that Cecil Rhodes built) F.W. de Klerk and Nelson Mandela sat at the same table and talked about a new constitutional order for the country, something that was hardly expected to occur then. It was as if the ideology and infrastructure that strangled people's minds for nine decades had collapsed overnight.

The symbolism of the place where the talks took place was as important as the substance of the talks. It was the "first truly serious meeting" between the white government and the ANC in 78 years, Mandela observed. The event, he went on, was "freighted with deadly weight of the terrible tradition of a dialogue between master and servant".

To overcome that burden, Mandela requested "all who are hostages of the past to transform [themselves] into new men and women who shall be fitting instruments for the creation of a new South Africa".

These developments had no obvious precedent in history. It was the first time that a ruling racist regime of any white settler country had begun what would lead to a fundamental change in the constitutional structure of such a country. This actually was "Part 2" of the South Africa Act of 1909, which had led to the creation of the dominion of the Union of South Africa in 1910. It was also an admission that South Africa was not and could not remain a "white man's country" but, in the words of the Freedom Charter of the ANC, must belong to all who live in it. In May 1990, the ruling National Party (NP) and the ANC began the tedious process of negotiating the modalities for dismantling white minority rule. Difficult as the process would be, the people of South Africa needed to create a new constitutional formula in order to escape the crippling legacy of colonial conquest and its distorted psychological legacy.

The very acknowledgement that the ANC could not be ignored was a major achievement. From 1912 the ANC had been the chief custodian of the national aspirations of the African people under the most difficult circumstances. The unbanning of the Communist Party of South Africa (CPSA) was a surprise. One of the first measures taken by the NP after it came to power in 1948 was to pass the notorious Suppression of Communism Act in 1950. The chief reason for the Act had been to defend "white" South Africa from the twin dangers of black nationalism and "communism". Now all that fear seemed to have been jettisoned.

The event of Mandela's release was transmitted around the world by satellite. The celebration that followed, especially Mandela's whirlwind visit to the United States, underlined the scale of the defeat of De Klerk and the international forces of imperialism that supported the Afrikaner regime in its forty years of brutality. The man the regime had sought to condemn to oblivion in 1964 had not only survived, but had come out a world statesman, and the organisation whose politics he had been convicted for had emerged as a major negotiating partner. In its revised strategy, the ANC stated in 1991 that:

All these developments represent a major victory for the forces, led by the ANC, which have struggled for many decades for the destruction of the system of white minority domination and the transformation of South Africa into a united, democratic and non-racial democracy. The immediate issue on the agenda was the question of political power. To effect the transfer of power into the hands of the people as a whole was and still is the most crucial and immediate challenge facing the national democratic movement.

However, even with the start of the negotiations, the ANC could not lose sight of the fact that the regime still retained the capacity to implement counter-revolutionary measures on a whole range of fronts. "The white ruling group", the 1990 *Guidelines on Strategy* stated, "has entered the negotiations process with its own agenda: a radically reformed system of apartheid which will retain the essentials of white domination of economic, political, and social institutions of our country". Developments in South Africa from 1990 to the eve of the 1994 election somewhat vindicated this conclusion.

The Meaning of 1994

Looking back at the period 1910 to 1994, one is struck by the monumental efforts of white settlers to reduce Africans to nothing but labour power. This effort involved domination unmediated by any compassion. Almost 84 years after Britain created the edifice of white minority rule, those whom Fanon called the "damned of the earth" woke up from the dead under the leadership of the ANC to rejoin the living. As Nadine Gordimer (1994, p. 4) put it, the election of the African National Congress as the head of the transitional government in May 1994 was not just a new beginning.

> It was a resurrection; this land rising from the tomb of the entire colonial past shared out among the Dutch, the French, the British, and their admixture of other Europeans, this indigenous people rising from the tomb of segregated housing, squatter

camps, slum schools, job restrictions, forced removals from one part of the country to another; from burial of all human aspirations and dignity under the humiliation of discrimination by race and skin; this people rising, for the first time in history, with the right to elect a government: to govern themselves. A sacred moment is represented in the act of putting a mark on a ballot.

The triumph of the ANC and its allies was a watershed between the period of colonial dominance in Africa. The 1913 Land Act made 87% of South Africa a "white man's country" where Africans were allowed only if they came to sell their labour power. The NP, which was formed in 1914 to represent the national aspirations of the Afrikaners who had suffered defeat in the Anglo-Boer War, assumed power in 1948 and began a programme to finally solve the "native problem". If 1948 marked the apogee of Afrikaner nationalism, 1960 marked the nadir for African hopes. In 1960, the ANC and the Pan-Africanist Congress were summarily banned because of their demand to share power in a unified South African state. The then Minister of Justice interpreted this demand as follows: "What they want is our country" (Fine & Davis, 1990, p. 220).

In 1966, during the fifth anniversary of the declaration of South Africa as a republic, Prime Minister Verwoerd declared: "Although we are young, we are a nation in South Africa to whom all belong, and all of us can say with pride, this is our country" (Hepple, 1967, p. 185). At another occasion Verwoerd declared that "South Africa is a piece of Europe at the tip of the African continent" (1966, pp. 705-706). In other words, the apartheid system was more than an oppressive and exploitative legal structure with far-reaching social and economic consequences; it refused to accept Africans as legitimate inhabitants of the country. Segregation and its successor, apartheid, became state policies for mobilising the force and violence necessary to regiment black labour for the economic advancement of whites.

When the Dominions Office became the Commonwealth Relations Office in January 1947, *The Times* remarked the following in a lead article:

The historic word Empire, however it may have been misrepresented abroad, calls for no apology...It commemorates the
centuries in which the British have striven, first to work out the
conception of political liberty for themselves, and then to
communicate that liberty to all the peoples who share their
allegiance. The goal and achievement are now summed up in a
title that is proof against detractors, the British Commonwealth
of Nations. (Grierson, 1972, p. 298.)

What did the establishment of the British Commonwealth of Nations
amount to? According to Grierson (1972, p. 298),

[a]ny photograph of a Commonwealth Conference in the
immediate aftermath of the Second World War will supply the
answer—a small group of white men standing protectively
around the British monarch on the Buckingham Palace lawns.
"The Commonwealth is a closed group, said the Honourable
D.F. Malan, Prime Minister of the Union of South Africa, in the
spring of 1951. "The Commonwealth can...exist only as a result
of an essential identity of interest between all its members."

The irony of ironies is that Malan, a racist to the core, could define the
nature of the Commonwealth! South Africa, having been forced to leave
the Commonwealth, would, after the triumph of Mandela, rejoin it with a
markedly different perspective from that of Malan and kindred spirits.

The Inauguration of the Government of National Unity

"On 10 May 1994, amid an atmosphere that was joyous, moving and
solemn", writes Judd (1996, p. 410), "Nelson Mandela was sworn in as the
State President of the Republic of South Africa". The ceremony ended 350
years of white domination in South Africa. Mandela, in his calm and
dignified bearing, sometimes dissolving into small and spontaneous
displays of pure pleasure, swore "to be faithful to the Republic of South
Africa, so help me God". In his inaugural speech, the new State President
announced: "The time for healing of wounds has come. The moment to

bridge the chasms that divide us has come. The time to build is upon us."
He concluded with this promise: "Never, never and never again, shall it be
that this beautiful land will again experience the oppression of one by
another" (Judd, 1996, p. 410)

The end of white domination had enormous international significance. The event itself was witnessed by one of the largest gatherings of
world leaders of all political persuasions. President Fidel Castro of Cuba
(the long-time Achilles heel of the United States) received the loudest and
most prolonged ovation. He shared the stage with the United States first
lady, Hillary Clinton, and Vice President Gore. So did Libya's Moammar
Gaddafi and Yassar Arafat of the Palestinian Liberation Organisation—
two other Achilles heels of the United States. President Mandela shared
the stage with what seemed (to those who formulated the Nixon and
Reagan policies) a lost generation of "freedom fighters" if they were
charitable, or "terrorists" if they expressed their true feelings. The freedom
fighters included Walter Sisulu, Govan Mbeki, Joe Slovo, etc.

In the background were grim-faced, uniformed pillars of the soon to
be discarded Anglo-Afrikaner white supremacist state who stood "like
undertakers or godfathers" (Judd, 1996, p. 410) at the burial of the old
order.

> In a sense, the inauguration of Nelson Mandela, based on the
> irrefutable triumph of the African National Congress in the
> preceding general election, may be seen as one of the last and,
> arguably, one of the most dramatic and moving transfers of
> power within a country which had formerly been among the
> most prosperous, controversial, valued and bitterly contested
> within the British Empire and the Commonwealth. (Judd, 1996,
> p. 411.)

The "new" South Africa was born amidst profound relief, a palpable desire
for reconciliation, overwhelming optimism and genuinely high hopes for
the future. Even with all the birth pangs, the Government of National
Unity managed the transition with remarkable success. How did South
Africa escape what President Mbeki, on the occasion of the adoption of

The Republic of South Africa Constitution Act, called an "immoral and amoral past"? It has to do mainly with the character of the ANC and the nationalism that it represents, that is, the long tradition of building a "broad church" or "hegemonic organisation" that does not seek to define itself in exclusionist or narrow ideological terms (ANC, 1998, p. 4).

Furthermore, in 1990, when De Klerk released Mandela and un-banned all "subversive" organisations, neither side had defeated the other. "The corollary of this was that both sides continued to dispose of sufficient strength to inflict casualties on each other."

> Equally important, each side understood clearly that because the other had these possibilities, continuation of the conflict meant that whoever sought to assume a militant posture, summarised in the slogan "The Struggle Continues", would have to accept that they too would be severely bled and weakened, to the point where any victory they secured might very well result in them as victors having to preside over a wasteland. (Mbeki, 1998, p. 54.)

This then was the context of the much-maligned policy of reconciliation. Does reconciliation mean ignoring the injustices of the past and present? The answer to this question raises even more questions. For instance, could reconciliation have taken place without compromises, some of which are extremely painful to the victims? In an interview with the *Cape Times* (24 February 1997) Mbeki underlined the problem:

> Within the ANC, the cry was to "catch the bastards and hang them". But we realised that you could not simultaneously prepare for a peaceful transition while saying we want to catch and hang people. So we paid a price for the transition. If we had not taken this route, I don't know where the country would have been today. Had there been a threat of Nuremberg-style trials over members of the apartheid security establishment we would never have undergone the peaceful change.

Are these just excuses of a regime that has lost its way and betrayed the revolution? This issue was recently highlighted by Marais (1998, pp. 2, 5), who pronounced the negotiated transition of 1994 a failure because the ANC, instead of transforming the state, itself became assimilated into the status quo. "Already ossifying within the ANC", he wrote, "are trends that ally it to an agenda which conflicts fundamentally with the hopes and aspirations of the majority of South Africans". Even worse, Marais (1998) described the ANC as having sold out to neo-liberal policies.

> The neo-liberal features of the ANC government's macro-ventures and *supine postures* struck before the demands of corporate South Africa are, in such a reading, not anomalies. Spurring these developments is the tendency to judge the possibilities of national development on the basis of a deeply conservative and empirically questionable interpretation of globalization. Indeed, the post 1994 development seems to amplify Ellen Meiskin Wood's lament that: "it is not only that we do not know how to act against capitalism but that we are forgetting how to *think* against it".

According to Marais (1998, pp. 2-5):

> a survey of the ANC's history reveals telling legacies, which though submerged during the anti-apartheid struggle, have been pushed to the fore during the transition. Indeed, they raise the question whether a process of change centring on the deracialization of power and privilege (but without dismantling the structural foundations of inequality) might not be compatible with the organisation's historical discourse.

Has the ANC become an instrument of the African petty bourgeoisie? In a discussion document, *The Character of the ANC*, the ANC shows its awareness of the shifting class alliances:

> While the overwhelming majority of the poor, unemployed and marginalised are black, the last few years have seen the rapid development of a new black, upper middle-class. The gap

between the richest ten percent of blacks and the majority has grown very rapidly. Many ANC leading cadres have benefited directly from these new realities. The promotion of tens of thousands of formerly oppressed is a progressive development, but it does need us to be thoughtful on this issue. We must ensure that the ANC continues to represent the interests of the great majority, and not, narrowly, those of an emerging new elite. What is now needed is not a "the poorer the better" moralising outlook. Rather, we must ensure that both ideologically (in the values and policies we develop) and organisationally, the new powers, wealth and privileges do not become an end in themselves, but are used in the service of the national democratic struggle. The best means for ensuring this strategic objective is keeping the mass participatory character of the ANC. This is the best antidote to the danger of our organisation being transformed into a narrow, professionalised machine, enjoying support, but not empowering mass participation. (*Umrabulo* no. 3.)

Conclusion

This chapter was aimed at putting South Africa's transition to democracy into historical perspective. The task of transition is enormous. The travails of nation building in the modern world are well known. Following the end of white minority rule in 1994, the Government of National Unity began to define the character of the "new South Africa". A new flag and a new anthem, both made up of symbols of the former and the current regime, have been accepted. In building a nation, many traditions have to be taken into account. Many wounds are to be healed. In a multi-ethnic country like South Africa there are many sacred traditions and "illustrious" forebears to be taken into account. Nation building is a common project for the present and the future. The tragedy caused by the white minority was very much in the minds of those who crafted the South Africa Constitution, as evidenced by the institution of the Truth and Reconciliation Commission. The rationale was simple—*the capacity to feel shame for the crimes of the past had to be part of any healthy national consciousness.*

Looking at the achievements of the Government of National Unity one has to agree with Anthony Lewis who recently visited South Africa. He wrote in *The New York Times* of 16 August 1999:

> Of all countries, South Africa cannot be separated from its past. Not long ago it was a country where people were tortured and murdered because of their politics. A country where, because of their race, husbands were systematically separated from their wives. A country where a small minority, defined by race, held all economic and political power. Given that history, it is some-thing of a miracle that South Africa today is a normal country with social and economic problems. The problems are large, but they can be debated in freedom. Tyranny is only a memory.

Lewis touches on two important issues: that South Africa cannot forget its past and that though it is now a "normal" country, it has enormous socio-economic problems. The black-white economic disparities are a case in point. They are not an act of nature but were created by humans. Those who wished to create capitalist relations of production chose as their foundation stone the restriction of land ownership to the white minority and the exclusion of the black majority from any share in property. A similar sentiment was expressed in 1910 when the author of the *Gloucestershire Survey* stated without embarrassment the forth-right opinion that the "greatest evils to agriculture would be to place the labourer in a state of independence [i.e. by allowing him to have land] and thus destroy the indispensable gradations of society". "Farmers like manu-facturers", said another writer of the time, "require constant labourers—men who have no other means of support than their daily labour, men whom they can depend on" (Dobb, 1963, p. 222).

That wealth and poverty are two sides of the same coin in a capitalist society may have been forgotten in the developed world. But in South Africa the concentration of poverty amongst Africans is a constant reminder that white wealth was achieved through economic pressure, monopoly, political repression, usury and the expropriation of land of the indigenous owners. The South African white capitalist class is a creation, not of thrift and abstinence, as economists have traditionally depicted it, but of unconscionable hunger for African land and the attached economic and political benefits.

This raises the question of the suitability of affirmative action to create a just society. Since 1994, the ANC government's pursued an aggressive policy of equity in the labour market and passed new legislation to ensure that those who had been discriminated against in the past obtained a fair deal. The Employment Equity Act of 1999 is the cornerstone of the new affirmative action policy. Nevertheless, until the economy is democratised, South Africa's newly born freedoms will remain a chimera. This central truth has been obfuscated in South Africa in particular and in capitalist countries in general.

Indeed, the *capitalist market* is seen as the panacea of all economic ills. Moreover, after the collapse of communism in the Soviet Union, *socialism* was pronounced dead and *globalisation* became the new mantra. However, *globalisation* is emerging as the ideology of a new phase of unchecked capitalist hegemony. Indeed, current globalisation with its challenge to the nation state highlights that *under capitalism democracy has always been restricted to the political domain, while economic management has been held hostage by non-democratic private ownership of the means of production.* Such a democracy is incomplete, even by Western standards. Moreover, capitalist economic management is predicated upon the cultivation of egotistical and individualistic human functioning in a market place that crushes the sense of community and comradery.

References

Adam, H. (1971), *Modernising Racial Domination: South Africa's Political Dynamics,* Berkeley, University of California Press.

Adam, H. et al. (1997), *Comrades in Business: Post Liberation Politics in South Africa,* Cape Town, Tafelberg.

Allighan, G. (1961), *Verwoerd: The End*, Johannesburg, Purnella & Sons.

Arendt, H. (1962), *The Origins of Totalitarianism*, New York, Meridian Books.

Bryce, J. (1969), *Impression of South Africa,* New York, The New American Library.

Davenport, T.R.H. (1987), *South Africa: A Modern History,* 3rd ed., Johannesburg, MacMillan.

Dobb, M. (1963), *Studies in the Development of Capitalism,* New York, International Publishers.

Cairns, H. & Alan, C. (1965), *Prelude to Imperialism: British Reactions to Central African Society,* London, Routledge & Kegan Paul.

Calpin, G.H. (1968), *At Last we have Got our Country Back,* Cape Town, Buren Publishers.

De Kiewiet, C.W. (1943), *A History of South Africa: Social & Economic,* London, Oxford University Press.

Dutt, R.P. (1953), *The Crisis of Britain and the British Empire,* New York, International Publishers.

Farüredi, F. (1998), *The Silent War: Imperialism and the Changing Perception of Race,* New Brunswick, Rutgers University Press.

Fine, R. & Davis, D. (1990), *Beyond Apartheid: Labour and Liberation in South Africa,* Johannesburg, Ravan Press.

Gregory, T. (1962), *Ernest Oppenheimer and the Economic Development of South Africa,* London, Oxford University Press.

Grierson, E. (1972), *The Imperial Dilemma: The British Commonwealth and Empire 1775-1969,* London, Collins.

Houston, G. (1988), "Capital Accumulation, Influx Control, and the State in South Africa, 1970-1982", *Journal of Contemporary African Studies,* vol. 7, no. 1/2.

Huttenback, R.A. (1976), *Racism and Empire, White Settlers and Coloured Immigrants in the British Self-Governing Colonies 1830-1910,* Ithaca, Cornell University Press.

James, L. (1994), *The Rise and Fall of the British Empire,* London, Arbacus Press.

Jay, R. (1981), *Joseph Chamberlain, A Political Study,* Oxford, Clarendon Press.

Johnson, R.W. (1977), *How Long Will South Africa Survive?* New York, Oxford University Press.

Judd, D. (1997), *Empire: The British Imperial Experience from 1765 to the Present,* London, Fontana.

Kuper, L. & Smith, M.G. (1969), *Pluralism in Africa,* Berkeley, California University Press.

Kuper, L. (1977), *The Pity of it All: Polarisation of Racial and Ethnic Relations,* London, Duckworth.

Krüger, D.W. (1969), *The Making of South Africa; A History of the Union of South Africa 1910-1961,* Johannesburg, MacMillan.

Magubane, B.M. (1969), *The Political Economy of Race and Class in South Africa,* New York, Monthly Review Press.

Magubane, B.M. (1989), *From Soweto to Uitenhage: The Political Economy of the South African Revolution,* Trenton, Africa World Press.

Magubane, B.M. (1997), *The Making of a Racist State. British Imperialism and the Union of South Africa, 1875-1910,* Trenton, Africa World Press.

Marais, H. (1998), *South Africa: Limits of Change, the Political Economy of Transformation.* London, Zed Press.

Mbeki, T. (1998), *The Time Has Come,* Cape Town, Tafelberg Publishers.

Milner, L. (1933), *The Milner Papers,* Vol. II, (ed.), Cecil Headlam, London, Casell & Co.

Moore, B. Jr (n.d.), *Social Origins of Dictatorship and Democracy: Lord and Peasant in the Making of the Modern World,* Boston, Beacon Press.

Morris, J. (1978), *Farewell to the Trumpets. An Imperial Retreat,* London, Farber & Farber.

O'Dowd, H. (1978), "South Africa in Light of the Stages of Economic Growth", in Schlemmer, L. & Webster, E. (eds), *Change, Reform and Economic Growth,* Johannesburg, Ravan Press.

Plaatje, S.T. (1916), *Native Life in South Africa,* Johannesburg, Ravan Press.

Proudhon, P-J. (1924), quoted in *Demanding the Impossible. A History of Anarchism,* (ed.), Peter Marshall, London, Fontana.

Pryer, S.H. (1955), *Imperial Policy in South Africa 1902-1910,* London, Oxford University Press.

Quigley, C. (1981), *The Anglo-American Establishment. From Rhodes to Cliveden,* New York, Books in Focus.

Robinson, R. & Gallagher, J. (1961), *Africa and the Victorians: The Climax of Imperialism,* New York, Anchor Books.

Simpson, A. (1987), *Tycoons, Revolutionaries, and Apartheid,* New York, Pantheon.

Slovo, J. (1976), "South Africa—No Middle Road", *Southern Africa, the New Politics of Revolution,* (eds), Basil Davidson, Slovo & Wilkinson, Penguin Press.

Trollope, A. (1878), *South Africa, a Report of the 1878 Edition with Introduction and Notes by J.H. Davidson,* Cape Town, Balkana Press.

Van den Berg, P. (1967), *South Africa: A Study in Conflict,* Los Angeles, California University Press.

Williamson, J. (1933), *A Short History of the British Expansion,* New York, MacMillan.

Wilmot, A. (1895), *The Story of the Expansion of South Africa,* 2nd ed., London.

Wolpe, H. (1972), "Capitalism and Cheap Labour-power. From Segregation to Apartheid", *Economy and Society,* vol. 1, no. 4.

Wolpe, H. (1988), *Race, Class and the Apartheid State,* Amsterdam, Unesco Press.

Chapter 3

South Africa: A Transformative State?

Gregory Houston and Yvonne Muthien

"Transformation is this Government's reason for existence …" ("State of the Nation" address by President Mandela to parliament, 6 February 1998, quoted in Mandela, 1998.)

Introduction

The scale and depth of social transformation in South Africa in the 1990s can be gauged by comparison with the chilling reality of the 1980s: South Africa was on the brink of civil war, social infrastructure including schooling had collapsed, youths in the townships were rendering the country ungovernable, children watched the horror of burning "collaborators" alive in the streets and suffered the trauma of apartheid atrocities, security forces were lashing out in fear as the old order was falling apart and the regime could no longer rule in the old way, and the liberation forces were battle weary and the casualties were high. This political stalemate set the scene for the negotiated political settlement and historic compromise in the 1990s.

The democratic state that was born in South Africa in 1994 evolved through four transitional phases: the *pre-colonial state* characterised by the politics of conquest and incorporation, followed by the brutal land dispossession of the *colonial state* (1652-1909), the Constitution of the *segregationist state* premised on cheap labour (1910-1947) and the *apartheid regime* (1948-1993) characterised by the systematic destruction of indigenous social capital and black family and community life.

These transitional phases provide the landscape for a formidable challenge: the fundamental transformation of both state and society. This challenge sets apart state building in the democratic South Africa from state building elsewhere.

This chapter therefore focuses on the role of the state in social transformation, and the variety of ways in which the state carries out this particular role. The chapter further examines the construction of the necessary institutional capacity to fulfil the hegemonic project of transformation. The transformative state is thus a state whose programmatic activities are geared towards social transformation and is of necessity a strong and extended state. Examples of other transformative states include the post-revolutionary state in Russia, many post-colonial states and states undergoing transitions from authoritarianism to democracy.

The State as an Instrument of Social Transformation

The word "transformation" is found in virtually all African National Congress (ANC) documents, many speeches of ANC and government leaders, and most policy documents of the new government. These range from the ANC's policy guidelines for a democratic South Africa adopted at its 1991 national conference, *Ready to Govern*; an ANC discussion document released in November 1996, *The State and Social Transformation*; the ANC's draft strategy and tactics released before its December 1997 national conference, *All Power to the People*; to the speeches of former President Mandela and President Thabo Mbeki.

There are clear references to the important role of the state in social transformation in these documents and speeches. For example, the ANC declared that its policy document, *Ready to Govern*, was "structured so as to highlight the strong relationship between the creation of a political democracy and social and economic transformation". In this regard, the document outlines the ways in which the state could transform the state system, the economy, land ownership, the living conditions of all South Africans, education, the security apparatuses, and so on. Thus, the first step in the transformation of South Africa was the creation of a democratic state, through which political power could be used to transform state, society and the economy.

Likewise, in the opening sentence of *The State and Social Transformation* the ANC (1996) states the following: "The struggle for the social and economic transformation of the South African society is essentially the task of replacing the Apartheid state with a democratic one." It later adds that "the collective strengths and means concentrated in the democratic state to bring about the transformation of society" should not be destroyed by measures that "weaken the democratic state". In this document, the ANC clearly points out that the democratic state has a transformative responsibility.

The ANC's 1997 *Draft Strategy and Tactics* identified "the current period as one in which all levers of power must be transformed to serve the interests of the people". For the ANC, success in transformation will depend critically on the role of the state. The document points out that "by assuming the leading position in government, the democratic movement took formal control of the state machinery, with the possibility of starting, in earnest, to transform it to serve the new order".

The ANC (1997) identified the following main features of the new democratic state:

> All citizens should be guaranteed the right to elect a government of their choice, freedom of expression, freedom from discrimination, and other rights entrenched in the Constitution. They should have a government not only formally based on their will; but also one that is open and transparent, and one that consults and continually involves the people in policy formulation and implementation.

The ANC (1997) further characterised the new democratic state on the basis of specific tasks:

> It is a state which should mobilise the country's resources to expand the wealth base in the form of a growing economy. It is a state which should continually strive to improve people's quality of life. Such a state should ensure that all citizens are accorded equal opportunities within the context of correcting the historical injustice (of apartheid).

The *Draft Strategy and Tactics* also pointed out that this gives the democratic movement "immense possibilities to use the new situation as a beachhead to fundamentally transform society". One section of the draft, entitled "Programme of National Democratic Transformation in the Current Phase", outlines four main transformative tasks for the democratic state:

- *Democratisation and governance*: here the central aim is to create a democratic state underpinned by principles of "good governance".
- *Transformation of state machinery*: here the central aim is to change the doctrines, the composition and the management style of the civil service, judiciary, army, police and intelligence structures.
- *Economic transformation*: here the central aim is to promote growth and development in order to effect the redistribution of wealth and income in favour of those previously excluded from the economic mainstream.
- *Meeting social needs*: here the central aim of transformation is to improve the living conditions of the people, especially the poor.

The central role of the state in social transformation was acknowledged by President Thabo Mbeki in his address to the ANC Youth League congress in 1996:

> We consider the attainment of political democracy as a precondition for the continuing struggle aimed at the achievement of full social [and] economic emancipation for all the people. Commendable progress is already being made in putting building blocks aimed at ensuring the democratisation of the political order, the deracialisation and rebuilding of the economy, the public service, security organs of state, social services and cultural institutions. The success of our policy of reconciliation, national unity and nation-building also depends on the progress we make in addressing the political and socio-economic divisions in the conditions of life of the people.

Nelson Mandela's report to the 50th conference of the ANC in 1997 made reference to the need for a democratic state for the transformation of state, society and the economy in South Africa:

Having been elected into government, one of the first things that was very clear to us is that we cannot effectively use our access to political power to effect a fundamental transformation of our society by relying on the old apartheid state machinery. One of the central tasks of the democratic revolution is the abolition of the apartheid state and its replacement by a democratic state.

The transformative role of the state is also acknowledged in the speeches of various cabinet ministers. Former Labour Minister Tito Mboweni, for instance, stated the following in his speech on the labour budget vote in 1997:

> The government as a whole faces major tasks before it. ... The critical issue for us is that on an hourly, daily, weekly, monthly and yearly basis, we have to be hard at work, *laying the foundations for continuous processes of change and progressive transformation*. Achieving a better life for all is therefore not an event but a process. *That process has been joined by this first democratic government.* (Emphasis added.)

Likewise, at the launch of Curriculum 2005, the former Minister of Education, Sibusiso Bengu, stated:

> Because education and training are central activities of our society and are of vital interest to every family and to the health and prosperity of our national economy, the government is committed, as a matter of national importance, to changing education and training in South Africa.

The former Minister of Justice, Dullah Omar, pointed out at a media briefing in February 1997 that the mission of his department is directed at, amongst others, the following aim:

> To establish and maintain, in the spirit of the Constitution, and through a democratic process of transformation, a legitimate administration of justice which is efficient, accessible, accountable, just, user-friendly and representative of the South African community.

Finally, the transformative role of the state is explicitly recognised in most policy documents of the new democratic state. This is reflected in two ways. First, a number of these policy documents include the term "transformation" in their titles. These include the White Paper of the Department of Health, *Transformation of the Health System*, the *White Paper on Transformation of the Public Service*, the *White Paper on Transforming Service Delivery*, and *A Programme for the Transformation of Further Education and Training* (Education White Paper No. 4).

Second, a clear indication of the priority given to social transformation is found in most policy documents of government departments. For instance, in the introduction to the *White Paper on Education and Training in a Democratic South Africa,* the Minister of Education stated:

> This policy document describes the process of transformation in education and training which will bring into being a system serving all the people, our new democracy, and our Reconstruction and Development Programme.

He added that

> ... a priority for the national and provincial Ministries of Education is to create a transformative, democratic mission and ethos in the new departments of education which can completely supersede the separate identities of the former departments.

The Minister acknowledged that his "Ministry is acutely aware of the heavy responsibility it bears for managing the transformation and redirection of the system of education and training ...".

In the same vein, the focus of the defence force is clear. The *Defence in Democracy White Paper on National Defence for the Republic of South Africa* considers "transforming defence policy and armed forces in the context of the Constitution, national security policy, the RDP [Reconstruction and Development Programme], and international law on armed conflict" as the "overarching challenge". Transformation is seen as essential because of the history of the armed forces in the country, new strategic considerations in the international, regional and domestic environment and, most important, the advent of democracy in South Africa.

These examples clearly demonstrate the programmatic vision of various organs of the transformative state.

Implementing Social Transformation

The next section in this chapter is to examine the nature of the transformation of state and society in South Africa in terms of the four transformative tasks set for the state by the ANC.

Establishing Democratic Governance

The first challenge of transformation faced by the democratic state was democratisation and democratic governance. The starting point for an analysis of policy frameworks for transformation in these areas must be the ANC's Reconstruction and Development Programme, "an integrated, coherent socio-economic policy framework", which underpinned most government policies during the first years of the democratic state (ANC, 1994). Here the ANC included the *democratisation of state and society* among the main priorities of the democratic government. The ANC envisaged, amongst others, the following activities:

- Extending access to power and the right to exercise that power to all South Africans through the enfranchisement of all;
- Empowering the population through expanded rights, meaningful information and education, and an institutional network fostering representative, participatory and direct democracy;
- Creating a wide range of institutions of participatory democracy in partnership with civil society to facilitate direct democracy;
- Transforming the Public Service to make it more efficient, responsive, transparent and accountable while increasing the capacity of the public sector to deliver improved and extended public services to all South Africans; and
- Transforming the security apparatuses (defence force, police and intelligence services) from agents of oppression into effective servants of the community (ANC, 1994, pp. 120-121).

The Democratic State

The first democratic election on 27 April 1994 brought into being the first democratic state in South Africa. The first stage of democratic governance in South Africa was informed by the provisions of the interim Constitution. The interim Constitution set out the nature of citizenship and extended universal franchise to all citizens and permanent residents of the country. It also contained a Bill of Rights that enshrined the fundamental rights and freedoms of the subjects of the state. It established the Government of National Unity (GNU), run by a president, two executive deputy presidents and a cabinet drawn from the leading parties in the election. Political parties holding at least 80 seats (at least 20% of representation) in the national assembly were entitled to an executive deputy president, and all parties holding at least 20 seats (5% of representation) in the national assembly were entitled to ministers and deputy ministers (Venter, 1994; Basson, 1994).

The interim Constitution provided for a bicameral Parliament (a national assembly consisting of 400 members and a Senate consisting of 90 members, ten from each province). These two houses jointly functioned as a constitutional assembly with the task of drafting and passing a new Constitution. Parliament had to make laws in accordance with the Constitution. This represented a fundamental change from earlier Constitutions based upon the principle of parliamentary supremacy. The Constitution is regarded as the supreme law of the country and would bind all organs of state at all levels of government, including Parliament. The Constitutional Court had jurisdiction to inquire into the constitutionality of any bill or act.

The members of the legislature were elected on a proportional representation basis, half from national lists and half from provincial lists of party candidates. This system restricted voters to choosing the political party of their choice, which contrasted with the racially exclusive constituency-based electoral process of the previous era.

Initially, the Senate under the interim Constitution functioned as a legislative organ. However, its transformation into the National Council of Provinces promoted a second broad function: intergovernmental co-operation and co-ordination. Hence members of the council became responsible to the provincial and the national legislatures, since they participated at both levels.

Nine provinces were established under the interim Constitution. Each had its own legislature that, as the legislative authority in the province, had the power to make laws for the province in accordance with the interim Constitution. The provincial legislatures were not empowered to infringe upon the provisions of the Constitution. The laws made by a provincial legislature applied only within the territory of the province concerned. The interim Constitution provided for provincial legislatures of between 30 and 100 members elected in terms of the system of proportional representation. The premier was the head of the executive council, which comprised members holding portfolios from all parties holding at least 10% of the seats in the provincial legislature.

Metropolitan, urban and rural local governments, each category having differentiated powers, functions and structures, could be established under the provisions of the interim Constitution. Local governments were not autonomous and could regulate their affairs only within the limits prescribed by law. Consequently, Parliament and provincial legislatures could prescribe the limits to local government powers and functions. The elections for the first democratic local government structures were held on 1 November 1995, bringing into being the third tier of democratic government in the new South Africa.

One of the most significant changes from the previous era was the introduction of a Constitutional Court. The Constitutional Court had jurisdiction as a court of final instance over all matters relating to the interpretation, protection and enforcement of the provisions of the Constitution. It had to determine the constitutionality of national and provincial laws as well as defend the fundamental rights of individuals. Furthermore, the interim Constitution empowered the Constitutional Court as well as ordinary courts of law to test all actions of the executive as well as acts of Parliament. These powers of the Constitutional Court abolished the supremacy of Parliament as a law-making body as well as placed a limit on the power of government in exercising a governance role.

Public Participation

The new political environment led to the introduction of a political culture radically different from that which marked the apartheid era. Perhaps the most significant example of the new political culture was the Constitutional Assembly Project (CAP), which aimed at drawing the bulk of the population into Constitution writing. Underlying the CAP was the ANC's earlier commitment to democratic participation. It enabled non-governmental institutions and organisations to participate in decision making.

The aim of the CAP was to make Constitution writing as inclusive as possible. This was done in a number of ways. Six theme committees were set up by the Constitutional Assembly to consider and collate submissions from a wide variety of stakeholders, including organs of civil society, ordinary individuals, political parties and all those who had an interest in contributing to the new Constitution. Popular participation in Constitution writing was made possible by encouraging the population to make submissions in their own languages, resulting in some 2,5 million written submissions. This was supplemented by thousands of public meetings in almost every town and village to give people an opportunity to express their views on what should be included in the new Constitution. People were encouraged to attend these meetings through advertisements on television and radio. Popular awareness of the issues involved was further encouraged by the distribution of a regular newspaper, *Constitutional Talk*, a television talk show by the same name, and numerous radio programmes dealing with Constitution making (Hlophe & Naidoo, 1996).

Public Accountability

Public accountability is central to democratic governance. In the system of parliamentary democracy, the legislature constitutes the supreme authority as the elected representatives. The executive derives its authority from the legislature and is accountable to the legislature for its actions. The effectiveness of the legislature in holding government accountable depends on the quality of the elected representatives in terms of professional expertise and direct accountability to constituencies.

Specialised committees (e.g. portfolio committees) and the opening of hearings and proceedings of parliamentary committees to the public as well as the provision of research support enhance the capacity of the legislature to scrutinise government. The interests of governance and public scrutiny have to be balanced, though. In the first two years of democratic rule in South Africa, the Portfolio Committees tackled their responsibility of holding government accountable with considerable fervour. The newly elected representatives also distrusted the old guard civil service as the initiators of legislation. Legislation was therefore duly scrutinised, leading to considerable delays and constraining the ability of the new executive to enact new policy. The pressure of the parliamentary time schedule together with appeals to comradely support improved co-operation between the executive and the legislature in the same party. This set the stage for classic oppositional politics within the legislature, with the opposition spearheading the drive for public scrutiny and the majority party in the legislature "defending" the interests of the executive.

That there is robust opposition to and scrutiny of government actions cannot be doubted. Overall the transparent functioning of portfolio committees and the dedication of a key number of parliamentary activists in committee work bode well in terms of accountability.

Institutions Supporting Democracy

The South African Constitution has enshrined a number of institutions supporting constitutional democracy. These include the Public Protector, the Auditor-General, the Public Service Commission, the Human Rights Commission, the Commission for Gender Equality, the Independent Electoral Commission and the Commission for the Promotion and Protection of the Rights of Cultural, Religious and Linguistic Communities. The independence and impartiality of these institutions are enshrined in the Constitution.

The Auditor-General has the standing and resources to fulfil its functions, and has elicited unqualified parliamentary support. Indeed Parliament sanctioned the behaviour of the executive in infringing on the autonomy of the Auditor-General on two occasions. In both instances the ministers were cautioned by Parliament against contravening rule 99. This level of parliamentary protection has not been demonstrated with the other commissions, who equally battle to gain government co-operation and compliance in the exercise of their functions.

The provisions of the Promotion of Access to Information Act, which safeguards whistle-blowing and independent access to public information as well as institutions buttressing democracy, bode well in terms of accountability.

Transforming State Machinery

The second challenge of transformation, the transformation of state machinery, is to change the doctrines, composition and management style of the civil service, judiciary, army, police and intelligence structures. Because of space constraints, we will focus on the transformation of the Public Service Commission (PSC) and the South African National Defence Force (SANDF).

Civil Service Reform

A number of policy documents were developed to address the transformation of the Public Service and to increase the capacity of the public sector to deliver improved and extended public services to all South Africans. The *White Paper on the Transformation of the Public Service* (WPTPS), published in 1995, identified

> the need to reverse the systematic exclusion of Black people and women from positions of influence within the public service that had characterised the apartheid system, as well as the systematic exclusion of people with disabilities from positions at all levels within the service (Presidential Review Commission (PRC), 1998, para. 4.2.5.1).

The WPTPS included among the main requirements for reform and transformation a change in the racial and gender composition of the workforce in the Public Service, and the equitable inclusion of people with disabilities. It stipulated that in order to address this, within four years at least 50% of managers in all departments must be from the black communities and 30% of new recruits to the middle and senior management echelons should be women; and within ten years, people with disabilities should comprise 2% of public service personnel. In addition, the *White Paper on a New Employment Policy for the Public Service* (WPNEPPS), published in October 1997, stipulated that

> [a] professional, impartial Public Service which is representative of all sections of society is essential to efficient and effective government and the achievement of South Africa's democratic, economic and social goals (WPNEPPS, para. 1.1).

A representative public service is also necessary because it will include public servants who are "able to relate closely to every section of South Africa's diverse society; public servants who are familiar with people's needs, can communicate in their languages, and can respond to their concerns" (WPNEPPS, para. 3.13).

At the beginning of 1994, only 2%, 1%, 3% and 5% of the managers in the Public Service were African, coloured, Indian or women respectively (PRC, Table 4.1). White males dominated the management echelons while African workers, who constituted 70% of public sector workers, were located largely in categories defined as unskilled. However, the Presidential Review Commission (PRC), charged with conducting a review of the Public Service, stated in 1997 that despite the challenges facing the new government, remarkable progress had been made in transforming the Public Service, including national and provincial structures which had "become remarkably more representative in a relatively short space of time" (para. 2.1.3). Equal access to employment opportunities and affirmative action strategies were the main measures for increasing the social mobility of previously disadvantaged communities.

In late 1997 black people accounted for 79% of the Public Service while 49% of public servants were women. Thirty-eight per cent of managers at director level and above were black, and 11% were women, of whom four were employed as directors-general (WPNEPPS, para. 3.9). Yet the various departments emphasised different aspects of transformation: representivity, accountability, service delivery or institutional change (paras. 2.5.1 and 4.2.1).

The PRC points out that the Department of Health (DoH) has emphasised changes in human resource management, leading to a change in the profile of managers in the department from 99,6% white males prior to 1994, to 50% in 1997. All the finance-related departments (Finance, State Expenditure and the South African Revenue Service) have experienced difficulties in transforming the racial, gender and occupational profiles of their personnel. The ratio in the Department of Finance, for example, is approximately 60% white and 40% black, with most of the latter falling below the managerial echelons. This profile is also evident in other departments that require "professional" skills for which they compete with the private sector. The departments of Justice and Foreign Affairs have avoided the introduction of well-articulated affirmative action policies and strategies, preferring instead to rely on a "flexible approach" or "placement guidelines", which have resulted in few changes to the profile of their departments.

Finally, the *Batho Pele* (meaning "people first") *White Paper on Transforming Service Delivery* commits public servants to consultation, service standards, fairness, efficiency, courtesy, access, information, transparency, redress and value for money at customer desks, and to an annual departmental report to citizens on meeting service delivery targets. This contrasts sharply with the apartheid-era civil service, which was, essentially, "constructed and managed for the purpose of regulation, control and constraint, and not for those of community empowerment and development".

The most far-reaching act of reform in the civil service was the unbundling of the PSC and the separation of its executive and oversight functions.

The PSC role of checking on administration and the political executive finds its origins in the English civil service of the mid-19th century. Its task was to uphold the merit principle and guard against cronyism and nepotism, as well as to protect civil service employees from arbitrary political abuse. The South African Public Service Commission, however, assumed both the functions of establishing the rules of administration and checking the exercise thereof (Muthien, 1996; Motala, 1997). Moreover, the commission held all executive powers in administration, with the power to refuse ministerial requests for staff and salary increases, and for changes to conditions of service and organisational design.

The unbundling of the PSC was an attempt to democratise the state from within. Policy functions were located with a line-function ministry; executive decision making was devolved to cabinet ministers and greater managerial autonomy was afforded to line-function agencies; and the PSC assumed a purely oversight function. The contradictions of its previously fused functions, however, created confusion, with neither the executive nor the legislature accepting guardianship of the body. The ability of these institutions to serve as a check on the executive is dependent on the levels of co-operation it secures and the ultimate sanction that Parliament can exercise to secure public accountability.

There can be no doubt that a professional civil service, insulated from political power, serves democracy best and that the distance from direct democracy in itself constitutes part of accountability and constraint of political power. The inherent problem of democratising state administration is vested in reconciling the political imperatives of public accountability with the managerial imperatives of administrative flexibility and responsiveness (Balfour, 1997; Ruscio, 1997).

Security

Various government departments set out policy frameworks to transform the security apparatuses from agents of oppression into effective servants for empowerment. For example, among the main transformative priorities of the SANDF are the consolidation of democracy, the achievement of social justice, economic development and a safe environment as well as a substantial reduction in crime, violence and political instability. Civil-military relations, under the terms of the defence white paper, are to be transformed by making the SANDF a non-partisan military force, subject to control and oversight by a duly elected and appointed civilian authority, and obliged to perform its functions in accordance with the law. The white paper also committed the SANDF to reflect the composition of the country by encouraging affirmative action and introducing equal opportunity programmes.

The challenge of transforming the defence force has been steered by the need to ensure that the military's role and conduct are consistent with democracy, the Constitution and international norms, and consistent with the need to develop an approach to security that is not reliant on the use of force, but places emphasis on the achievement of social justice, economic development and a safe environment (Nathan, 1995). Therefore, in order to instill democratic values throughout the SANDF, the military and the civilian functions were separated through the establishment of the Defence Secretariat and the Civic Education Programme. The SANDF has also become more representative of the South African population: It has 69% black members, including 13 black generals, one of whom is the first black female general, and 19% female members.

Among the objectives the Department of Safety and Security set out in its white paper was "the development of appropriate policing services in South Africa" through "a shift from an inheritance of authoritarian law and order responses, to a broader concept of safety and security for all citizens". In particular, it was recognised "that policing in a democracy requires professional law enforcement which does not infringe upon human rights".

Public Policy Making

A significant feature of transformation during the first term of office of the democratic government has been the democratisation of public policy-making processes. In particular, a shift occurred from semi-secretive, technocratic and authoritarian policy making to more public and accountable policy making.

The new policy-making approach was a result of the new government's active interest in transforming the relationship between organs of civil society and the state. Introducing participatory democracy, accountability and transparency, the approach was aimed at bringing about fundamental changes in the policy environment in South Africa. Policy making/formulation was to be substantially more open to public input than under the racist and authoritarian apartheid state. The substantive change in policy formulation and implementation penetrated several other areas. Examples of a broadening base for public input in policy making include the manner in which ministries develop policies and processes through public participation in the legislative process. These include the publication of green and white papers to encourage public submissions, and the holding of conferences and workshops to include a wide variety of stakeholders in discussions on specific policy issues. The legislative process provides for a wide range of opportunities for the public to participate in policy making. These include the consideration of written submissions, the holding of public hearings and the public's interaction with parliamentary committees.

Perhaps one of the most significant features of the new policy making is the proliferation of statutory and other consultative bodies that aim at involving civil society in policy making. Examples of these at the local level include local development forums, local water committees and community police forums. What these demonstrate is a transformation from top-down decision making to a process driven from the bottom.

An important new consultative body is the National Economic Development and Labour Council (NEDLAC). A statutory body, it was established as a forum for consensus seeking and inclusive decision making on national economic and social issues by representatives of organised labour, business, community organisations and the government. The government is committed to placing all issues or laws relating to labour, social or economic policy before NEDLAC prior to introducing them in Parliament or implementing them. NEDLAC's main objectives are to reach consensus and conclude agreements which increase participation of all major stakeholders in shaping policy on economic, labour and development issues, and which promote sustainable economic growth and greater social equity in the community and the workplace.

Economic Transformation

The third challenge of social transformation is economic transformation. However, the ANC has not been consistent in its policy on the role of the state in economic transformation. It has moved from initial commitment to public ownership, albeit in a limited form in the Freedom Charter, compromise around a "mixed economy" and "growth through redistribution" to the current emphasis on growth as a necessary condition for both employment and redistribution. The ANC's Freedom Charter included a number of clauses that were aimed at economic transformation. For example, it proposed that "the mineral wealth of our country, the banks and monopoly industry shall be transferred to the ownership of the people as a whole". By the time the ANC entered into negotiations, however, it had moved away from a commitment to nationalisation to accept a limited role for the state in a mixed economy. Thus, neither the RDP nor the government's Growth, Employment and Redistribution (GEAR) macroeconomic policy framework, unveiled in June 1996, provided a policy framework for economic transformation. Indeed, the focus shifted from redistribution so as to promote growth, to growth and development so as to effect the redistribution of wealth and income. The changed focus led to the introduction of policy initiatives around affirmative action, black economic empowerment, support for small and medium-sized enterprises and support for black farmers.

GEAR emphasises the redistributive thrust of the reprioritisation of government expenditure and the role of social and sectoral policies in meeting basic needs, improving services available to the poor and building social infrastructure. GEAR affirms that growth needs to be translated into redistribution of incomes and opportunities through appropriate social development policies and programmes, and deliberate promotion of employment creation. GEAR envisages increased state expenditure on infrastructure as a growth enhancer. Privatisation is seen as a means of reducing debt. At the same time, the government must play a central redistributive role through such policies as land reform and the provision of basic social services (Donaldson, 1997; Nattrass, 1996).

GEAR, however, indicates a commitment to market-orientated economic reform in line with what has been termed the "Washington consensus", a type of economic reform demanded by the World Bank and the International Monetary Fund. These include fiscal discipline, to which the government has responded by reducing the budget deficit, reallocating state expenditure to health, education and infrastructure, broadening the tax base and reducing marginal tax rates, abolishing the dual exchange rate in 1995 and phasing out exchange controls, securing property rights, increasing deregulation, trade liberalisation and privatisation, and removing barriers to direct foreign investment and financial liberalisation. In short, it appears that the government has restricted its role to setting the framework within which a free market can operate (Calitz, 1997).

The poor track record of GEAR in delivering on economic growth, job creation and social upliftment led to severe criticism by the ANC's alliance partners, COSATU and the SACP. By the end of 1998 the ANC was forced to concede that GEAR failed to live up to its promise and to re-introduce the RDP as the government's primary development agenda.

Affirmative Action

The apartheid legacy of racial and gender discrimination is also evident in private sector employment patterns. Over one-third of women is self-employed and 70% of women workers in the formal sector earn less than R500 a month. Only 1% of disabled people are employed in the formal sector of the economy. African and women workers are concentrated in low-wage, low-skill employment, while white men dominate the high-paying managerial and executive positions. The average ratio of the salaries of managing director to the wages of the lowest paid worker is about 100:1. In addition, there are huge disparities in the gradations between unskilled workers, semi-skilled workers and artisans; blue and white-collar workers; and production and technical/professional employees.

The main measure introduced to promote affirmative action in the private sector is the Employment Equity Act. This Act has two objectives: to implement measures to eliminate discrimination in employment and to pro-vide guidelines for companies to promote occupational equity by encoura-ging the equal representation of black and women workers and the disabled. The Act calls on companies to draw up "equity plans" that include numerical goals (for increasing the number of blacks, women and disabled workers so as to approximate their proportional representation in the total South African population), a timetable for implementing "equity plans", mecha-nisms to bring about equity and union-management consultation procedures (Ray, 1998).

Black Economic Empowerment

The government has facilitated black economic empowerment through the Affirmative Procurement Policy according to which government contracts under R2 million are allocated to firms owned by disadvantaged groups. This has resulted in an increase in the share of procurement by affirmative enterprises to an estimated 37% of the total value of government contracts at the end of 1997. The government also committed itself to the establishment of a National Empowerment Fund to provide funds for the previously disadvantaged groups to acquire a stake in restructured public enterprises. However, the fund is only expected to have a visible impact in 2001.

The state has also developed a policy framework for assisting small, medium and micro non-farm enterprises (SMMEs), which are generally dominated by the historically disadvantaged communities. SMMEs are viewed as key vehicles for attaining a number of objectives, including job creation and income redistribution. The government has established a number of institutions to implement the national SMME development strategy by means of the Ntsika Enterprise Promotion Agency and Khula Enterprise Finance. Ntsika focuses largely on the establishment of a network of local business service centres to deliver non-financial support to SMMEs, including support to strengthen their competitiveness. Khula began its operations at the beginning of 1997, but the value of loans made has not been sufficient to meet SMME needs.

Government initiatives for redressing racial imbalances in access to agricultural opportunities are largely mentioned in the *White Paper on Agriculture* published in 1995. The White Paper recommends that special attention be given to the needs of small-scale farmers to ensure equitable access to markets; that access to agricultural financing be broadened to include previously disadvantaged and beginner farmers; and that access to existing institutional infrastructure such as the co-operative system be broadened to include those previously denied access. However, one such initiative, the Broadening Access to Agriculture Trust (BATAT), envisaged as a supply-side initiative aimed at widening access to agriculture for those who previously lacked access, failed to materialise. Two of the main development finance institutions, the Land Bank and the Industrial Development Corporation (IDC), have committed themselves to putting greater emphasis on small and medium-firm development and black empowerment in industrial agricultural concerns.

Meeting Social Needs

The fourth and final challenge of transformation, namely meeting social needs, is geared towards improving the living conditions of the people, especially the poor. The eradication of racial inequalities in access to social services is particularly evident here.

Lack of basic amenities such as electricity, flush toilets and piped water can be linked to poverty. In 1993, only 22,7% of poor households had access to electricity, 19,5% had access to flush toilets and 28,4% had access to piped water. At the end of 1994 almost 50% of poor households still had no electricity supply. The backlogs in education infrastructure were enormous, with just under half of all schools having no electricity and 24% having no access to water in 1996. The total shortage of classrooms countrywide in 1996 was 57 499. Large backlogs exist in the provision of health care facilities, requiring a sustained average 3,3% annual increase in the health care budget for ten years (or 6,9% for five years), over and above the increase necessary to service the needs of the growing population who use the existing hospitals. The housing backlog at the beginning of 1994 was estimated at three million units.

The RDP provides the basis for various policy frameworks aimed at meeting social needs. The ANC hoped to meet the need for jobs, land, housing, water, electricity, telecommunications, transport, a clean and healthy environment, nutrition, health care and social welfare. This was to be achieved through programmes to redistribute land to landless people; ten years of compulsory education for all school-goers; building over one million houses; providing clean water and sanitation to all; electrifying 2,5 million homes; and providing access for all to affordable health care and telecommunications (ANC, 1994, pp. 7-8). Many of these programmes were covered in policy documents of various government departments.

For example, the *White Paper on South African Land Policy* introduced three major land reform programmes: the redistribution of land to meet the need for land and to reverse the racial geography of the country; the restitution of land rights to restore land which was forcibly taken from people during the apartheid era; and tenure reform to provide secure land tenure and to resolve conflicting rights and claims to the same land.

Apartheid accounted for unequal access to land asset and resources. Hence the overwhelming majority of people were restricted to owning land in approximately 13% of the country. Land redistribution, which has been facilitated by the R15 000 subsidy per household for the acquisition of land, resulted in the transfer of 324 486 hectare of land to just over 20 000 households and 100 000 people by the end of 1997. The ANC promised to redistribute 30% of agricultural land within the first five years of the implementation of the land redistribution programme. By September 1998, however, only 1% of all agricultural land had been redistributed, leaving the government with just under a year to redistribute the remaining 29% (Tilley, 1998). Restitution of land rights proved even more difficult to effect and only 18 restitution claims had been resolved by the end of 1997. This resulted in approximately 27 000 people recovering about 150 000 hectares that had been taken from them during the apartheid period. Finally, the Extension of Security of Tenure Act was passed in 1997 to provide secure tenure for the approximately six million black households located on white-owned farms (Bond & Khosa, 1999). Among the most important constraints on delivery in this area were administrative capacity, particularly at the local level, an inadequate budget to implement the policies and the limited availability of state land and the difficulty to dispose of it.

The Department of Housing aimed to approach the housing challenge by:

- stabilising the housing environment in order to ensure maximal utilisation of state housing expenditure and mobilising private sector investment;

- facilitating the establishment or directly establishing a range of institutional, technical and logistical housing support mechanisms to enable communities to improve their housing circumstances on a continuous basis;

- mobilising private savings (whether by individuals or collectively) and housing credit at scale and on a sustainable basis, and simultaneously ensuring adequate protection for consumers;

- providing subsidy to disadvantaged individuals to assist them to gain access to housing;

- rationalising institutional capacities in the housing sector within a sustainable long-term institutional framework;

- facilitating the speedy release and servicing of land;

- co-ordinating and integrating public sector investment and inter-vention on a multi-functional basis.

In the area of housing delivery, the 1994 *White Paper on Housing* aimed to give all South Africans access to a permanent residential structure with secure tenure and adequate water, sanitation, waste disposal and electricity services. A core element of the housing programme was the subsidy scheme for land, housing and infrastructure to those earning less than R3 500 per month. This was supplemented by the expansion of housing credit to the poor, with the government assuming some of the risk inherent in lending to low-income groups (mortgage indemnity schemes) (Bond & Khosa, 1999). By the end of 1997 over 400 000 houses had been completed or were under construction, while approximately 700 000 housing subsidies had been allocated. This has resulted in the provision of housing to 1,2 million South Africans since 1994 (*President's Report to the Nation*, 1998). There was, however, shortfall on the government's target of one million new houses by the end of the first term of the ANC-led government in 1999.

The Department of Health hoped to meet basic needs by, amongst others, promoting equity, accessibility and utilisation of health services; extending the availability and ensuring the appropriateness of health services; and developing health promotion activities. To these ends the department aimed, first, to increase access to integrated health care services for all South Africans, focusing on the rural, peri-urban and urban poor and the aged, with an emphasis on vulnerable groups; establish health care financing policies to promote greater equity between people living in rural and urban areas, and between people served by the public and private health sectors; and distribute health personnel throughout the country in an equitable manner. Second, the department aimed to establish a district health system in which all communities are covered by a basic health unit which offers an essential package of care; ensure a functioning referral system at the primary, secondary and tertiary levels; improve access to comprehensive health services; ensure the universal availability of high-quality, low-cost essential drugs; and ensure that every South African develops his or her potential fully, with the support of community-based nutrition promotion activities (Bond & Khosa, 1999).

The Department of Health has transformed access to health care, where discrimination was still rife. It also extended health care to rural populations. This included the amalgamation of 14 health departments into a single health system; the reduction of disparities in health service delivery; increased access to integrated services based on primary health care principles; and prioritising the care of children and women. Government spending on health increased by 24% in 1996/1997, 6% in 1997/1998, and 1% in 1998/1999 (Bond & Khosa, 1999). Among the main priorities of the democratic government's health budget was a clinic-building programme, the strengthening of primary health care and the elimination of charges at clinics.

The Constitution guarantees the right of equal access to public primary health care services for every South African. The principle of equal access to primary health care services requires the equalisation of geographical access and quality of services throughout the country. This has led to the building of 504 new clinics in previously under-served areas since 1994, thereby expanding access to a further five million people. Primary health care services are provided free of charge although people who can afford to pay for prescribed medicines are required to do so. On the negative side, however, hospitals are being closed and rationalised and their health workers retrenched. This is in large part due to the reprioritisation of budget allocations in favour of primary health care. In addition, clinics are still not widely used, probably due to lack of easy access and the poor quality of services, while a significant proportion of poor households continue to use hospitals and private doctors (May, 1988). Furthermore, the reprioritisation of funding was initially implemented by diverting health resources from better-served provinces to under-served provinces. This has been replaced by unconditional block grants to provinces and thus the termination of central control over health resource allocation.

The apartheid era accounted for unequal racial access to education and training in the form of separate education and training systems and unequal funding of these systems. During the apartheid era, for example, government expenditure on education was also allocated disproportionally to benefit first whites, then Indians and coloureds and, lastly, Africans. For instance, in 1983/1984 the government spent R234 per African pupil, or 14% of the subsidy of R1 654 per white pupil. In 1993/1994 primary school pupils in the former homelands received only 21% of the average amount spent on white primary school pupils.

Education is a right guaranteed by the Constitution. Hence the new government committed itself to providing free and compulsory education for all children up to Grade 7. Public expenditure on education increased by 25% in 1996/1997, 7% in 1997/1998 and 4% in 1998/1999. In part, the increase was directed at addressing the racial backlog in education expenditure. Education policies are designed, amongst other things, to redress the legacy of racial inequalities in education provision, and to build a new and unified national system based on equity and redress. Among the most important policies and programmes are those which deal with norms and standards for school funding and the specific needs of the schools of previously disadvantaged communities. Public schools range from the historically well-resourced suburban schools to sparsely equipped and overcrowded rural and township schools. Almost all the pupils in the well-resourced schools succeed in obtaining their senior certificates, and an impressive proportion qualifies for admission to higher education. The majority of pupils at the under-resourced schools drop out prematurely or fail to obtain senior certificates, and only a small minority win entrance to higher education. The result is gross inequalities in access to employment opportunities. Providing equal access to education is one way of reducing barriers to the social mobility of members of the previously disadvantaged communities. The development of norms and standards for school funding is aimed at ensuring that the well-resourced suburban schools carry some of the costs that used to be met through public funding. However, the richest 12,5% of the population continue to utilise

23,4% of public education resources while the poorest 53% of the population receive about 40% (Creamer, 1998).

Government expenditure is a reflection of political priorities and objectives. With its focus on redistribution, the current government enhances the welfare of disadvantaged groups in the society through its provision of goods and services to these groups. In this way a close link is established between the budget and policies towards redistribution, poverty alleviation and the eradication of inequalities between gender, racial and ethnic groups and regions (PRC, para. 5.2.1). Thus the provision of access to basic services in previously disadvantaged groups has become a major directive in public expenditure.

Since taking power in 1994 the ANC-led government has increased expenditure on social services. Expenditure on welfare and social grants increased to R19 million in the 1998/1999 budget, and expenditure on health services increased to R23 billion and that on education to R45 billion, but expenditure on housing programmes and subsidies remained at R3,5 billion. Total government social expenditure increased by 15,3% in the 1998/1999 budget (Bond & Khosa, 1999).

Social grants reach some three million South Africans, and in many cases provide the sole source of income for poor households. Public expenditure on welfare and social grants increased by 13% in 1996/1997, 13% in 1997/1998, and 7% in 1998/1999. In part, the increased expenditure was due to the introduction of parity in grants for the previously disadvantaged communities. These included old-age pensions, child maintenance grants and disability grants, which were previously set at different levels for the different racial groups. In addition, the Department of Welfare extended the application of child maintenance grants to blacks in rural areas, who were previously excluded from the system.

Despite these efforts, material and social inequalities still largely follow racial lines. The most glaring indication of the persistence of racial inequalities is income inequality. The poorest 40% of households (mostly African), equivalent to 52% of the population, account for less than 10% of total income, while the richest 10% of households (mostly white), equivalent to 6% of the population, account for 40% of total income. The

Human Development Index (HDI) can be used to demonstrate racial disparities in human development. In mid-1998 the HDI of the black population was equal to that of the poorest performing countries, while whites scored on a level equal to that of the best performing countries.

Conclusion

South Africa has been a transformative state since 1994. This is demonstrated by the recognition of the transformative role of the state in ANC documents, by ANC and government leaders, as well as in policy documents of the ANC; the development of policy frameworks designed to bring about the transformation of state, society and the economy; and the activities of the state which led to social transformation.

However, in assessing the sustainability of South Africa's fledgling democracy, it may be worthwhile to reflect on the country's institutional and social strengths as well as weaknesses. The fledgling democracy has delivered the franchise to the majority of South Africans, so brutally disenfranchised under colonialism and apartheid. The key challenge for the new democratic government is to deliver on the promise of economic empowerment by improving the material well-being of the impoverished majority.

The new South Africa augurs well in terms of formal democracy, i.e. the key pillars of democratic consolidation are in place:

- A multi-party parliamentary system is operative and its election processes are considered to be procedural and substantially free and fair.

- A strong sense of constitutionalism and the rule of law prevail, supported by various institutions buttressing democracy, including the Constitutional Court, the Human Rights Commission, the Commission on Gender Equality, the Auditor-General, the Public Service Commission and the Public Protector.

- Mechanisms of accountability, which enshrines the right to public information, force government to be transparent and expose acts of corruption among public officials. The Constitution moreover enshrines the values of good governance and clean administration in public affairs.

- There is a professional civil service, which functions on the basis of constitutional values such as impartiality, dedicated service delivery and fiscal accountability.

- Mechanisms for citizen participation in government are in place, including public hearings of parliamentary committees and public participation in policy making, though effective citizen participation requires both an informed public and a vibrant civil society.

- An integrated and highly developed economic infrastructure with considerable potential for economic prosperity has been established.

However, the continuation of systematic inequality and material deprivation prompts us to revisit current debates on state-civil society relations, in particular debates on economic democracy. The imperatives of development in highly unequal societies demand a democratic state that is strong, expansive and committed to a clear development trajectory, a notion which rests somewhat uncomfortably with the values of a liberal democracy and free market ideologies.

Among the challenges facing the new democratic state are the following:

- The new democracy needs to institutionalise transformation and reform. A plethora of new policy statements in the form of green and white papers has been issued, but in many instances institutional infrastructure and budgetary measures need to be aligned with the new policy objectives and the concomitant programmes.

- Economic empowerment has been limited to a few beneficiaries, the so-called "transitory bourgeoisie". Hence the base of economic empowerment needs to be widened.

- Reconciliation cannot be achieved without social justice, which includes redress and improving the material well-being of the majority. While the country is well endowed in terms of democratic institutions and infrastructure, the lack of delivery in terms of economic democracy could well jeopardise the newly found democracy.

References

African National Congress (1991), *Ready to Govern*, African National Congress, Johannesburg.

African National Congress (1994), *The Reconstruction and Development Programme*, Umanyano Publications, Johannesburg.

African National Congress (1996), *The State and Social Transformation*, African National Congress, Johannesburg.

African National Congress (1997), *All Power to the People*, African National Congress, Johannesburg.

Balfour, D. (1997), "Reforming the Public Sector: The Search for a New Tradition", *Public Administration Review*, vol. 57, no. 5, September/October.

Basson, D. (1994), *South Africa's Interim Constitution: Text and Notes*, Juta, Cape Town.

Bond, P. & Khosa, M.M. (1999), *An RDP Policy Audit*, Pretoria, HSRC Publishers.

Calitz, E. (1997), "Aspects of the Performance of the South African Economy", *The South African Journal of Economics*, vol. 65, no. 3, September.

Creamer, K. (1998), "Participatory Budget Planning Process Needed — COSATU", *IDASA Budget Watch*, September.

Department of Agriculture and Land Affairs (1995), *White Paper on South African Land Policy*, Department of Agriculture and Land Affairs, Pretoria.

Department of Agriculture and Land Affairs (1998), *White Paper on Agriculture*, Department of Agriculture and Land Affairs, Pretoria.

Department of Defence (1996), *Defence in Democracy White Paper on National Defence for the Republic of South Africa*, Department of Defence, Pretoria.

Department of Housing (1995), *Department of Housing White Paper: A New Housing Policy and Strategy for South Africa*, Department of Housing, Pretoria.

Department of Public Service and Administration (1997), *White Paper on a New Employment Policy for the Public Service*, Department of Public Service and Administration, Pretoria.

Department of Safety and Security (1998), *White Paper on Safety and Security: "In Service of Safety, 1999-2000"*, Department of Safety and Security, Pretoria.

Donaldson, A.R. (1997), "Social Development and Macroeconomic Policy", *Development Southern Africa*, vol. 14, no. 3, October, p. 447.

Hlophe, D. & Naidoo, K. (1996), "The Constitutional Assembly Project: An Exercise in Participatory Democracy", in *Aspects of the Debate on the Draft of the New South African Constitution dated 22 April 1996*, Collected papers of an International Conference on the Draft Constitution held at Umtata, 24-26 April

1996, Konrad-Adenauer Institute, Johannesburg.

Lundhal, Mats (1999), *Growth or Stagnation? South Africa Heading for the Year 2000*, Ashgate, London.

May, J.D. (1998), *Poverty and Inequality in South Africa.* Report prepared for the office of the Executive Deputy President and the Inter-ministerial Committee for Poverty and Inequality, Praxis Publishers, Durban.

Motala, Z. (1997), "Towards an Appropriate Understanding of the Separation of Powers, and Accountability of the Executive and Public Service under the New South African Order", *South African Law Journal.*

Muthien, Y. (1996), "The Restructuring of the Public Service Commission: An exercise in Democratising the South African State?", *Journal of Public Administration*, vol. 32, no. 1, March.

Nathan, L. (1995), *The Changing of the Guard: Armed Forces and Defence Policy in a Democratic South Africa*, Human Sciences Research Council, Pretoria.

Nattrass, N. (1996), "Gambling on Investment: Competing Economic Strategies in South Africa", *Transformation*, vol. 31, p. 26.

NEDLAC (1998), *Report on the State of Social and Economic Matters in South Africa*, Johannesburg, NEDLAC.

Presidential Review Commission (1998), *Developing a Culture of Good Governance: Report of the Presidential Review Commission on the Reform of and Transformation of the Public Service in South Africa,* Pretoria, Presidential Review Commission.

Ray, M. (1998), "Skills Development", *South African Labour Bulletin*, vol. 22, no. 1, February.

Republic of South Africa (1995a), "White Paper on Education and Training", *Government Gazette*, no. 16312, Pretoria, 15 March.

Republic of South Africa (1995b), "White Paper on the Transformation of the Public Service", *Government Gazette*, no. 16414, Pretoria, 15 May.

Republic of South Africa (1996a), "Transformation of the Health System", *Government Gazette*, no. 17910, Pretoria, 16 April.

Republic of South Africa (1996b), "White Paper for Social Welfare", *Government Gazette*, no. 18116, Pretoria, 8 August.

Republic of South Africa (1998a), "Education White Paper 4, A Programme for the Transformation of Further Education and Training", *Government Gazette*, no. 19281, Pretoria,

Republic of South Africa (1998b), *The Building has Begun! Government's Report to the Nation*, Government Printer, Pretoria.

Ruscio, K. (1997), "Trust in the Administrative State", *Public Administration Review*, vol. 57, no. 5, September/October.

Tilley, S. (1998), "South Africa's Policy Implementation: A Grim Fairy Tale?", *IDASA Budget Watch*, September.

Venter, A. (1994), "The Executive: A Critical Evaluation", in De Villiers, B. (ed.), *Birth of a Constitution*, 1st ed., Ndabeni, Cape, Rustica Press, pp. 172-188.

Chapter 4

Democratising the South African State: The Challenge of Democratic Accountability and Public Sector Reform

Yvonne Muthien

Introduction

Public accountability constitutes the pivot of democratic governance and public administration. The centrality of democratic accountability is aptly captured in this quotation by James Madison in the *Federalist*:

> If men were angels, no government would be necessary. If angels were to govern men, neither external or internal controls on government would be necessary. In framing a government which is to be administered by men over men, the great difficulty lies in this: you must first enable the government to control the governed; and in the next place oblige it to control itself (cited in Schwella, 1991, p. 5).

Accountability is embedded in the system of liberal democracy, premised on the election of public representatives and the separation of the powers of the legislature, executive and the judiciary. Moreover, accountability is exercised through a complex system of institutional checks and balances which limit political authority. The sustainability of democracies can in part be tested against the strength of their institutions of accountability (Diamond, 1992; Weingast, 1997; Huntington, 1997). The history of liberal democracy has been one of setting limits on government. These limits are enshrined in constitutionalism and the upholding of a rule of law through an independent judiciary.

This chapter sets out to examine government accountability through the prism of institutions established to serve as a check on the executive, namely the legislature and "institutions supporting democracy". The chapter also provides an insider exposition of the transformation of a central state agency, notably the Public Service Commission, during the first few years of transition to democracy in South Africa, and reflects on some theoretical perspectives on the exercise of democracy and power.

Accountability through the Legislature

In the South African system of parliamentary democracy, the legislature constitutes the supreme authority as the elected representatives of "the people". In South Africa's constitutional state, the legislature, executive and judiciary are subjected to the Constitutional Court as the final authority and arbiter on constitutional rights. The executive derives its authority from the legislature and is accountable to the legislature for its actions. As the law-making authority, the legislature assumes the role of final arbiter of government policy and has the task of balancing the diverse interests of the broader society. The effectiveness of the legislature to hold government accountable depends on the quality of the elected representatives in terms of professional expertise and direct accountability to constituencies. Both of these conditions have been compromised with the exodus of skilled professionals from Parliament and the party-list electoral system. The degree of democratic accountability in South Africa (and other modern states) is further compromised by three factors:

- the complexity of modern public administration which often requires technical expertise that is not available among the lay representatives in the legislature;

- the volume, complexity and time constraints in enacting legislation; and

- the fact that legislation originates in the executive and is seldom initiated by the legislature, thereby reducing the supremacy of the legislature.

Specialised committees, e.g. portfolio committees on public accounts and finance, the holding of open public hearings and proceedings of parliamentary committees, as well as the provision of research support, enhance the capacity of the legislature to scrutinise government accountability. However, the interests of governance and public scrutiny have to be balanced. In the first five years of democratic rule in South Africa, the portfolio committees tackled their responsibility of holding government accountable with great fervour. The newly elected representatives distrusted the old guard civil service as the initiators of legislation. Legislation was duly scrutinised, leading to considerable delays and constraining the ability of the new executive to enact their new policies. The tension in the majority party between the executive and legislature was eventually dissipated by

- the pressure of the parliamentary time schedule;
- appeals to comradely support;
- the departure of many talented professionals from Parliament;
- improved co-operation at policy level.

This set the stage for classic oppositional politics within the legislature, with the opposition spearheading the drive for public scrutiny and the majority party in the legislature "defending" the interests of the executive. Portfolio committee chairs thus also called the civil service to task, especially scrutinising their commitment to the goals of the majority party.

A recent study revealed that by and large the majority of parliamentarians feel that they do not add great value to this scrutiny (Alence, 1998). They feel that the executive has the most dominant role in policy making and law making. That there is however a robust opposition and scrutiny of government actions cannot be doubted. Overall the transparent functioning of portfolio committees and the dedication of a number of key parliamentary activists in committee work bode well in terms of public accountability.

Institutions of Accountability

The South African Constitution has enshrined an elaborate array of institutions supporting constitutional democracy, which serve as a check on political and administrative authority. These include the Public Protector, Auditor-General, Public Service Commission, Human Rights Commission, Commission for Gender Equality, Electoral Commission and Commission for the Promotion and Protection of the Rights of Cultural, Religious and Linguistic Communities. Moreover, the independence and impartiality of these institutions are enshrined with an injunction to be impartial and "perform their functions without fear, favour or prejudice". Furthermore, "other organs of state must assist and protect these institutions to ensure the independence, impartiality, dignity and effectiveness of these institutions", and "no person or organ of state may interfere with the functioning of these institutions" (RSA Constitution, 1996). A powerful set of protections, indeed quite necessary for South Africa, has emerged from a history of violation of human rights and the rule of law by a bandit state machine! However, the novelty of exercising political power produces major constraints in setting limits on government. Furthermore, the strength of the watchdog institutions and their ability to set limits on the arbitrary exercise of power are dependent on a number of factors:

- their location, standing and status within the system of governance;
- the standing of their champion/guardian/protector within government, i.e. minister or president;
- the unqualified support of the legislature in the exercise of their functions;
- their level of resourcing and ability to fulfil their constitutional mandates.

On this scoreboard, the Auditor-General has the best standing and resources to fulfil its functions, and has recourse to parliamentary rules when its authority is challenged. This was demonstrated on two occasions. In the first case the Minister for the Public Service and Administration challenged the sweeping statements made by the auditor-general that the "public service was like the Titanic heading for an iceberg". The minister challenged the Auditor-General on his silence on both apartheid mis-management and the extent of reform initiatives, pointing out that the auditor-general had himself been a beneficiary of guaranteed job security by the new democratic government. In the second instance the Minister of Mineral and Energy Affairs challenged the auditor-general for allegedly covering up past secret transfers of funds in his department. Parliament sanctioned the behaviour of both ministers for infringing on the autonomy of the Auditor-General. This level of parliamentary protection has not been demonstrated with the other institutions, who equally battle to gain government co-operation and compliance in the exercise of their functions.

Accountability in Public Administration

This section will examine the restructuring and reform of the Public Service Commission, i.e. the centralised state agency which has governed the public service since 1910.

The Public Service Commission as Statutory Institution

The public service operates in a political environment which poses unique challenges to effective administration. The universal principles on which public administration is based, include career pathing, merit, efficiency and public accountability. These principles generally underpin the profes-sionalism, impartiality, experience and standards of ethical conduct neces-sary for efficient public administration and are duly enshrined in the South African constitutional law. Constitutional Principle 30 of the interim Con-stitution laid the foundation for the new civil service in a democratic South Africa:

> There shall be an efficient, non-partisan, career-orientated
> public service broadly representative of the South African com-
> munity, functioning on a basis of fairness and which shall serve
> all members of the public in an unbiased and impartial manner,
> and shall, in the exercise of its powers and in compliance with

its duties, loyally execute the lawful policies of the government
of the day in the performance of its administrative functions.

The quality of public life is dependent on the quality of public
administration and the quality of the public service. Effective legislative
drafting, policy formulation, budget determination, policy execution and
service delivery are all dependent on a professional and efficient public
service.

Role of Public Service Commissions

The institution of an independent and impartial public service commission
to act as a check on the executive in the administration of the public
service, finds its origins in the English civil service of the mid-nineteenth
century. From there the concept was "exported" to many Commonwealth
and other countries. The specific roles of public service commissions have
since been adapted to suit specific local needs and circumstances. Nevertheless, their basic function has remained that of protecting the public service from undue political interference.

Essentially, public service commissions were empowered to protect
the merit principle and to eliminate nepotism or favouritism, and to protect
civil servants from unfair dismissal and arbitrary political abuse.

The powers conferred on public service commissions differ from
country to country, ranging from purely advisory powers to powers of
monitoring and inspection, to executive powers whereby the recommendations of public service commissions are binding on the executive.

Interim Statutory Role

Since its inception in 1910, the South African Public Service Commission
had a much more extended mandate compared to the traditional mandates
of classical public service commissions. The Public Service Commission
set up under the interim Constitution (Act No. 200 of 1993) functioned in
terms of three Acts of Parliament:

- the Public Service Commission Act, 1984;

- the Public Service Act, 1994; and
- the Public Service Labour Relations Act, 1994, replaced by the general Labour Relations Act of 1996.

Section 210 of the interim Constitution conferred for reaching powers and functions on the Public Service Commission, including

- making recommendations, issuing directions and conducting enquiries into the organisation, abolition and administration of government departments;
- the conditions of service of members of the public service including salary scales;
- appointments, promotions, transfers and discharges in the public service;
- the promotion of efficiency and effectiveness in the public service; and
- issuing a code of conduct to govern the public service.

The Public Service Act, 1994 further empowered the commission to issue directives on age, educational, language, health and security requirements for appointment, promotion and/or transfer in the public service; training requirements in the public service; information technology; and grievances and appeals of public servants.

The personnel function of the commission was cumbersome and an impediment to efficient administration. The commission had to approve all management level appointments. The commission would approve, but the actual appointment, promotion, transfer or discharge had to be implemented by the department.

The commission's power of recommendations and directions was therefore not conventional, i.e. it was not merely advisory in the sense of "take it or leave it". The interim Constitution stipulated that a "recommendation" or "direction" of the commission had to be implemented by the appropriate authority within six months. The only exceptions were cases which required treasury approval, or if the president rejected a recommendation of the commission (President Mandela never rejected or referred back any recommendation/direction of the commission), or a recommendation or direction was withdrawn or changed by the commission itself.

The Public Service Labour Relations Act, 1994 dealt with collective bargaining in the public service and the settlement of disputes between the state as employer and trade unions. The Act provided that "all matters of mutual interest" between the employer and employee had to be negotiated in the relevant chambers of the Public Service Bargaining Council. The commission implemented the agreements reached in the bargaining chamber.

The statutory powers of the Public Service Commission were exercised over most of the national departments. Some national departments such as the Intelligence Service and the Department of Posts and Telecommunications and Broadcasting, have their own service acts and were therefore partially excluded from the commission's powers.

The interim Constitution provided for the establishment of nine provincial service commissions established by provincial legislation with jurisdiction only over provincial employees.

In addition, the provincial service commissions had to adhere to national norms and standards set by the national Public Service Commission. The determination of conditions of service and personnel practices were excluded from the ambit of the provincial service commissions. It is thus quite clear that the National Public Service Commission had become the "supreme authority" governing the public service. The constitutional drafters maintained a curious continuity in the structure and function between the former Commission for Administration and the Public Service Commission, ostensibly to centrally manage the amalgamation and rationalisation of the public service with maximum stability and minimum disruption of service delivery. This centralised commandism would also constitute a major obstacle to public service reform and efficiency.

Support Structure

A line-function office provided support to the commission in the execution of its powers and functions. The Office of the Public Service Commission had the status of a fully fledged national department with a director-general as chief executive officer. Aligned to the commission's constitutional mandate under the interim Constitution, the office was structured to render support functions in terms of organisational design in the public service policy on information technology procurement in the public service; remuneration systems and salary grading; labour relations policy for the public service; fringe benefits, including pensions and medical aid; human resource policy and practices; public service training and employment equity.

Reform of the Public Service Commission

The tension between institutions of accountability and government departments is not unexpected as the former are often considered a nuisance and an impediment to administration. The critical question remains who places a check on these institutions? This question was highlighted during the fusion of the "referee and player" roles of the Public Service Commission.

During 1995 the Public Service Commission fundamentally reviewed its statutory role in the context of the emerging new system of democratic governance. In a historically unprecedented move, the Public Service Commission devised a new system of state administration and governance for the public service, beginning with a dramatic unbundling of its powers and functions, transferring its policy functions to the newly created Department for Public Service and Administration and extensively delegating its executive functions to line-function departments, thereby vesting them with considerable managerial autonomy. This system was adopted by cabinet in February 1996 and pre-empted as well as paved the way for Chapter 10 of the new Constitution.

Constitutional Principle 29 of the interim Constitution required that the independence and impartiality of the Public Service Commission had to be safeguarded by the new Constitution in the interest of effective administration and a high standard of professional ethics in the public service.

In clarifying the functions of the new Public Service Commission, the traditional role of safeguarding the merit principle through a fully fledged central personnel agency was thoroughly considered. However, such cen-

tralised agencies were rather anachronistic and posed a number of problems.

First, their task was to uphold the merit principle and guard against
cronyism and nepotism, as well as to protect the civil service from arbitrary political abuse. In the case of the South African Public Service Commission, many more functions were actually devolved to it. The functions
of the commission indeed became so diverse that the impartiality and independence of the commission was questioned. The commission's impartiality and independence from the political executive was guaranteed by
law. However, in the execution of its functions the commission assumed a
contradictory role. On the one hand the commission was expected to protect officials from undue political interference in appointments, promotion
and discipline. On the other hand the commission was expected to
represent the state as employer in negotiations against trade unions on
remuneration and conditions of service. This dual role of the commission
brought the independence and impartial status of the commission into
question.

Second, there was a general perception that the powers and functions
of the commission were so wide that they actually infringed on the
political responsibilities and prerogatives of the government. This was
especially true where policy matters were concerned. Moreover, the
commission held all executive powers in administration, such as the power
to refuse ministerial requests for staff and salary increases, and changes to
conditions of service and organisational design.

The third major problem area concerned the extensive involvement of
the Public Service Commission in executive functions/decision making.
The commission set policy and norms and standards in the public service.
If departments needed to deviate from these, they had to approach the
commission for a ruling. This state of affairs became untenable, as it was
administratively inefficient and curtailed the managerial autonomy of
departments, as well as allowed departments to escape full accountability.
The commission assumed both the functions of establishing the rules of
administration and checking the exercise thereof (see Muthien, 1996;
Motala, 1997). It is interesting that the segregationist and apartheid states

ceded all executive powers in administration to this over-centralised, omnipotent and omnipresent body. It enabled those regimes to escape accountability for executive decisions and allowed for the scapegoating of the commission. Control over the commission was exercised through appointment mechanisms and the fact that the commission had to implement the policy of the government of the day. The commission was thus the monolith that both operationalised the objectives of the segregationist and apartheid state machinery and regulated it. It is also ironic that the ANC government, as part of the constitutional compromises, enshrined this institution largely intact in the interim Constitution, ostensibly to manage a centralised command-driven transition and to amalgamate the 15 apartheid administrations with maximum stability. However, the contradictions of maintaining this authoritarian structure within a new democratic order became increasingly untenable.

A New Model of State Administration

The commission's essential role as a check on the political executive thus had to be transformed into a purely monitoring and ombud function. The new model enabled government policy on public administration to be determined centrally by the executive, through the Minister for the Public Service and Administration. In this new model the Minister for the Public Service thus assumed responsibility for formulating national policy frameworks, norms and standards and administrative practices, as well as representing the state as collective employer. The establishment of the Department of Public Service and Administration emanated from the unbundling and transfer of powers by the Public Service Commission. All day-to-day administrative and executive functions which previously required a decision of the commission, were transferred to ministers and their departments. The commission itself would act as an independent body primarily to promote the basic values and principles of public administration as enshrined in the new Constitution.

The impact of this profound change in the system of public administration required that all role players in the public service had be critically positioned and equipped to assume their new roles when the new

Constitution and other relevant amended legislation came into effect. Thus therefore, in preparation for the new Constitution, a series of interim arrangements were effected in April 1996.

First, staff and other resources were divided between the Office of the Public Service Commission and the Department of Public Service and Administration according to their envisaged new functions.

Second, the Public Service Commission delegated its executive functions to the Department of Public Service and Administration and other line-function departments.

Constitutional Hiccups

At the time of the unbundling of the Public Service Commission in April 1996 the final chapter on the transformation of the commission had not been concluded. The new draft Constitution was submitted to the Constitutional Court for certification in compliance with the constitutional principles contained in the interim Constitution. The provisions on the commission were among those that were not certified by the Constitutional Court.

According to the Constitutional Court's judgement, Constitutional Principle 29 of the interim Constitution, which deals with the Public Service Commission, required that there be an independent and impartial commission. Implicit in the insistence upon independence and impartiality is the ability of the commission to constitute a check upon political executive power in the administration of the public service, and more especially in the making of appointments based on merit, equity and professionalism, to prevent nepotism, cronyism and patronage. The draft Constitution did not spell out the functions of the Constitution in any detail. Without knowing what the functions and powers of the commission would be and what protection it would have in the discharge of its constitutional duties, the Constitutional Court was unable to certify that the requirements were complied with.

The Public Service Commission provided the Constitutional Assembly with substantial inputs on the powers and functions of the new Public

Service Commission, and as required by the Constitutional Court clarified its role in safeguarding merit and equity in the public service.

The New Mandate

The new Constitution (Act No. 108 of 1996) made provision for a single independent and impartial public service commission. Clause 195(1) of the new Constitution established the basic values and principles of public administration:

(a) A high standard of professional ethics must be promoted and maintained.

(b) Efficient, economic and effective use of resources must be promoted.

(c) Public administration must be development orientated.

(d) Services must be provided impartially, fairly, equitably and without bias.

(e) People's needs must be responded to, and the public must be encouraged to participate in policy making.

(f) Public administration must be accountable.

(g) Transparency must be fostered by providing the public with timely, accessible and accurate information.

(h) Good human resource management and career development practices, to maximise human potential, must be cultivated.

(i) Public administration must be broadly representative of the South African people, with employment and personnel management practices based on ability, objectivity, fairness and the need to redress the imbalances of the past.

The new Public Service Commission has to promote the basic values and principles set out in the Constitution by

•   pursuing the promotion of a high standard of professional ethics in the public service;

•   issuing and promoting a code of conduct for the public service;

- monitoring, inspecting and evaluating the application of merit, equity and other related principles by departments and executing authorities and providing advice where necessary;

- monitoring, inspecting and evaluating the application of human resource practices, including management practices, and providing advice and issuing directions where necessary;

- investigating, monitoring, evaluating and providing advice on effective management and administration of the public service to departments and executing authorities;

- evaluating performance in the public service and proposing measures to improve efficiency and effectiveness;

- reporting to Parliament on all of the above matters;

- investigating grievances of officials and recommending redress; and

- conducting applied research in support of the above functions.

The national and nine provincial commissioners were appointed to the new Public Service Commission.

Support Structure

To support the commission in its new role, the Office of the Public Service Commission was initially reorganised into two broad line-function terrains: Merit and Equity, and Effectiveness and Efficiency. These divisions included functions such as

- investigation of grievances,

- appraisal of human resource practices, including recruitment, training and probationary practices, and advice on the promotion of merit and equity in the public service,

- support on the promotion of professional ethics in the public service,

- structural or organisational effectiveness of the public service,

- operational efficiency and the promotion of the efficient, economic and effective use of resources, and

- technological innovation.

With the appointment of the new commission in 1997/98 the office was again reorganised.

Reflections on Reform

The new role of the Public Service Commission differs substantially from the past one. In the process of re-engineering, the commission ceded many of its policy and executive powers. The unbundling of the commission and the separation of its executive and oversight functions was an attempt to democratise the South African state and have been criticised as both too far-reaching, but also hailed as a major achievement of administrative reform. Some observers have concluded that the new Public Service Commission no longer resembles a typical central administrative institution. In addition, many observers have argued that the unbundling of the commission was unconstitutional as it deviated fundamentally from the constitutional mandate bestowed on the commission by the interim Constitution.

The Public Service Commission took a bold step in unbundling its powers and functions from within and timed the transition in anticipation of an early adoption of the new Constitution. This radical step could be contextualised against the following considerations:

First, it coincided with international trends to introduce modern management principles and practices into the public service. One of the basic principles of modern civil service reform is greater managerial autonomy for departments, with greater emphasis on accountability of line managers for the achievement of results. The unbundling of the commission's executive functions was in line with this trend.

Second, the Public Service Commission followed another international trend—the establishment of specialised units and programmes aimed at developing and modernising public administration practices, including the Malaysian Administrative Modernisation and Management Planning Unit, the English Next Steps Programme, Singapore's "Public Service for the 21st Century" programme and Hong Kong's Efficiency Unit.

Third, the unbundling placed responsibility for policy and execution of policy squarely in the hands of the government of the day and should, at least theoretically, increase public accountability. The unbundling also crystallised the role of the commission as a check in the system of governance and has safeguarded its independence and impartiality.

However, the unbundling of the commission had been criticised in international reform circles as perhaps too far-reaching in that no mechanism of recourse was left to intervene or redress the violation of the merit principle. The provisions of labour legislation and recourse to the public protector and the courts nevertheless provide further checks and balances. The ability of these institutions to serve as a check on the executive is ultimately dependent on the levels of co-operation it secures and the ultimate sanction that Parliament can exercise to secure public accountability.

Unlike other international reform initiatives through which such extended functions were devolved three to four different agencies, the South African case demonstrated a remarkable economy in creating only two central agencies. Against the grain of the Weberian logic of bureaucracies which tend to expand and consolidate themselves, the Public Service Commission reduced its structure and transferred its powers. In a Foucauldian sense the commission surrendered its omnipotent, omnipresent control and power for a microscopic reach throughout the public service. The unbundling of the commission was intended as a first exercise in democratising the state, and set an example to other spheres of government. The transformation of the commission passed as a "silent revolution", but on whether the restructuring will deepen democracy, Foucault (1984) has this chilling reminder:

> I would say that the state consists in the codification of a whole number of power relations which render its functioning possible, and that revolution is a different type of codification of the same relations. This implies that there are many different kinds of revolution, roughly speaking as many kinds as there are possible subversive recodifications of power relations, and further that one can perfectly well conceive of revolutions which leave essentially untouched the power relations which form the basis for the functioning of the state.

The Public Service Commission has been enshrined in the new Constitution as the guardian of democratic values and principles in the public service, the custodian of the merit principle and the champion of equity and ethical conduct in government. The Constitutional Court re-affirmed this important role of the commission. The contradictions of its previously fused functions brought it under fierce attack, with neither the executive nor the legislature accepting guardianship of the body. The reach of its oversight function will have to be established, as well as its protection by the legislature, as it pursues its new mandate of securing public accountability. The recently completed report of the Presidential Review Commission on the Reform of the Public Service reinforced the need for an even leaner but independent Public Service Commission. To safeguard its autonomy, the commission recommended the transfer of the Public Service Commission to the President's Office to advise the president on the upholding of the merit principle in government. Hitherto this recommendation has not been implemented. Hence the Public Service Commission remains in the uncomfortable interstices between the executive and the legislature.

Conclusion

The pervasive question remains: how can the public service, thrice removed from the people, through its professional and career embeddedness, technocratic command and command over resources and hence the innate ability to dispense patronage, be made to function in a manner compatible with democracy? The history of the Public Service Commission demonstrated that excessive control of public institutions does not imply increased effectiveness. Quite the contrary, it can serve as a brake on efficient administration. Furthermore, the creation of multiple accountability mechanisms and institutions does not in itself increase accountability. The new South African public service administration has evolved by condensing broadly four models of state administration into a peculiar mix of contradictory identities, i.e:

- from the upper echelons of the civil service as agency specialists and technocrats,
- to these echelons as an elite style corps of civil service mandarins,
- to the upper echelons of civil service as a political machine,
- to the upper echelons of civil service as corporate managers.

There can be no doubt that a professional civil service, insulated from political power, serves democracy best and that the triple distance from direct democracy in itself constitutes part of the system of accountability and limitations on political power. The inherent problem of democratising modern state administration is vested in reconciling the democratic imperatives of public accountability with the managerial imperatives of administrative flexibility and responsiveness (Balfour, 1997; Ruscio, 1997).

Thus far we have concentrated on the accountability of government to the legislature through institutions supporting constitutional democracy. These forms of accountability, whilst public in nature, are nevertheless considerably removed from the majority of the population. A more direct form of accountability is exercised through "citizen charters", which render public officials accountable at the point of service delivery. The *Batho Pele* (meaning "people first") White Paper on Transforming Service Delivery commits public servants to values of consultation, service standards, fairness, efficiency, courtesy, access, information, transparency, redress and value for money, at customer desks, together with the requirement of an annual departmental report to citizens on meeting service delivery targets. As in other instances, the promise of this policy depends on a citizenry informed of their rights and with the necessary public confidence to assert these rights. Otherwise, like elsewhere, it can easily fade into social amnesia. The introduction of constituency representation would greatly enhance direct political accountability to the citizens.

Finally, attempts to set limits on political authorities, whilst under pressure to deliver, have produced major tensions in the political administrative interface. The sustainability of democracy and the rule of law require that both political authorities and public officials accept limits to the exercise of their authority, as well as subject themselves to public scrutiny, either through incentive or sanction (Weingast, 1997). To apply effective public scrutiny of public figures requires an informed citizenry, which will counter habitual corruption. This in turn requires a commitment to the democratic value of clean government. When the political economy of corruption becomes embedded in the social fabric of communities or localities and particular citizens become the beneficiaries of corruption, the sustainability of democracy is fundamentally compromised. Hence public education must forge a shared value commitment to democracy and clean government as ends in themselves.

Other central agencies of democratic accountability are the judiciary, especially the Constitutional Court, independent commissions of enquiry and the independent press. The government has expressed discomfort with press scrutiny but it challenges the press in terms of fair and accurate reporting rather than threatening its right of independent enquiry. Clearly the most demonstrable commitment to democratic accountability is vested in the subordination of political rule to constitutionality through the operation of the Constitutional Court as the ultimate safeguard and recourse of citizens in the protection of individual civil rights and liberties. The vibrancy of statutory institutions which buttress and safeguard democracy remains the acid test of a mature democratic system of governance.

Note

The author was appointed as a commissioner to the Public Service Commission by President Mandela, 1994-1997, and currently serves on the President's Advisory Council on National Orders.

References

Alence, R. (1998), *The Economic Policy-Making Process in South Africa*, unpublished report, Human Sciences Research Council, Pretoria.

Balfour, D. (1997), "Reforming the Public Service: The Search for a New Tradition", *Public Administration Review*, vol. 57, no. 5, Sept./Oct.

Diamond, L. (1992), "A Constitution That Works—Some Options", *South Africa International,* July.

Dommen, E. (1997), "Paradigms of Governance and Exclusion", *Journal of Modern African Studies*, vol. 35, no. 3.

Farazmand, A. (1997), *Modern Systems of Government: Exploring the Role of Bureaucrats and Politicians*, Sage, California.

Foucault, M. (1984), "Power, Sovereignty and Discipline", in Held, D. *States and Societies*, Martin Robertson, Oxford.

Hill, M. (1996), *Social Policy: A Comparative Analysis*, Prentice-Hall, London.

Hirst, P. (1997), *From Statism to Pluralism*, UCL Press, London.

Huntington, S. (1997), "After Twenty Years: The Future of the Third Wave", *Journal of Democracy*, vol. 8, no. 4, Oct.

Motala, Z. (1997), "Towards an Appropriate Understanding of the Separation of Powers, and Accountability of the Executive and Public Service under the New South African Order", *South African Law Journal*.

Muthien, Y. (1996), "The Restructuring of the Public Service Commission: An Exercise in Democratising the South African State?", *Journal of Public Administration*, vol. 32, no. 1, March.

Republic of South Africa (1993), *Interim Constitution of the Republic of South Africa*, Act No. 200 of 1993, Government Printer, Pretoria.

Republic of South Africa (1994-1997), *Annual Report of the Public Service Commission,* Government Printer, Pretoria.

Republic of South Africa (1996), The *Constitution of the Republic of South Africa*, Act No. 108 of 1996, Government Printer, Cape Town.

Republic of South Africa (1998), *Developing a Culture of Good Governance: Report of the Presidential Review Commission on the Reform and Transformation of the Public Service in South Africa*, Government Printer, Pretoria.

Ruscio, K. (1997), "Trust in the Administrative State", *Public Administration Review*, vol. 57, no. 5, Sept./Oct.

Schwella, E. (1991), "Selected Aspects of Democratic Accountability in South African Public Administration", *Perspectives*, vol. 1, no. 1.

Weingast, B. (1997), "The Political Foundations of Democracy and the Rule of Law", *American Political Science Review*, vol. 91, no. 2, June.

Chapter 5

Reflections on Provincial Government in South Africa since 1994

Thabo Rapoo

Constitutional Framework for Provincial Governance

Unlike the pre-1994 provinces that were a mere product of legal statute, the post-1994 provinces in South Africa are provided for in the Constitution (Khosa & Muthien, 1998). They are entities with original powers and functions entrenched by the Constitution. Chapter 3 of the Constitution defines and elaborates on a clear formal framework of relations between the national, provincial and local spheres of governance. For instance, the Constitution states that these spheres "are distinctive, interdependent and interrelated" (RSA, 1996, s40(1)).

The use of the term "spheres" in the current Constitution is not a random occurrence. It is due to a deliberate decision deriving from a political history dominated by authoritarian political regimes at the centre and, consequently, emasculated sub-national entities within a unitary Constitution. The choice of the term "sphere" was therefore based on a theoretical construct of "equality" and the ideal of "equity". The aim of this choice of term was to avoid entrenching the sense of hierarchy usually associated with the more traditional notion of "tiers". The term "tiers" is traditionally germane to unitary political systems where sub-national entities are politically subordinated to the centre due to the lack of an original constitutional basis for them.

One of the most contentious issues during the constitutional negotiations of 1992 to 1994 in South Africa was to allocate constitutional power and authority equitably between the spheres of government in order to prevent the concentration of power at the centre. Institutionally, this objective was to be achieved by, amongst others, devolving constitutional power and authority from the centre to the provinces, which were expected to countervail the power of central government. Many proponents of this view argued that devolving power to the provinces would act as a "check and balance" on the growth of the power of central government. To underpin perspective, the Constitution enumerated the concurrent and exclusive legislative and policy-making powers and functional responsibilities of the provinces in Schedules 4 and 5.

The enumeration of specific powers and functional responsibilities of the provinces in the constitutional document was also to serve as a constitutional "check and balance" to enhance the security and the autonomy of provinces vis-à-vis central government. In practice the operation of the post-1994 system of provincial government has challenged the ideals contained in the Constitution. The relationship between the provincial and national spheres of government has become very complex and poses serious difficulties to the central objective of establishing equity between these spheres of government.

The spheres of government are not only vested with original constitutional powers with regard to legislative and executive functions within their spheres of competence. They are also constitutionally guaranteed an equitable share of fiscal resources collected at national level. The equitable distribution of fiscal resources constitutes the single most critical category of disputes between spheres of government around the world. Virtually all decentralised political systems have also attempted to put in place institutional arrangements and objective formulae to resolve this problem. For instance, s214(1)(a) of our Constitution states that "an Act of Parliament must provide for the equitable division of revenue raised nationally among the national, provincial and local spheres of government". To give this provision a concrete institutional foundation, an independent Finance and Fiscal Commission was established to make recommendations to the National Assembly and provincial legislatures on the equitable distribution of revenue (RSA, 1996, s220). This was yet another constitutional device to serve as a "check and balance" to underpin the autonomy of provinces vis-à-vis central government.

The current Constitution therefore goes a long way towards providing more constitutional security for the political integrity and autonomy of the provinces, unlike other Constitutions in the history of this country. However, despite all these carefully crafted constitutional "checks and balances", the Constitution still contains certain critical features that ensure that the national government retains overall constitutional supremacy over the provinces. A number of examples will serve to illustrate this. First, the Constitution appears to imply, if not directly reserve, residual powers (i.e. those powers not defined and specified in the Constitution) (Zimmerman, 1992, pp. 35-36) for the national government. It does this in at least two ways: vesting authority in the National Assembly "to pass legislation with regard to any matter, including a matter within a functional area listed in Schedule 4, but excluding, subject to subsection (2), a matter within a functional area listed in Schedule 5"; (RSA, 1996, s44(1)(A)ii) and specifying only those powers over which the provinces can exercise legislative responsibility either exclusively or concurrently with central government. The exclusive functional responsibilities of the provinces are clearly enumerated in Schedule 5, while those of central government are not expressly defined beyond those it can exercise concurrently with the provinces in Schedule 4. The significance of this is that any function not expressly allocated to any sphere of government by the Constitution becomes a central government responsibility by default. In theory and in practice, this gives central government potentially enormous authority over a wide range of matters which could impinge upon the autonomy and functional responsibilities of the provinces.

Second, central government has the constitutional responsibility to make laws in terms of s44(2), amongst others to maintain national security; economic unity; essential national standards; minimum standards for service delivery; and preventing actions by provinces which are deemed prejudicial to the interests of other provinces. Added to this is the "necessary" and "incidental" powers provided for under s44(3). This provision states that the national Parliament may pass "legislation with regard to a matter that is *necessary* for, or *incidental* to, the effective exercise of a power concerning any matter listed in Schedule 4 ...". This gives central government enormous undefined and unspecified powers of intervention in those areas over which it exercises concurrent responsibilities with the provinces.

Third, central government is provided with overriding powers, defined within sections 146 to 148, over provinces in cases where conflict arises between national and provincial legislation. This is an indication that despite the ideal of equality between the spheres of government, the Constitution clearly establishes a hierarchy of authority, which places national legislative competence above that of the provinces. This is critical in the practical operation of the current system, particularly where it places a great deal of political premium on the notion of autonomy.

Fourth, s100 of the current Constitution empowers the national government to supervise the provinces and "intervene by taking any appropriate steps to ensure fulfilment" when a province "does not fulfil an executive obligation in terms of legislation or the Constitution". This means that the national government may intervene and take over, under clearly defined conditions, the administration of an entire functional responsibility if a province fails to fulfil its obligations in this regard. On several occasions since 1994 the national government was called upon to use this power of intervention in the Northern Province, KwaZulu-Natal and the Eastern Cape in respect of the administration of social pensions and financial management when these provinces were unable to execute these responsibilities properly.

What these provisions indicate is that, despite the ideals of equality and provincial autonomy, the Constitution has established a hierarchy of authority and hence unequal political status between the provinces and central government. Constitutionally, therefore, central government occupies an extremely powerful position relative to the provinces in respect of legislative and functional responsibilities. This matter has remained a constant problem in the ongoing attempts by the provinces to establish equitable relations between the spheres of government as provided for in Chapter 3 of the Constitution.

Provincial Governance in Practice

The next section will assess the practical operation of the current system of provincial government in the light of the parameters provided for in the Constitution.

National-Provincial Conflicts after 1994

The constitutional hierarchy of authority and power that underlies the predominance of central government within the current system of government in South Africa is critical for understanding the experience of provincial governance in South Africa after 1994.

The unsavoury political machinations of previous regimes resulted in political mistrust of overbearing central governments. This mistrust combined with the desire of many political groupings for security and political survival in a post-apartheid era provided the basis for the creation of a decentralised system of government. For instrumental purposes, a decentralised system of authority in South Africa was also unavoidable. Due to the vastness of its territory, it would be cumbersome to run this country by a centralised government. The interests of socio-economic, ethnic and political groupings in particular regions also served as a rationale for devolving power from the centre to allow some functional responsibility and authority to be exercised at the provincial sphere. It is generally acknowledged that a decentralised system of governance gives a stake to minority political elites that are not able to achieve power at national level by allowing them the opportunity to contest for power at provincial level (Friedman, 1999, pp. 44-46).

However, the political and instrumental considerations that warranted the introduction of a constitutionally entrenched system of decentralised authority and hence autonomous provincial governance in South Africa do not necessarily guarantee the viability and sustainability of the system in practice. This has been underscored by ongoing public debates regarding the apparent inefficiencies and institutional weaknesses of the post-1994 provinces. A rift characterises the system of government in South Africa, deriving from disagreement on the fundamental question of how best to divide powers and functions between the centre and the provinces. This problem was never resolved by the constitutional settlement and continues to cause conflict between the spheres of government.

Within the first year of the current system of provincial government being put to practice, the relationship between central government and the provinces came to be characterised by divisions and conflicts over demands by the provinces for more political authority over and greater responsibility for many functional areas (Humphries & Rapoo, 1994, pp. 3-15). At the forefront were the two opposition-controlled provinces of the Western Cape and KwaZulu-Natal on the one hand, and the two ANC-controlled provinces of Mpumalanga and Gauteng. It appears that the demands of the provinces were caused mainly by the perceived imperative on the part of the provincial political leadership to demonstrate, if not search for evidence of, their newly acquired constitutional, legal and political status vis-à-vis the central authority.

However, the demands for central government to speedily devolve more responsibilities to the provinces occurred in many instances within the context of weak institutional structures and underdeveloped political and administrative leadership (Rapoo, 1995, p. 6). This was not entirely surprising. After all, political considerations more than economic, developmental and institutional considerations were the driving force in the struggles between the protagonists and opponents of greater decentralisation of power during the constitutional negotiations, as well as between central government and the provinces during the early stages of the system. The perceived imperative to realise their constitutional power and political authority as quickly as possible appeared to preoccupy many provincial leaders while simultaneously facing the enormous challenge of establishing functioning systems of governance to deliver social services to their impoverished constituencies. This early preoccupation with questions of greater constitutional power and political authority led to the dissatisfaction with and the abolition of the former Senate which was replaced with the current National Council of Provinces (NCOP).

While the former Senate was criticised for its inability to represent and articulate the interests of the provinces adequately at central government level, the NCOP has also been severely criticised by the provinces, amongst others for failing to enhance their influence significantly in national legislative and policy formulation processes (South African Institute of Race Relations (SAIRR) 1998, p. 468; IDASA, 11 August 1997). It appears that the NCOP has not yet established its authority as the primary national political institution through which the political status and interests of the provinces could be articulated and promoted. Wide-spread reports of national cabinet ministers failing to appear before the NCOP over the past four years have tended to fuel further debates about the role of this institution within national policy making.

The Era of Pragmatism after 1996

Initially the provincial system was characterised mainly by dogmatic debates on the nature of South Africa's federalism as well as an overly quantitative approach to the division of powers and functions between central government and the provinces. Many problems acquired an overly party-political character, with notions such as "autonomy", "self-determination", "asymmetry" and so on dominating the demands of political parties such as the IFP, the NP and DP, which tended to take up the cause of provincial autonomy vis-à-vis the centre.

The period following the launching of the National Council of Provinces in 1997 saw a marked shift in the nature of intergovernmental disputes. The reality of governing the newly created provincial authorities—with their untried institutions and processes—bore down heavily on many protagonists on both sides of the divide. This was particularly so with those in charge of the provinces. The provinces, particularly the poor ones, began to better appreciate their institutional limitations against the backdrop of rising popular expectations for rapid social service delivery and limited fiscal resources. It became clear that irrespective of all the constitutional guarantees provinces had in respect of their political autonomy, some were still so poor and institutionally weak that they would virtually be unable to fulfil their constitutional responsibilities without the technical and financial assistance of central government. Only two provinces, the Western Cape and Gauteng, were financially and economically able to sustain some of their activities with less intervention from the centre.

The period after 1997 was therefore characterised by less strident and crude calls for more devolution of powers and responsibilities to the provinces. The debate on the devolution of powers and responsibilities to the provinces became more nuanced, increasingly emphasising the need for institution building, capacity building, civil service transformation and staff training. As the sheer scale of problems such as corruption and lack of financial resources increased, more attention shifted towards questions of financial accountability and quality of services delivered by provinces. These issues troubled political leaders at provincial and at national level.

The predominance of central government in fiscal and financial matters as well as its responsibility for setting the overall national economic policy and legislative framework in a range of policy areas has given a centralist orientation to processes of governance in South Africa. This orientation is likely to persist for some time due to a number of structural factors: many provinces still lack the administrative and technical capacity to fulfil many of their responsibilities; the economic and fiscal weaknesses of many provinces lead to dependence on fiscal transfers from central government; and central government has the constitutional responsibility to ensure fiscal discipline and determine overall national development policy priorities to which the provinces have to conform to ensure macro-economic stability (Van Zyl, 1998, p. 32).

New Wave of Discontent within the Current System

During 1998, the chorus of discontent about the current provincial system of government has grown. Although other political parties and commentators joined the main complainants, namely the ANC, much of this has been unco-ordinated. The discontent seems to signal that restructuring might be necessary. Some political leaders have suggested that the entire system needs to be radically overhauled or even abolished.

A number of factors triggered this new development. First, many provinces have struggled since 1994 to transform or rationalise their administrative institutions and systems to handle the increased socio-economic and developmental responsibilities. This is particularly so with the poorer provinces such as KwaZulu-Natal, the Eastern Cape and Northern Province, which have also inherited remnants of the old "homeland" civil services, parastatals and personnel who continue to drain fiscal resources.

Second, a report published in August 1997 by the Public Service and Administration revealed widespread problems. These included severe lack of institutional capacity, administrative leadership and management skills; absence of financial control systems; inadequate accounting mechanisms as well as too many under-performing civil servants. Many provincial civil servants were untrained and unskilled, which in many cases led to maladministration, corruption, large-scale waste and mismanagement of provincial resources. These problems have prompted the national government and several provincial authorities over the past two years to establish numerous investigative commissions of inquiry into official corruption throughout the country (The South Africa Report, 1998a, pp. 5-8; The South Africa Report, 1998b, pp. 4-9). Mpumalanga, the Northern Province, Eastern Cape and KwaZulu-Natal have been among the most severely affected in this regard.

Third—and very important—national government has had to intervene and "bail out" provinces such as KwaZulu-Natal and the Eastern Cape for overspending their budgetary allocations (Naidoo & Pintusewitz, 1998, pp. 37-40). In both cases, the financial assistance from central government does not come without strings attached and many see these preconditions as detrimental to the cause of provincial autonomy. For instance, Finance Minister Trevor Manuel's adjustment budget in 1998 outlined central government's intention to make available R1,5bn to assist both the Eastern Cape and KwaZulu-Natal to overcome their severe financial difficulties, but performance-related conditions were attached to this assistance. These included a requirement for the two provinces to balance their books under supervision of officials from the national Department of Finance.

In theory, central government's financial "bailing out" of and even technical assistance to provinces have not created a more receptive attitude to national government intervention in provincial governance. One example of this occurred in the Eastern Cape in January 1998 when central government, through the Department of Social (Welfare and Population Development), intervened in the pensions crisis in the province. Central government provided R800m to assist the province when it was unable to pay pensions to 632 000 pensioners (South African Institute of Race Relations, 1998, p. 485). In 1997, the Presidential Review Commission also urged central government to invoke s100 of the Constitution, which empowers it to take over the administration of any provincial function if the provinces concerned are unable to execute their constitutional responsibilities. The commission recommended that the government invoke this section in relation to the Northern Province and Eastern Cape due to financial mismanagement and lack of qualified financial managers there (Presidential Review Commission, 1998).

The cumulative effect of all this has been to nurture a less favourable attitude towards provincial political autonomy among the general public as well as among senior members of government at both national and provincial levels. For instance, former Minister of Constitutional Development and Provincial Affairs, Vali Moosa, argued early in 1998 inside the NCOP that the current provincial system needs reforming (*Financial Mail*, 19 June 1998).

Northern Province premier Ramatlhodi in a speech to a conference echoed this sentiment in early 1998 where he called for "a fundamental re-evaluation of the powers and functions of provinces". He indicated four future options: greater devolution of powers—favoured by KwaZulu-Natal and the Western Cape; reduction of provincial powers; the deployment of skilled personnel and administrative resources to poorer provinces; and the asymmetrical assignment of powers to provinces based on existing capacity. He seemed to indicate a preference for the latter option, arguing that the Northern Province would prefer a more visible presence of central government in certain areas of provincial responsibility such as financial management and skills development. Ramatlhodi believed that more latitude was needed in other areas, such as cross-border trade relations, migration and labour policy, agriculture and security. He also contended that central government was able to use the national/provincial sectoral policy co-ordinating bodies such as the minister members of the executive council (MINMECs) to issue directives to provincial members of the executive council (MECs) who shunned their accountability to provincial premiers. He argued that such shunning of accountability was an unconstitutional encroachment upon the responsibilities of provincial premiers.

Ben Turok, convenor of the National Assembly's finance committee, expressed the view that the transfer of power and functional responsibilities to the provinces between 1994 and 1996 was carried out at a time when many provinces still had inadequate technical and administrative capacity. He suggested that provincial powers over functions such as finance should be withdrawn (The South Africa Report, 1998a, p. 6).

This view appears to command some support within the ANC (The South Africa Report, 1998b, p. 5), and is likely to be popular among bureaucrats, senior managers inside national ministries and others who are more concerned with questions of resource management, financial accounting as well as technical and pragmatic aspects of social service delivery.

Former Gauteng premier Mathole Motshekga also echoed these sentiments in a document presented to the provincial cabinet in 1998. He found the overlapping powers and responsibilities between the spheres of government to be responsible for the national/provincial conflicts over the past five years. He asserted that the current intergovernmental relations' structures were failing to mediate the rivalry and tensions between national ministers and provincial MECs (*The Star*, 2 September 1998). Motshekga argued that the current system had to be co-ordinated from inside the deputy president's office. Interestingly, this statement came from a premier of one of the two economically strong and well-run provinces. Politically, a province like Gauteng would gain from a less interventionist role for central government in respect of the functional relations between the provinces and the centre. A co-ordinating role for the deputy president's office would only enhance the dominance of central government over sub-national entities, which many campaigners for provincial rights would find unacceptable. However, some commentators argued that the role of central government in the development of the current provinces is critical at least in the short to medium term.

The early stages of the implementation of the current system of provincial government saw provincial authorities and proponents of provincial rights routinely demanding the wholesale transfer of powers and functional responsibilities to the provinces as a right and panacea for the ills afflicting the system. In contrast, current sentiments seem to demand a more nuanced approach, which might include withdrawing some critical provincial responsibilities in order to improve the system's effectiveness. It is quite clear therefore that an instrumentalist approach to improving the performance of the provinces has surreptitiously emerged. The period leading to the 1999 national election also served to bring into sharp relief the issue of government's inability to deliver on its social services programmes, especially at provincial levels. Limiting provincial autonomy could therefore become an extremely attractive option for politicians for whom turning the provinces into mere administrative tools for central government presents an easy solution to the problems of inefficiency, corruption and lack of delivery on basic services at provincial level.

In the long term though, the current receptiveness to a more dominant and interventionist role for central government in the affairs of provinces is likely to strengthen the hands of those politicians who, for ideological reasons, have always opposed the idea of constitutionally entrenching the political and administrative autonomy of provinces.

Prospects for the Future

In terms of the Constitution, the institutional integrity of provinces in South Africa is guaranteed and their powers and functions are entrenched. However, in practice many of them have struggled to establish themselves in respect of their institutional character, particularly in the context of weak administrative capacity and inadequate fiscal resources. Many provinces have not yet been able to command enough fiscal resources to determine their own developmental priorities and develop their own socio-economic agendas as constitutionally autonomous governments. Many of them have spent the first five years of their existence putting in place or getting to grips with new systems of government as well as implementing various programmes of structural transformation.

Provincial governments face debilitating problems such as inability to reduce expenditure on personnel salaries and large numbers of civil servants (both of which can only be solved at national level), and raising sufficient own revenues to reduce dependence on central government transfers. These problems have resulted in permanent crisis management at provincial level; thus preventing the provinces from experimenting with programmes to enhance their socio-political and economic well being. Provinces therefore have yet to consolidate institutionally and carve a high political profile for themselves among their constituencies. For instance, only two opposition-controlled provinces have ever attempted to design their own provincial Constitutions and only one—the Western Cape—has succeeded in having its own Constitution adopted.

Politically, the provinces have yet to constitute a strong and united interest group that regularly lobbies for its collective welfare within the national political structures and policy-making processes. In terms of political structures in general, all the provinces have their governance institutions in place. However, many legislatures have struggled to define their roles properly within the entire system of provincial government (Rapoo et al., 1997). Many members of provincial legislature (MPLs) still have inadequate law-making and policy-making skills as well as lack of capacity to scrutinise the activities of government agencies and hold provincial governments to account effectively. This has, in many cases, created a power vacuum that has gradually led to a concentration of power and authority in the hands of provincial premiers, provincial executive councils and their departments.

Many provincial legislatures have thus evolved as weak institutions, sometimes serving as little more than rubber stamps for domineering provincial executives. This derives mainly from the current electoral system, which does not allow for MPLs to represent geographic constituencies. There is therefore a weak representative relationship between legislatures and their electorates, which creates a "democratic deficit". This occurs when political institutions at provincial level do not competently represent and articulate the interests of their electorates at all levels of policy making. Such non-representative political structures are a serious challenge for democratising countries like South Africa.

The fall out from all this is that the public have little confidence in provincial governance compared to the levels of confidence in central government, as evidenced by public opinion surveys (see Chapter 10). The results of the 1999 national and provincial elections and patterns of voter preference for political parties are interesting. For instance, the bad performance of region-based minority political parties during the elections, compared to the overwhelming victory of the ANC at both national and provincial levels, appears to reflect low levels of voter identification with either the individual provinces or the entire system of provincial government. These parties have struggled to translate the regional proximity of their power bases into greater political support against the ANC during the 1999 general election. Even the IFP and the National Party, which achieved impressive victories in the 1994 election against the ANC in KwaZulu-Natal and the Western Cape respectively, were unable to repeat their victories during the 1999 election. Moreover, many political parties, including regional minority parties, tended to conduct their provincial electioneering based on national policy issues and agendas rather than province-specific policy problems. However, the outcome of the provincial elections has nevertheless created more political diversity within provincial legislatures than was the case during the first five years of the new democracy. For instance, unlike in the past when opposition benches at national and provincial levels were dominated by the National Party and the Democratic Party, the current era sees more parties such as the United Democratic Movement (UDM) and the United Christian Democratic Movement (UCDM) added to the opposition benches in provinces such as the Eastern Cape and North West.

Conclusion

All the difficulties experienced at provincial level, however, should be placed within context. The provinces in South Africa are still evolving in terms of institutional and political identity, administrative capacity, technical effectiveness and political influence (Khosa & Muthien, 1998). Valuable experience is being gained—through trial and error—on the practice of running provincial political institutions where, in some cases, none existed before. This experience will contribute towards improving the operation of provinces in the future, based on the unique circumstances of this country. In the meantime though, a new non-partisan consensus on the need for a balance between the political and constitutional autonomy of the province vis-à-vis the centre and the need for efficient and effective delivery of basic services will be critical in improving the current system.

As a new set of developmental priorities are being determined for the period 1999-2004 by the newly elected national and provincial governments, the institutional and political development of the provinces in the medium to long term will be placed on the national agenda. Both the national and provincial political leaderships need to focus on technical and administrative capacity building for the provinces, with proper monitoring and evaluation to ensure that the objectives of these activities are achieved. Consensus or political readiness seems to be developing regarding the visible presence of central government in some areas of provincial responsibility, particularly financial management. This, at best, would be a short-term measure accompanied by vigorous financial management and skills-training programmes for key provincial departmental managers. In the meantime though, effective systems are necessary to ensure internal financial accountability in the provinces to deal with mismanagement of public resources and corruption. At the same time, the provinces have to be externally accountable to the electorate for the use of public resources.

Finally, the issue of allocating own and independent sources of revenue to the provinces remains a source of serious intergovernmental conflict and national political priority (Naidoo & Pintusewitz, 1998, pp. 37-40; Van Zyl, 1998). The Finance and Fiscal Commission has already lent its weight to the allocation of independent sources of revenue, but some provinces, particularly the poor ones lacking substantial revenues bases, apparently indicated aversion to this. Hence a co-ordinated national strategy is required to address the short and long-term fiscal needs of the provinces. The strategy would have to ensure that capacity exists to effectively utilise already existing provincial sources of revenue (e.g. vehicle licensing; taxes on horse racing and gambling; rates; service charges; etc.) before exploring the addition of other sources such as sur-charges on personal income tax as well as corporation tax. It is also important that the intergovernmental fiscal relations system in South Africa is revamped to deal effectively and efficiently with critical fiscal transfers to the poorer provinces with weak revenue bases and great social needs (Van Ryneveld, 1996; Van Zyl, 1998, p. 36). The long-term objective would be to build administratively and politically strong and account-able provinces with adequate fiscal resources to fulfil their constitutional responsibilities.

References

Financial Mail, 19 June 1998.

Friedman, S. (1999), "Power to the Provinces", *SIYAYA*, Issue 4, pp. 44-46.

Humphries, R. & Rapoo, T. (1994), "Some Remarks on Governing the Regions", in Humphries, R. & Rapoo, T. (eds), *Governing the Provinces*, Proceedings of a conference convened by Centre for Policy Studies on forming new govern-ments and administrations in South Africa's regions, pp. 3-15.

IDASA (1997), *Provincial Whip*, 11 August.

Khosa, M. & Muthien, Y. (1998) (eds), *Regionalism in the New South Africa*, Ashgate, Aldershot.

Naidoo, K. & Pintusewitz, C. (1998), "Are the Provinces Overspending?: Budgeting in the New Intergovernmental Fiscal System", *Indicator*, vol. 15, no. 1, pp. 37-40.

Presidential Review Commission (1998), *Developing a Culture of Good Gover-nance*, Report of the Presidential Review Commission on the Reform and Transformation of the Public Service in South Africa, 27 February.

Rapoo, T. (1995), "A System in Dispute: Provincial Government in Practice", *Policy, Issues and Actors*, vol. 8, no. 10, September, p. 6.

Rapoo, T. et al. (1997), *Democracy In-action: Democratic Institutions and Policy-making Capacity in Gauteng*, Centre for Policy Studies, Research Report No. 53.

RSA (1996), *The Constitution of the Republic of South Africa, 1996, Act 108*, as amended.

South African Institute of Race Relations (1998), *South Africa Survey 1997-1998*.

The South Africa Report (1998a), no. 1.

The South Africa Report (1998b), no. 2.

The Star, 02/09/98.

Van Ryneveld, P. (1996), "The Making of a New Structure of Fiscal Decentralisation", pp. 4-24, in Helmsing et al., *Restructuring the State and Intergovernmental Fiscal Relations in South Africa*, Graduate School of Public and Development Management.

Van Zyl, A. (1998), "Financing the Provinces in South Africa", *Indicator*, vol. 15, no. 1.

Zimmerman, J. (1992), *Contemporary American Federalism: The Growth of National Power*, Leicester University Press, Leicester.

Chapter 6

The Gauteng Legislature: The First Five Years

Eddy Maloka

The establishment of the nine unicameral provincial legislatures is one of the achievements of South Africa's new democracy. Aimed at bringing government closer to the people, it is unlike the provincial administrator and executive council of the previous unitary system. Indeed, post-apartheid provincial legislatures represent a constitutionally protected sphere of government with powers to pass laws in certain spheres and influence the national legislative process through the National Council of Provinces (NCOP).

In his discussion of parliamentary scrutiny as well as prospects and problems facing the Australian Parliament in the 1980s, Ian Sinclair (1982, p. 70) summed up the work of the provincial legislature as follows:

> ... the main opportunities or procedures for the Parliament to scrutinise and criticise the government are through the debate on the address in reply; the budget process; debates on particular bills ... private members' notices of motion and private members' bills; debates on matters of public importance and censure of a minister, member or government. Along with these procedures are the debates on government statements, petitions, and, of course, Question Time.

Clearly, the emphasis here is on holding government and the executive accountable.

The Gauteng legislature (1997/98, p. 4), for its part, has a vision of "a society including its government, arriving at a consensus on the passage, and implementation of its laws as contained in the spirit of the Constitution" of the country. Its mission, therefore, is "the effective and efficient development of policies, enactment of legislation and ensuring that those policies are implemented with the participation of the public and its elected representative". Emphasis here is on the law-making function of the legislature through consensus amid the process of the repeal of apartheid laws and the transformation of apartheid institutions over the last five years. However, entailed in Gauteng's vision and mission are issues of democracy, transparency, accountability, sustainability, efficiency and effectiveness.

The Gauteng legislature as an institution had to be created from scratch and, indeed, at the time of writing, had managed to develop structures and systems to tackle the tasks identified by Ian Sinclair above. During the first three years of its existence as a legislature, focus had to be on the following:

- the organisational development of the legislature, including the development of its vision and mission, as well as the determination of its spending priorities;
- the development of the infrastructure and human resources to support members in carrying out their work; and
- the development of systems to enable the legislature to accomplish its mission (The Speaker's Budget Vote, 1997/98, p. 2).

By 1997, the physical and the organisational structure of the institution were in place, and so were the systems and procedures essential to the work of a legislature. The first annual report of the legislature was even published in that year. The remainder of this chapter will focus on these structures, systems and procedures.

Procedures and Practice

In terms of the Constitution, a provincial legislature can make laws for, amongst others, agriculture, abattoirs, housing, health services, casinos, cultural affairs, the environment, education (excluding technikons and universities), airports (excluding international and national airports), public transport, regional planning and development, tourism and welfare services. The activities of a provincial legislature are, therefore, centred on passing laws for the province, exercising oversight over the executive and the administration and electing a premier for the province.

The Gauteng legislature had 86 MPLs (members of the provincial legislature) in 1994. The African National Congress (ANC) was the majority party with 50 MPLs (59% of the total) and the New National Party (NNP) was the official opposition with 21 MPLs. The Democratic Party (DP) and the Freedom Front (FF) came second after the NNP with five MPLs each, with the Inkatha Freedom Party (IFP) with three MPLs. The African Christian Democratic Party (ACDP) and the Pan-Africanist Congress of Azania (PAC) were the smallest parties with one MPL each.

The Gauteng legislature has its own office bearers who are responsible for the day-to-day work of the institution. The speaker is the presiding officer who, while being a member of the majority party, is expected to be impartial when conducting the proceedings. The Speaker has a deputy speaker (a position currently held by a female MPL). Other office bearers are: the chairperson of committees, who co-ordinates the work of the committees and acts as the presiding officer in the absence of both the speaker and the deputy speaker; the leader of the house, who acts as a link between the legislature and the executive; party whips, who are responsible for the discipline of their members and the organisation of their party caucuses; the chief whip, a member of the majority party, who is the most senior whip; the leader of the official opposition; and the secretary to the legislature, who is the head of the legislature's administration.

The sittings of the Gauteng legislature are usually on Tuesday and Thursday afternoons (14:15), with Wednesdays occupied by cabinet and cabinet sub-committee meetings that are usually followed, in the case of the ANC at least, by a party caucus in the afternoon.

Each Parliament has rules that govern procedures and practices around the work of members. The British parliamentary rules, for example, are made up of four elements: the common law which evolved in the House of Commons for centuries; standing orders which followed the codification of certain practices; parliamentary case law which was the result of the interpretations of and rulings on traditional practices and standing orders by successive speakers; and customs and conventions which are mere agreements and arrangements that facilitate the business of the house (Laundy, 1989).

Within a period of less than five years, the Gauteng legislature had managed to develop its own standing rules. Each member has a copy of *Gauteng Legislature: Guide for Members* which acts as a reference book in addition to the standing rules. These rules evolved from the speaker's house rules and the provisional standing rules, both of which were adopted on 17 May 1994, as well as the standing rules adopted on 5 December 1994. These were then refined and revised over time. Today, the ten chapters of the standing rules deal with aspects ranging from "Order in Meetings and Rules of Debate" and "Interpellations and Questions" to "Committees" and "Public Participation".

In addition to the standing rules, the legislature has a Rules Committee consisting of ten members (including the speaker as the chairperson and the deputy speaker), appointed by the speaker. Each party with at least 5% of the seats in the house is allocated at least one seat in the committee.

The Gauteng legislature has been able to build administrative machinery aimed at supporting members and the parties in doing their work. Important in this regard was the review of the administrative system which began late in 1996 and culminated in the creation of four directorates the following year. This development was accompanied by the increase of the administrative staff component to 116, which increased the staff member: MPL ratio from 1:1 to 1.4:1.

The Directorate: Parliamentary Operations is responsible for the plenary of the house as well as standing committees. In addition to ensuring the security of the legislature and taking charge of international exchanges and other protocol matters, this directorate is also responsible for the public participation and petitions office discussed later in this chapter. The Directorate: Operational Support is responsible for the logistical and technical support to the plenary of the house. It is this directorate that ensures that the four-language (Sotho, Zulu, Afrikaans, English) translation is available to the members, and that the proceedings are captured verbatim in the Hansard and later archived. The public relations work of the legislature is done by the Directorate: Information and Liaison Services. Research support to committees and office bearers is provided by this directorate. The Directorate: Institutional Support is in charge of all administrative, financial and human resource matters.

Thanks to these support systems and structures, parties and members are able to carry out their work. Documents are distributed daily to members, and those that are needed for a particular sitting are put on tables in the chamber before the sitting commences. Members receive order papers with details on orders, questions submitted, legislation before the house and the schedule of committee meetings.

Arranging of the business of the house, however, is the work of the Proceedings Committee that is chaired by the leader of the house. The speaker and his/her deputy are ex officio members of this committee, with parties represented by their leaders. The leader of the house, in consultation with the Proceedings Committee, ensures that the business of the house is placed on the order paper which is then distributed to members.

A member can introduce a private bill or a motion in the house. Such a motion may be a subject for discussion, a draft resolution or a substantive motion for approval as a resolution of the house with respect to, amongst others, censuring a person or body. As in many other Parliaments, "Question Time" is an important part of the work of the legislature, especially with regard to holding the executive accountable. Members can ask four types of questions: interpellations, that is, questions intended for debate; questions for oral reply in the house; questions to the executive requiring a written reply; and oral questions to the premier without notice.

Despite restrictions on when, how and how many questions can be posed in respect of standing rules by a member per given time, these questions are an important tool for keeping the executive accountable. However, "question time" has been utilised more by the opposition than by members of the majority party, the latter being disinclined to subject their party colleagues to embarrassing questions. (Indeed, replies to these questions are often used by the opposition to issue press statements or call for enquiries.) In addition to being "monopolised" by the opposition, "question time" generates little public interest when compared to the British and Australian Parliaments, for example.

Standing Committees

Committees are the backbone or the "engine room" of any parliamentary system. It is in committees that members become thorough and develop specialisation in scrutinising bills or calling the executive to account. The core functions of committees are to develop and scrutinise legislation; exercise oversight over the executive and administration; and develop policy. These include the power to introduce a bill; deal with or consider a bill or any matter referred to them by the speaker; monitor, investigate and even make recommendations regarding any matter they consider relevant; summon any person to appear before them; and request any information they consider necessary for its work.

The Gauteng legislature has 15 standing committees and one ad hoc committee, all of which meet fortnightly, or weekly if necessary. Ten of the 15 standing committees are portfolio committees that correspond to the ten executive portfolios. That is: Housing and Land Affairs; Education; Finance and Economic Affairs; Social Welfare and Population Development; Public Safety and Security; Sports, Recreation, Arts and Culture; Public Transport, Roads and Works; Health; Agriculture, Conservation and Environment; and Development Planning and Local Government. The other committees are the Rules Committee, Petitions and Public Participation Committee, Internal Arrangements, Public Accounts Committee and the Privileges Committee. All the committees have ten members except the Finance and Economic Affairs Committee which has 13 members.

There is a fair representation of minority parties on all committees, especially with regard to their speaking and voting rights. All the committees are chaired by the ANC as the majority party except the Public Accounts Committee which is chaired by the official opposition (NNP) because of the crucial role it plays in terms of keeping the executive and administration accountable with regard to financial and administrative matters. At least five of the 16 committees are chaired by women. In fact, the deputy speaker, a female MPL, deputises the speaker as the chairperson of the Rules Committee, and is also the chairperson of the Privileges Committee in terms of the standing rules. Two of the five female chairpersons were white ANC members in the period 1994-1999. This fair representation of the opposition and women in the committees was in line with the ANC's commitment to democracy, transparency as well as gender and racial representativity in the structures of government.

This fairness notwithstanding, the speaker allocates votes to each committee member in proportion to the number of seats his/her party has in the house and the size of the committee itself. The ANC, inevitably, has a majority in all committees. However, according to "Guide for Members", emphasis is on deciding the business of committees through consensus, voting only being used as a last resort.

Committees have two key support pillars in the form of committee co-ordinators and researchers. Each committee is allocated a committee co-ordinator who supports the chairperson of the committee, co-ordinates the work of the committee and ensures that rules are adhered to in the committee. This work by committee co-ordinators involves, amongst others: sending out notices of meetings; drawing up the committee meeting agenda with the help of the committee chairperson; actioning committee meeting minutes; handling submissions from individuals and/or groups; liaising with provincial departments; attending public hearings convened by the committee; filing and keeping a record of committee documents and meetings; and helping with the drafting of committee reports.

The Research Services Unit provides research support to the committees and this includes the following services:

- Conduct empirical research
- Co-ordinate, facilitate and monitor commissioned research
- Provide advice and information on policy matters
- Provide reports and summaries on national bills
- Provide speech-writing services to office bearers

- Analyse and process public comments on bills and other matters of public interest.

Committees dealing with budget-related matters are crucial to any parliamentary system. It is for this reason that Gauteng's Finance and Economic Affairs Committee has three more members than any other committee. Every beginning of the year each member of the executive, including the premier and the speaker, present his/her proposed budget to the house. These are then referred to relevant committees for thorough scrutiny. The purpose of this exercise is to ensure that the legislature oversees the spending of provincial money. The speaker and chairperson of the Finance and Economic Affairs Committee, for that matter, attend the budget *lekgotla* convened by treasury as part of an inclusive budget process.

Whereas the Finance and Economic Affairs Committee is involved proactively in the policy-making process and holding the executive accountable, the Public Accounts Committee acts as a watchdog to ensure financial control and detect any irregularity. Indeed, in some provinces, there is no distinction between this committee and the Finance and Economic Affairs Committee because of the complementary role the two committees play. In Gauteng these committees operate separately to ensure efficiency and effectiveness.

All in all, the work of committees has increased significantly both in terms of the number of meetings and the quality of input into the legislative process. Between January 1997 and March 1998, for example, 538 committee meetings were held and 44 days were spent in public hearings of the committees.

National Council of Provinces (NCOP)

Provinces participate in the national legislative process through the NCOP. Gauteng is represented at the NCOP by six permanent delegates—three from the ANC, with the NNP, FF and the DP each allocated one delegate. Four special delegates (three from the ANC, and one from the NNP) are designated by the premier, with three temporary delegates sent in addition to represent the legislature on a particular bill.

Bills before the NCOP are classified as "Section 75" and "Section 76" bills. The former are bills that do not affect the provinces and are voted on at the NCOP on party basis. Section 76 bills affect the provinces and voting on them is by province. Therefore, for provinces to vote, provincial mandates must be formulated and given to the provincial delegation.

The mandating process is one of the complex aspects of the NCOP and the Gauteng legislature in particular. The NCOP follows a four-week legislative process that begins when a bill reaches the NCOP from the National Assembly. After a week of processing this bill at the NCOP, it is referred to the provinces. The second week, known as "provincial work week", is occupied by the work of delegates in their provinces, together with the relevant provincial committees. In fact, in addition to the speaker and the leader of the house, chairpersons of committees also play an important role during these two weeks in ensuring that the committee deliberate on the bill as well as maintain contact with the NCOP.

When the NCOP bill arrives at the Gauteng legislature, the Proceedings Committee sits to decide whether to classify it as "important", "ordinary" or "technical". If it is considered "important", a simple majority in the house can confer the mandate after a relevant committee has completed its work. If a bill is considered "ordinary" and the house is not sitting, the report of a relevant committee is distributed by the speaker to all members, and unless four written objections are received by midday of the next day, the decision of the said committee is taken as a mandate.

The whole mandating process and the selection of special delegates are monitored by the chairperson of committees. The provincial delegates then head for Cape Town in the third week to participate in the NCOP committees and engage other provinces on their mandate. The NCOP plenary sits on the fourth week.

For the mandating process to succeed the programme of the provincial legislature must be synchronised with that of the NCOP. In addition to that, Gauteng has an office in Cape Town which, amongst others, co-ordinates the flow of information and documents between the province and the NCOP; provides administrative support to delegates; and liaises with the NCOP administration for the province.

Public Participation

Ensuring active and effective public participation in the work of the legislature has been one of the objectives identified from the beginning. The Petitions and Public Participation (PPP) Office was created in the Directorate: Parliamentary Operations to facilitate public participation and provide administrative support to the petitions process (such as public hearings) initiated by the legislature itself.

"Petition" refers to a request or complaint from a member/s of the public, while "submission" refers to a written/oral suggestion from a member/s of the public. When a petition is received, it is forwarded to the Petitions and Public Participation Committee; a submission is referred to a relevant standing committee.

Besides petitions and submissions the public can participate in the work of the legislature by attending public hearings on legislation, a sitting of the house or a meeting of a standing committee. In fact, the legislative process itself is structured in such a way that no law is passed without public input. After a bill has been introduced by either the provincial cabinet, an MPL or a standing committee and published in the provincial gazette, notices are put in the newspapers calling for public response within 14 days. When a standing committee sits to deliberate on a bill, it can invite organs of civil society or even convene a public hearing.

The PPP Office has been proactive in empowering and encouraging the public to take part in the work of the legislature. Between July 1997 and May 1998, for example, 38 workshops were organised in a number of communities. Plans are in place to incorporate public participation matters in the school curriculum, thanks to the collaboration of the legislature with the Gauteng Department of Education. Brochures and other forms of educational material on public participation are available to members of the public.

Additionally, the interior of the legislative chambers has been designed in such a way that they welcome members of the public. They also have anti-apartheid art displays on the walls.

Conclusion

The establishment of the Gauteng legislature as an institution with structures and systems to enable it to carry out its law making and oversight functions is one of the biggest achievements of South Africa's new democracy.

This achievement notwithstanding, the Gauteng legislature is still faced with a number of challenges. For example, the formulation of policy is still dominated by the executive as opposed to the legislature, especially the committees. The oversight role of the legislature is, for that matter, constrained by the imperatives of party politics, as ANC members are likely to protect their fellow members of the executive when under attack from the opposition.

References

Gauteng Legislature (1997/98), *Annual Report*.

Laundy, P. (1989), *Parliaments in the Modern World*, Dartmouth, London.

Sinclair, I. (1982), "Government, Parliament and the Administration", in Nethercote, J.R. (ed.), *Parliament and Bureaucracy: Parliamentary Scrutiny of Administration—Prospects and Problems in the 1980s*, Hale and Iremonger, New South Wales.

The Speaker's Budget Vote (1997/98).

Chapter 7

Local Government in Intergovernmental Relations: The Northern Cape[1]

Doreen Atkinson

Introduction

The Constitution makes provision for developmental local government operating within a new system of inter-governmental relations—a system of "co-operative governance". In terms of this vision, the three "spheres" of government will be "distinctive, interdependent and interrelated". They are meant to function in a mutually supportive fashion, and there is a positive obligation on the national government and provincial governments to "support and strengthen the capacity of municipalities to manage their own affairs, to exercise their powers and to perform their functions" (Section 154 of the Constitution).

The Constitution establishes a flexible approach to decentralisation, with the intention that powers and functions are to be performed by the sphere of government with the necessary capacity and competence to most efficiently perform each function. The flexibility inherent in the constitutional provisions dealing with decentralisation introduces ambiguity into the relationship between the municipal and the provincial and national spheres of government. According to Sections 151 and 156 of the Constitution, local government is a "sphere of government" that has executive and legislative authority and a "right to govern on its own initiative". The Constitution maintains that municipalities have a comparable status to the other spheres, and national and provincial government may not compromise any municipality's right to exercise its powers.

On the other hand, Section 156 stipulates that municipalities have executive authority and the right to *administer* functions listed in Schedules 4 and 5. Municipalities may make by-laws for the *admini-*

stration of these matters. Furthermore, national and provincial governments must "assign" the *administration* of matters listed in Parts B of the Schedules to municipalities. The tension between the two types of provisions concerns the level of discretion, authority and initiative that municipalities should enjoy. Words such as "govern" and "initiative" denote significant autonomy, discretion and choice. Words such as "administration" denote the deconcentration of functions, without any real autonomy or choice.

In the context of this ambiguity, different national and provincial line departments have taken different approaches with regard to municipal involvement in service delivery. The overriding impression is that the constitutional provisions have not, as yet, influenced line departments to engage in meaningful decentralisation. There have been large variations amongst provinces and amongst departments in their approaches to decentralisation to transitional municipalities.

A Testing Ground for "Co-operative Governance": The Northern Cape

The Northern Cape is one of the new provinces created by the 1993 interim Constitution. As such, it began with certain disabilities: the lack of an established provincial administration, the need to consolidate provincial governance in a newly defined area, and an untested revenue base. A further difficulty was the degree of politicisation in the local and provincial government sphere due to the fine balance of power between the African National Congress and the National Party. Furthermore, the Northern Cape is by far the largest province in terms of land area, but the smallest in terms of population. This poses another challenge for local and provincial governance in the province.

Simultaneously with the introduction of the new provincial dispensation, local authorities had to weather the storms of the local government transition.[2] Their performances varied from remarkably good to disastrous. In many towns, inexperienced councillors and frustrated town clerks experienced friction, sometimes leading to the resignation of key municipal personnel. In some towns, officials with no municipal experience replaced them; in others, their positions remained vacant. In a few towns, municipal management virtually collapsed. The deterioration of the financial position of many local authorities was both a cause and an effect of the deleterious situation. There is therefore a real need for assistance from the provincial and national government, and from other agencies. Such assistance should be forthcoming within the philosophy of "co-operative governance" , which is encapsulated in the Constitution.

A Helping Hand? The Department of Local Government and Housing

The Department of Local Government and Housing (DLGH), located in Kimberley, is meant to be the central supportive agency for local authorities in the Northern Cape. Its performance, however, has not been encouraging. Part of the problem is that the department had to build up its resources from the modest base of a regional office of the erstwhile Cape Provincial Administration. Hence the officials who were inherited from the previous order lacked the authority and experience to manage a provincial department.

In 1995, the department suffered a further setback due to an inappropriate appointment at chief director level. When the appointee left the department two years later, the department's meagre resources were in shambles, and the reputation of the department suffered incalculable damage.

A crucial problem for the department is its limited regional capacity. There are three regional offices, in De Aar, Springbok and Upington. These offices are at present primarily concerned with providing housing and infrastructure subsidies in the erstwhile "coloured reserve" areas, which are still administered under Act 9 of 1987. These regional offices have no authority to take decisions; all matters have to be referred to Kimberley.

The overall result has been a very inadequate performance on the part of the department, on various grounds. Officials were often ineffective in responding to the needs of local governments. Certain systemic forms of support were implemented, notably intergovernmental grants and the

Project Viability Programme, which was implemented on the initiative of the Department of Constitutional Development (now Department of Provincial and Local Government). However, in late 1998 the DLGH began to regain a sense of mission with regard to local government, and began putting its own house in order.

A Lack of Response

Between 1997 and 1999, local governments in the Northern Cape experienced intense frustration with the lack of response from the DLGH to their needs.[3] The town of Springbok, for example, had to wait four years for the department to approve its structure plan. Long delays led to local authorities' interpreting the situation in party-political terms, which in turn worsened relations between local authorities and the department.

The Bo-Karoo District Council mentioned another source of frustration with the DLGH—its sluggish implementation of the infrastructure development plan. The department had promised R50 000 to each District Council for designing IDPs in rural areas. However, this money never came through, and the predominant impression was that the department had run out of money.[4]

Local authorities believe that there are not sufficient local government skills in the DLGH, which causes enormous frustration. Very few departmental circulars or guidelines are made available, and letters remain unanswered. For their part, DLGH officials often seem overwhelmed by the massive task they have to perform, in the context of numerous small local authorities with capacity constraints. Furthermore, DLGH, like several other Provincial Departments, is chronically underfunded and understaffed.

The problems faced by the Northern Cape DHLG have been replicated in other provinces. The failure of provincial departments to provide adequate support has a number of causes. Firstly, it has proved difficult for provincial departments to adequately monitor municipal performance. Municipalities had no statutory requirement during the transitional phase to inform provincial government of their performance. Frequently, provincial departments have discovered that a council is close to financial collapse only when it is too late to implement effective remedial action. Secondly, even when provincial departments are aware of difficulties within municipalities, few provincial departments have experienced staff to provide the necessary assistance. Thirdly, these administrative capacity constraints are compounded by financial constraints, with most provincial departments lacking sufficient funds to mount rescue packages for ailing or non-viable municipalities. Fourthly, there remains a fundamental lack of clarity about what developmental functions local authorities are supposed to perform that makes support from provincial to local level difficult. Finally, there is often intense inter-departmental rivalry at provincial level that can prevent co-ordinated support for local government.

With the support of SIDA, the DLGH launched a programme of capacity building in its own ranks in November 1997. The following objectives were put forward:

- To improve the quality of public administration in municipalities;
- To build the role of the DLGH as enabler and facilitator;
- To cope with a declining budget and re-evaluate the scope and direction of services;
- To develop effective management information systems;
- To launch a local government development programme to enable local authorities to take on broader development objectives.

The Philosophy of "Forums"

The Northern Cape Provincial Government promoted the establishment of Local Development Forums (LDFs) or Community Development Forums (CDFs) as advisory bodies in the different towns. The results were mixed—some towns formed vibrant forums, while they collapsed in other towns.

The forums were established under the auspices of the RDP Office, situated in the Premier's Office. The DLGH in the province also strongly subscribed to the "forum approach". The impression is created that more effort has been put into promoting forums than in promoting the functioning of municipalities. In this sense, the forum idea distracted attention from the goal of building viable municipalities.

The forum movement hampered the functioning of local authorities in other ways as well. In towns such as Keimoes, Carnarvon and Springbok, the relationship between the forums and the Transitional Local Councils (TLCs) became positively hostile, at least partly because the forums were used as an alternative platform for local leaders, from which they could challenge the legitimacy of the TLCs. Strong party-political cleavages also contributed to tensions between the forums and the TLCs.

Mutual Distrust

Certain departmental officials have become aware of the problems of local government, such as its politicisation and the loss of key municipal personnel. However, key officials tend to blame much of the misfortunes of local government on conservative municipal officials. Town clerks, in particular, have come in for criticism from departmental officials. The fact that inexperienced councillors often rely on the advice of town clerks has made the latter's influence even more pernicious—at least in the eyes of some DLGH officials.

The relationship between the DLGH and the District Councils has become a particularly sore point. The deteriorating relationship between the Diamantveld District Council and the DLGH illustrates this problem.

The Diamantveld District Council, located in Kimberley, has been involved since 1994 in a dispute with the DLGH about the management of the two small towns of Campbell and Windsorton. Management in the pre-1994 dispensation was done on an agency basis, with the Cape Provincial Administration and the House of Representatives as principals.[5] The relationship continued after 1994, despite the fact that the Provincial Government never got around to sorting out the terms of the agreement and despite numerous appeals by the District Council.

In 1995, the DLGH acknowledged its responsibilities,[6] when it requested the District Council to continue to administer Windsorton on a contractual basis. However, the terms of the contract were never clarified, and no indication was ever given as to how the financial needs of the Windsorton TLC were to be addressed, whether District Council officials were to be transferred to the Windsorton TLC, or who was responsible for financial management. In the meantime, the District Council provided administrative services out of its own resources.

The situation became a very frustrating one for the District Council. For example, it submitted its budgets to the DLGH in July 1995; by July 1996, there was still no reply. In the meantime, the District Council had to continue with the administration function.

Negotiations eventually ensued between the two parties in June 1998, when the DLGH made it clear that it wanted the District Council to accept full responsibility for the administration of Windsorton, to provide bridging finance on a continued basis, and to use its levy revenue to defray the operating expenses of the Windsorton TLC. The DLGH was explicit that this would exclude financial help. This was totally in contrast with the inherited agency function, whereby the District Council performed administration in Windsorton on the express understanding that the principal would foot the bill.

For its part, the District Council maintained that "it is more than willing to perform this function, provided that certain legal requirements are met".[7] The District Council argued that, in terms of Section 10D(1) of the Local Government Transition Act, no power or duty will be imposed on a municipality without the provision of sufficient resources to perform such a duty. If the Provincial Government were to transfer responsibility for the administration of Windsorton to the District Council, it would have to provide the funding. Furthermore, legislation, budgetary constraints and fiscal discipline restrain the District Council, which means that levy revenue could not be applied to defray the operating expenses of another municipality. In particular, it should be kept in mind that the budgets of District Councils are scrutinised very carefully by the national Department of Finance, with specific attention paid to financial sustainability, recovery of costs and the prohibition on performing functions outside the mandate of the District Council. With regard to Windsorton, the Department of

Finance expressly informed the District Council that it had no mandate to use levy revenue to cover Windsorton's administrative expenses.[8]

While the dispute dragged on, the expenses incurred by the Windsorton administration accumulated. By March 1998, the province owed R900 000 to the District Council. The problem became so pressing that both the Auditor-General and the Public Accounts Committee of the legislature expressed their concern.

This issue had broader implications. District Councils in the Northern Cape have long experience of administering rural settlements.[9] The Diamantveld District Council intended appointing a regional town clerk; however, the uncertainty about the administration of Windsorton and Campbell prevented this post from being filled. In the meantime, the Windsorton TLC was undertaking various unauthorised expenditures, for which the District Council did not accept liability. Not surprisingly, the Auditor-General's office was becoming increasingly convinced that the situation was unacceptable.

Despite these pressures, the DLGH did not clarify the situation, and refused to enter into a formal contract regarding its responsibilities. The DLGH maintained that it could no longer provide funding as in the past, because of "constitutional provisions and the FFC directives".[10] The District Council rejected this argument. It stated:

> The Department has taken a very casual stance as far as their commitment to Council goes to reimburse these funds, even going as far as to state that no funds are available to be used for this purpose due to the changed method of intergovernmental assistance. This constitutes gross abuse of the Council's resources and good faith, which also raises the question of the Department's *bona fides* regarding reimbursement of these funds.[11]

The mud slinging worsened, with the DLGH accusing the CEO of the District Council of immoral behaviour and contravening the spirit of co-operative governance.

In the process, conflict ensued within the District Council itself. Many of the ANC councillors began to oppose the stance of their own CEO, despite the legal justification for his position. The councillors began to join forces with the DLGH itself, through ANC party channels. This put the District Council officials in a very invidious position, where their councillors were disinclined to listen to their advice. The officials believed, rightly or wrongly, that this was part of an ANC plan to remove key white officials, including the CEO, from their positions in the District Council.[12] If there was some collusion between provincial government officials and district councillors, against officials of the District Council, then it bodes ill for the future of "co-operative governance" in this region.

The Project Viability Programme

The most far-reaching attempt in South Africa to assist local authorities is the Project Liquidity Programme (PLP). Initiated by the DPLG, it was aimed at providing early warnings about impending problems within specific local authorities. In terms of the programme, provincial teams were established, consisting of experts in municipal finance, as well as DLGH officials.

The main purpose of the programme is to identify and assist those municipalities that show signs of becoming insolvent. The main elements of the programme are:

- Monitoring of all municipalities (in particular, their cash flow and payments rates). During each quarter, each local authority had to submit particular information about its financial position. The information would lead to the identification of local authorities that were encountering difficulties.

- The creation of provincial task teams to assist municipalities in trouble.

- Conducting municipal management audits. The PLP team undertook "walk-through audits" of troubled local authorities, to assess specific reasons for their situation.

- Implementing management support programmes (including financial restructuring, rationalising of local administration, personnel audits, implementation of credit control measures, and training of councillors).

This programme has had some success in reducing municipal insolvency and placing municipalities on a stable footing. However, the PLP assumed that a provincial government had sufficient capacity to act on the warning signs. In the Northern Cape, this capacity had not yet been established in the DLGH, although the groundwork was being laid for improved performance. During 1999, the support function was contracted out to private sector management companies, under the auspices of the Municipal Support Programme. This helped several municipalities to stabilise their performance.

Much more systemic intervention is necessary to institute an intergovernmental system capable of supporting developmental local government. In the words of the MEC for Local Government in the Northern Cape:

> Although various actions have been taken by government to address the current crisis situation in municipalities in the short to medium-term, long-term solutions are required to restore financial discipline, eliminate outstanding debts and generate the necessary cash flows.

Financial Assistance: Intergovernmental Grants

Until 1999, the most meaningful form of assistance which local authorities received from the DLGH, were the intergovernmental grant (IGG). IGGs have become an integral part of municipal finances in many towns; indeed, some towns rely on IGGs in order to stay financially afloat.

The DPLG intended the IGGs to be allocated according to two criteria: the poverty index and population figures.

The DLGH tried to set conditions for granting the IGGs. It requested proper financial statements from local authorities, as well as evidence that local authorities were trying to remedy their arrears situation. However, the department lacked the capacity to check up on the information provided by municipal officials. Furthermore, it was legally obliged to pay out the IGGs to local authorities, and therefore its prescriptions did not have much force in practice. The department was also concerned about the tendency of local authorities to use IGGs to pay for salaries, especially if they had severe cash-flow problems.

The amount of money allocated to provinces by national government to DLGH was steadily reduced. Between 1995/96 and 1996/97, the amount provided for Northern Cape IGGs was reduced by 15%, from R21 million to R19 million.

The IGG system was not well understood at local level. The complaint was frequently heard that IGGs were mainly given to those local authorities who were in dire straits, and that those who performed well, got less. This led to resentment about the allocation of IGGs: some towns believed that they got less because their payment situation was not as desperate as that of other towns. This was seen as " rewarding failure and penalising success".[13]

The system of IGGs was changed in March 1998. The system of IGGs was transformed into the system of "equitable share" payments, targeted specifically at the service charges of indigent families. This is administered directly from the Department of Provincial and Local Government (DPLG) in Pretoria, which means that provincial Departments of Local Government have lost their discretion regarding financial support for local governments' operating expenses. Effectively, the system has been centralised at national level.

Winning Friends and Making Enemies: Local Governments and Line Departments

Local authorities in the Northern Cape have had to deal with a wide diversity of new relationships, as well as with old relationships in a new key. With some departments, a co-operative relationship has flourished; with others, there has been conflict and bitterness. Some departments have welcomed the new "sphere" of local government, whereas others have regarded it as a challenge to the authority of the Provincial Government.

This section provides a brief overview of the kaleidoscope of post-transition relationships in the Northern Cape, which add up to the complex picture of "co-operative governance".

The Department of Water Affairs and Forestry: Champion of Local Government

The Department of Water Affairs and Forestry (DWAF) was one of the few national line departments that built significant relationships with local government in the Northern Cape. It invested a great deal of energy in building up District Development Co-ordinating Committees (DDCCs), of which there was one in each of the six District Council regions. These DDCCs helped TLCs and District Councils to come into contact with line departments and other service suppliers. The DDCCs built up a remarkable degree of momentum during 1998; however, they were taken over by the Provincial Government's RDP Office, and subsequently dwindled.

The Northern Cape DWAF office recently completed a thorough study of water issues in the province. Significantly, it included a large section on institutional issues, with specific emphasis on local government. This was because it realised the importance of local authorities as future Water Services Authorities (to be established in terms of the Water Services Act). DWAF in the Northern Cape has also compiled Water Services Negotiation Workbooks, to assist local authorities to amalgamate their water services administrations within the newly demarcated jurisdictions.

However, despite the DWAF's positive attitude to local governments, the latter sometimes experienced frustrations with the DWAF. According to the Water Services Act, District Councils had to become Water Services Authorities (WSAs). WSAs had to draft water services plans, for which R150 000 was made available for each District Council. The Diamantveld District Council expressed frustration about what it regarded as inadequate funding to draft a proper water services plan. The frustration went deeper—the District Council felt that DWAF should have negotiated this with the District Councils. Instead, DWAF laid down fixed conditions for them. Hence the District Council officials felt that agency relationships were becoming positively dangerous in practice, even though in principle they were a good idea.[14]

Furthermore, DWAF funding (for example, the Working for Water Project) was allocated untimely. Despite the success of water projects, the Bo-Karoo District Council felt frustrated that DWAF money was provided in December, and the District Council had to spend it by March. This caused procedural problems, with much less effective control than before.[15] The reason for such sudden spending spurts is because of DWAF's internal budgeting practices, which lead to the reallocation of resources just before the end of the financial year to ensure that annual budgets are spent. This practice requires local authorities to respond immediately to frantic last-minute project implementation.

The National Department of Finance

The Department of Finance has to approve the budgets of local authorities. In the Northern Cape, this led to recurrent and worsening conflicts, notably between the Department of Finance and the District Councils. One prescription by the Department of Finance, which reduces the autonomy and discretion of District Councils, concerns payments to the Local Authorities Loans Fund. The Department of Finance prohibits the provision of infrastructure funding to local authorities that are in arrears with their contributions to the Fund. In the Diamantveld area, three local authorities (Delportshoop, Jan Kempdorp and Warrenton) were negatively affected by this prescription.[16]

A matter of much greater magnitude, however, was the growing restrictions on the budgetary allocations to District Councils. This issue needs to be placed in historical context.

The District Councils were established on the basis of the erstwhile Regional Services Councils, which, in turn, derived from the Divisional Councils in the old "Cape Province". The Divisional Councils were important service delivery agents in the rural areas; they built rural roads, managed rural clinics, and administered rural settlements. This was funded by District Council rates, which were levied on rural inhabitants.

When the Regional Services Councils were established, these functions were continued on an agency basis for provincial departments, such as roads and health departments. Due to the legacy of the Divisional Councils, the Northern Cape District Councils also had a strong tradition of either administering rural settlements directly (now on behalf of the DLGH), and of assisting TLCs with regard to administration and financial management. This is very different from District Councils in the other parts of the country, where the emphasis was solely on providing funding for infrastructure.

These additional roles played by the Northern Cape District Councils came under increasing pressure from the Department of Finance, which adopted a very conservative policy with regard to District Council budgets. The Diamantveld District Council, for example, had significant items in its 1998/99 budget turned down,[17] notably:

- R1 996 138 budgeted for administration of rural councils, regional administration and treasury services;
- R291 569 budgeted for an emergency control centre;
- R350 000 for a public bursary scheme.

In each case, the Department of Finance insisted that the money be spent on "capital projects where the greatest need exists".

The Diamantveld District Council was deeply dissatisfied with these prescriptions,[18] and valiantly stated its objections. The issue of regional administration caused the greatest concern. The District Council noted the following factors, which need to be taken into consideration:

- **Historical background.** The District Council performed the financial administration of towns in the district on an agency basis for the provincial government for many years. The District Council required at least two full-time and two part-time officials. With the amalgamation of towns into TLCs in 1994, the demands on these officials increased markedly, as towns called upon the District Council for assistance.

- **Establishment.** The initiation of a regional administration component was approved in the 1995/96 budget as an allocation to participating bodies. Annual allocations were subsequently made in the same way, all of which were approved. The Diamantveld District Council could not reasonably terminate the treasury services unit, which evolved from this original concept. At the time, five municipalities were served in terms of their debtors, budgets, financial statements and routine internal control functions.

- **Precedent.** The concept of regional administration or treasury services was an established function of other District Councils, such as the Bloemarea District Council in the Free State.

- **Economies of scale.** The District Council could provide adequate services to several local authorities at a cost far lower than the combined cost if each municipality attempted to undertake these functions independently.[19]

- **Contractual obligations.** The District Council entered into contracts with three municipalities, in addition to the two towns traditionally managed by the District Council. These contracts provided for payment of services at a reasonable and affordable rate.

- **Infrastructure investment.** The District Council allocated R150 million in projects since 1991. Management of these facilities by recipient local authorities was generally inadequate, and the District Council was concerned that this would lead to deterioration of infrastructure. Provision of management support and administrative services was an important investment in the well being of these communities.

The District Council also took issue with the rejection by the Department of Finance of the emergency centre. It argued that the allocation was based on the withdrawal of the SANDF from this function, the transfer of the function to District Councils in the Eastern Cape (which created a precedent), the establishment of the facility in the District Council building before the previous election, and the needs of over 900 users of the 107 emergency system in the district. Ambulance, fire-fighting and other disaster management functions depended on this unit for effective communication.

The District Council did not let the matter rest, and proceeded to organise a meeting with the DPLG and the Department of Finance. It repeatedly stated its need to meet with the Department of Finance prior to finalising the budget.[20]

In the face of the intransigence of the Department of Finance, the District Council began the painful process of cutting its budget, including freezing posts in the Department of Environmental Health, reducing equipment for civil defence, and reducing regional tourism projects.[21] The post of internal auditor was frozen, which, as the District Council commented, ironically contradicted the emphasis of the Department of Finance on effective internal control. Numerous other functions had to be cut back, including publicity, conference attendance, computer facilities and equipment maintenance.

A meeting with the Department of Finance was eventually held on 18 November 1998, which led to some of the items being reinstated. Significantly, this included an additional R1 million being allocated to regional administration. However, the experience was a bitter one.[22]

A further unhappy consequence of these interventions by the Department of Finance was the effect on District Council infrastructure programmes. The Minister of Finance reduced the Bo-Karoo District Council's budget for 1997/98; subsequently, a revised budget had to be drawn up. Until it was approved, no capital expenditure could be made.

Relationships between Local Government and Provincial Departments

A general difficulty experienced by District Councils is the lack of co-ordination between them and provincial line departments on agency relations. District Councils already provide agency services to the Department of Health, the Department of Transport, and the Department of Water Affairs and Forestry. District Councils feel strongly that there should be a uniform contract between local governments and different line departments. Such an exercise was attempted before 1994—a contract was drafted after several years but was never signed. This process was then interrupted by the political transition after 1994. At present, departments seem to accept the old draft contract as a guide, but there is not enough uniformity.

Two or three times each year the CEOs and departmental heads of District Councils meet to discuss common problems. They have discussed the lack of a uniform contract, but believe that it will be difficult to draw up such a contract, because they perceive the provincial government as being negative towards District Councils.[23] This has meant that District Councils, in particular, have been involved in protracted negotiations with Provincial Departments on a one-to-one basis. This has meant that there has been no coherent provincial policy on the role of District Councils, giving rise to frequent disagreements on several policy questions.

The experience of the health sector illustrates this problem. Before 1994, Regional Services Councils performed health functions for the erstwhile Cape Provincial Administration on an agency basis. These focused on primary health care and ambulance services. After 1994, District Councils continued with these functions, while being remunerated for their services by the new Northern Cape Provincial Government. The Provincial Government paid a 100% subsidy, which covered not only staff, but also vehicle and equipment operating costs.[24] The local authorities operated as autonomous agencies.

However, the provincial health department became increasingly dissatisfied with the health system. It set about restructuring the health system in accordance with the National Department of Health's new District Health System (DHS) philosophy, in order to overcome fragmentation of existing services, and to promote efficient, effective and affordable service delivery.[25] In the delivery of ambulance services, for example, the provincial department became frustrated with labour problems between staff and local authorities. Also, certain responsibilities, such as staff training and vehicle maintenance, were unclear.[26]

In addition, the Health, Developmental Social Welfare and Environmental Affairs departments were facing considerable financial shortfalls as reflected in the medium-term expenditure framework for the next three years. The Department of Health maintained that the fragmented system of health services was financially unsustainable.

Consequently, the provincial health department gave local authorities a year's notice of the termination on 1 January 1999 of the agency relationship. The department would then take over the provision of health services. The temporary solution, the department believed, was to freeze municipal health posts, while seconding departmental staff to local authorities, as and where necessary. With this goal in mind, the department drastically cut financial provisions made to local authorities for health services. In the Diamantveld area, the reduction of financial support in May 1998 led to the closure of five clinics, and the reduction of ambulance services by 50%.[27]

A task team was set up, on which local authorities and municipal trade unions were represented. The task team had to investigate options regarding the implementation of the DHS. However, the MEC made it clear that the task team should consider no other options than provincialisation.[28]

There were practical difficulties in this approach. The first was that local authorities believed that they were responsible for municipal health (in terms of Schedule 5 of the Constitution). The second was that local authorities believed that Section 10D(1)(b)(i) of the Second Amendment Act of the Local Government Transitional Act (LGTA) obliged provincial government to provide resources to fulfil this function. The third difficulty was that the scales of remuneration of local authorities were in general more favourable than those of the department, with the result that local authority officials were reluctant to become departmental employees. There were other staff-related problems. There was no provision at the time for transfers into the public service, in terms of the Public Service Act, which meant that all staff would have to be newly appointed. There was a real possibility of staff opting for severance, which would in particular aggravate the shortage of trained ambulance men in the province. Furthermore, there was the prospect that clinic staff may receive packages and then re-apply for posts.

Not surprisingly, this matter aroused fierce opposition from District Councils, as well as the municipal trade unions. IMATU lodged an appeal to the Supreme Court, to set aside the department's decisions. The Hantam District Council backed this appeal. Their concerns were based on the unconstitutionality of the department's decision, as well as the fact that it was contradictory to the White Paper on the Transformation of the Health System.[29]

In addition, NOCLOGA appointed a health committee to investigate the matter, a decision that was boosted by the lack of response of the department to NOCLOGA's queries about the issue.[30]

Specific problems listed by District Councils included the following:

- The secondment of personnel, accompanied by financial cutbacks, would mean that local authorities themselves would have to pay the operating costs of vehicle maintenance, office accommodation, administration and insurance;
- Conflicting lines of authority in staff administration were created, leading to disciplinary problems.

The response of the department to the local authorities was frosty. Numerous requests for meetings to resolve the problem were ignored. On 2 July 1998, a meeting eventually took place, where the department agreed to reinstate its allocations for health services for the current financial year.[31]

The department did not, however, abandon its plans to provincialise health services. As far as ambulance services were concerned, the local authorities gave up the fight, especially because Schedule 4 of the Constitution lists ambulance services as a provincial function. Since 31 December 1998, ambulance services again became a provincial function. However, this only happened after two years of declining financial allocations from the department to local authorities—leaving a residue of bitterness. The Department is also proceeding with its programme of provincialisation of clinics.

The Provincial Department of Transport

The maintenance of rural roads by District Councils came under increasing strain. The fuel levy, which was a means to build commuter transport, streets and stormwater infrastructure, has been removed.

District Councils maintained certain roads as agents for the Department of Transport. They did the re-gravelling, scraping and normal maintenance of proclaimed roads.

According to Article 10D of the LGTA, no function could be devolved to local government without the resources being made available. At the time, there was no written agency agreement with a province, with the result that the budgetary allocations to District Councils were constantly revised. Provincial funding was totally insufficient for the maintenance of roads. The budget of the Provincial Department of Transport was cut repeatedly, due to the emphasis on social services in the Northern Cape.

Different District Councils had different experiences with the Department of Transport. Relations between the Diamantveld District Council and the Department of Transport were very good. Cabinet wanted to take the roads function back to the province, but the department fought to keep the District Councils as agents.[32]

The Bo-Karoo District Council, in contrast, regarded the department as very autocratic, and felt that there was not sufficient consultation with District Councils. This would be a disaster for the Bo-Karoo District Council, as 52% of its activities were transport related.[33] In addition to the decreases, there was a tendency to allocate additional funding just before the end of the financial year, which made planning difficult.

The Bo-Karoo District Council and the Department of Transport also had disagreements on road maintenance priorities. In July 1997, for example, the District Council sent a deputation to discuss the budgeting of roads with the MEC for Transport. For the District Council, ongoing repairs and maintenance to rural roads were more important than resealing roads. The MEC of Transport agreed to this; a few days later, however, a letter arrived from the MEC that contradicted the understanding reached at the meeting. This led to another deputation from the District Council (based in De Aar) to the department (based in Kimberley, 200 km away).

In the meantime, the financial situation of the Bo-Karoo District Council's Department of Technical Services was so bad that the re-gravelling team could not function. This occasioned another letter to the MEC. After another meeting, the MEC approved the re-allocation of funds. The department provided R800 000 from the re-sealing funds for the maintenance of roads.

Clearly, the relationship between the Department and the District Council has been undermined by the worsening budgetary situation of the Department. It would be difficult to create a positive relationship under such circumstances. In practice, it has contributed to the District Councils' sense of powerlessness and frustration.

The Role of the Northern Cape Legislature

The Portfolio Committee on Public Accounts of the Northern Cape Legislature regularly holds hearings, before which certain local authorities are required to appear. This committee is ideally situated to uncover management difficulties in local authorities, and to put pressure on officials and councillors to set matters right. For example, it investigated the problems of the Windsorton administration and the town's financial crisis. It analysed the administrative collapse in Port Nolloth, and summoned the suspended treasurer and the former town clerk to give evidence to the committee.[34] It also made recommendations regarding financial management in Groblershoop, and the accounting system in Keimoes.

The committee floated several suggestions for improving the support systems for local government:

- That the DLGH appoints employees to compile financial statements for smaller local authorities;

- That District Councils and larger local authorities assist smaller local authorities in the drawing up of financial statements;

- That accounting work be contracted out to private auditing firms;

- That smaller local authorities combine their resources to appoint joint treasurers.

The Local Government and Housing Committee of the Northern Cape Legislature has also begun to flex its muscles. For example, in June 1998, the committee discussed the protracted financial crisis in Warrenton; the ongoing conflict between the Diamantveld District Council and the DLGH about the administration of Windsorton; the problem of unauthorised loans in Noupoort; and the collapse of the Port Nolloth municipal administration.

The committee tried to make its activities more accessible to the public, and it therefore held six regional sessions throughout the province.

It is not yet clear what the impact of these legislative committees really was. It appears that relationships between the committees, the DLGH, NOCLOGA and the office of the Auditor-General were being consolidated. This was partially due to the assistance of SIDA, and the growing concern in the legislature about the extent of municipal mis-management.

The Role of the Auditor-General's Office

The Office of the Northern Cape Auditor-General has been very active in monitoring local government performance. The Office submitted reports on specific local authorities to the Public Accounts Committee of the legislature.

The record of the local authorities was a cause for concern. In 1994/95, 90% of local authorities did not submit their annual financial statements to the Auditor-General by the due date.[35] Some of the local authorities applied for extensions, on various grounds, such as vacant treasurers' posts, elections at local government level, intensive workloads, and inadequate skills. The amalgamation between white and black municipalities, and the chaotic financial affairs of the latter, also contributed to this situation. In its 1996 report to the committee, the Auditor-General noted that the financial statements of 25 Northern Cape local authorities for the 1993/94 financial year were incomplete, their accounting systems were deficient, and their records were incomplete.

The Auditor-General can also notify local authorities of shortcomings in their financial systems. It then sends similar notifications to the DPLG, which can take action in relation to troubled local authorities. The Auditor-General's Office in Kimberley has also tried to improve municipal performance by compiling a guide with criteria for effective management. These criteria fall into the following seven categories: strategic management, organisation, staff issues, operational planning, financial planning, control and management information.

The Northern Cape Local Government Association: A difficult birth

The Northern Cape Local Government Association (NOCLOGA) took several years to get established. During 1994, there was no Northern Cape Province, and therefore no inherited local government association akin to the Free State Local Government Association (FRELOGA).

NOCLOGA's revenue depends on contributions paid by local authorities. This revenue is slow in coming, partly because NOCLOGA had inadequate administrative capacity, and partly because local authorities often cannot yet see a record of action. Due to the three years of its relative inaction, NOCLOGA now faces a problem of credibility. Many CEOs and town clerks do not see any reason to support NOCLOGA, as they have not experienced any benefits from their membership.

NOCLOGA recently appointed its first CEO, a secretary and an administrative officer. The effectiveness of this leadership still remains to be seen.

One of the practical problems that NOCLOGA has to address, is its communication with its member local authorities. In such a vast province, effective telecommunication was crucial. NOCLOGA wants to encourage local authorities to install computers and electronic mail stations. However, not much has yet been achieved in this regard yet, due to the chronic shortage of funds.

NOCLOGA's immediate prospects improved significantly after establishing a co-operative relationship with the Swedish Association of Local Authorities (SALA). The main aims of the SALA programme are:

- To support NOCLOGA to identify the needs of its members, develop feasible strategies and mobilise resources;
- To assist NOCLOGA in dealing with other provincial local government associations, as well as the South African Local Government Association (SALGA);
- To assist NOCLOGA in drafting a three-year action plan;
- To build an organisational financial base for local funding, and to establish NOCLOGA as a legitimate training institution for local authorities in the Northern Cape.

During 1998, NOCLOGA established six working committees:[36]

- **Constitutional Matters and Legal Affairs**, to assist with the implementation of legislation, strengthen local authorities with regard to legal matters, and ensure that NOCLOGA is recognised as the effective local government association of the Northern Cape;
- **Health, Welfare and Community Services**, to devolve health functions to a district health system, and act as a channel through which the health concerns of local government will be brought to the attention of SALGA and the provincial and national health departments;
- **Human Resource Development**, to build the skills of councillors and municipal officials as regards financial management, local economic development, public relations and legislation, through the provision of training based on the modules devised for the Project Viability Training Programme;
- **Development and Facilitation**, to focus primarily on housing issues;
- **Electricity**, to promote the debate about the restructuring of the electricity distribution industry in the Northern Cape, and plan for an efficient, affordable and sustainable industry in that province;
- **Finance and Tourism**, to assist local authorities so as to make them financially sustainable and promote tourism in the Northern Cape.

In early February 1999, a training session was held for all local authorities. This was offered with the help of SIDA, to enable all local authorities to do a needs assessment, and to determine what they expect from NOCLOGA. At the time, NOCLOGA had no policies in place, as it had no resources.

NOCLOGA is still finding its feet in the community of local government associations. It is affiliated to SALGA, although this is a problematic relationship. NOCLOGA is for instance frustrated by the fact that it does not have a clear role vis-à-vis SALGA. For example, NOCLOGA often gets information from SALGA at very short notice. Notice of MINMEC meetings, usually held in Cape Town, is often so short that NOCLOGA cannot attend, and therefore has no opportunity to feed into the policy process.

NOCLOGA still owes SALGA its affiliation fee. In turn, SALGA still retains NOCLOGA's portion of the "equitable share" destined for local authority associations. This creates an invidious stand-off. SALGA will only transfer NOCLOGA's portion of the "equitable share" once NOCLOGA pays its affiliation fee. NOCLOGA, however, has no resources, and therefore finds it very difficult to raise the affiliation fee from its own members. A further frustration is that NOCLOGA believes that SALGA provides little service to provincial associations.

The relationship between NOCLOGA, the legislature and the National Council of Provinces (NCOP) is also unclear. NOCLOGA feels disgruntled with the fact that the NCOP has links with the legislature, but none with NOCLOGA. This is a very weak link in NOCLOGA's situation.

NOCLOGA has slowly begun providing support to local authorities, and it intends to focus on the following urgent problems:

- Most local authorities face labour problems. Smaller local authorities typically do not have a labour department, and have to depend on local lawyers who know little about municipal law. Trade unions, in contrast, have sophisticated lawyers, so that local authorities tend to lose their cases against trade unions. SALGA is supporting NOCLOGA to finance labour offices in each province. SALGA will advertise two posts in the Northern Cape, and will pay their salaries.

- NOCLOGA wants to overcome the tension between councillors and officials.
- NOCLOGA wants to assist groups of local authorities to co-operate so as to use their scarce resources effectively.
- NOCLOGA wants to have a meeting with the MEC to discuss the principles underlying financial allocations to local governments.
- In October 1998, NOCLOGA held a workshop about post evaluations and categorisation of municipalities (in association with the Northern Cape section of the Bargaining Council) in Kimberley.

NOCLOGA's credibility is slowly improving. During the protracted conflict with the Department of Health over the provincialisation of health services, the Bo-Karoo District Council decided to turn to NOCLOGA to approach the MINMEC for guidance.[37]

NOCLOGA is now poised for growth in influence and effectiveness. NOCLOGA's significance in the intergovernmental system is being increasingly recognised by the DLGH and SIDA, and by NOCLOGA's own membership. NOCLOGA's key weakness remains its poor financial base and its insufficient administrative corps.

District Councils to the Rescue?

Local authorities currently find themselves in a vacuum, with little effective support emanating from provincial government, national departments, NOCLOGA or SALGA. In this vacuum, the District Councils have stepped in to provide practical assistance to local authorities in distress. The Hantam District Council, for example, took over the administration of Nieuwoudtville after all the local officials resigned in that municipality. In Ritchie, after the erstwhile treasurer defrauded the local authority, the municipality then turned to the Auditor-General and the Diamantveld District Council for assistance.

These emergency interventions by District Councils have led them to conclude that more systemic district-based support systems can be provided. District Councils believe that there is a great deal of duplication of equipment and staff at TLC level. Local authorities need to learn how to share, and District Councils can help in this regard, because they function at a level that promotes economies of scale. District municipalities can have one engineer and one financial service.[38]

District Councils believe that administrative expenses cannot be recouped from TLCs, as they are financially too stressed. Rather, funding should be made available by province, as a subsidy to District Councils to deliver these district services.[39]

At present, the assistance of District Councils to local authorities takes various forms:

- Support to certain TLCs with the compilation of their annual financial statements;
- Computer support;
- Town clerk services in some cases.

In Delportshoop, for example, the Diamantveld District Council performed town treasurer services on a contractual basis. The District Council built up the Delportshoop municipal administrative capacity, including financial administration, record-keeping and the drawing up of financial statements. The District Council's computer system managed 2 500 monthly accounts in Delportshoop.[40]

However, the "Sir Galahad" role of District Councils, that is, their coming to the rescue of ailing local authorities, was severely circumscribed by the rigid prescriptions of the national Department of Finance, as outlined in an earlier section. The Department of Finance only measured District Council budgets against the criterion of infrastructure. This was counter to the philosophy of District Councils in the Northern Cape. In the Bo-Karoo District Council area (centred in De Aar), for example, the District Council only received about R4m in levies, compared to Diamantveld District Council's R30m. In the Bo-Karoo, only about R2m was available for capital projects, once overheads had been catered for. The District Council wanted an assessment of needs that transcended the exclusive focus on infrastructure. The skills base of the area needed to be built up, so that they could manage their capital projects.[41]

The role of District Councils remains ambiguous. This causes intense confusion and frustration. In the town of Loxton, for example, the Bo-Karoo District Council provided administrative services. When the Loxton TLC wanted to appoint their own town clerk, the initiative was stopped by the MEC. However, the MEC failed to give guidance about who should do financial and administrative services in Loxton. The MEC promised to discuss this with the District Council, although the meeting never materialised; hence the situation was never clarified. In the meantime, the District Council continued to supply administrative services in Loxton.[42]

The ambiguity in the role of the District Councils is worsened by the stand of the Department of Finance, which limits local authorities to a 6% per annum increase in their budgets, with the result that District Councils cannot develop new administrative departments. This means that District Councils are the only port of call for local authorities in distress, even though this takes place without the approval of national government and without much practical or financial support from the Provincial Government.

As a result, some District Councils have had to cease their efforts to assist local authorities. Until recently, the Bo-Karoo District Council provided administrative services in Petrusville, even though the Petrusville TLC could not afford to pay for these services. The Petrusville TLC owed the District Council R105 690 for administrative and financial services, for environmental health services, and for District Council levies. In desperation, the District Council decided that all services to Petrusville would be terminated.[43]

The role of the District Councils in supporting TLCs, and in providing administration on an agency basis to TLCs, is a crucial one. There are clearly strong forces pulling the District Councils simultaneously towards a strengthening of this role as well as towards a more conservative orientation.

The provincial DLGH still had to make up its mind on what it considered to be most important—to clip the wings of District Councils (a position which sometimes appears to have party-political considerations), or to utilise the District Councils to supply regional administrative services on a cost-effective basis. In this unstable climate, it would be foolhardy to predict the outcome.

Conclusion

Three generalisations can be made about the role of local government in the emerging system of intergovernmental relations:

- Some departments are seriously considering devolution of functions to local government level—and in particular, to district councils. Department of Water Affairs and Forestry is a notable case.

- This tendency is counter-balanced by the persistent failure of many municipalities to resolve their financial and administrative problems, despite four years of democratic local government and Masakhane campaigns. These constraints have made the transfer of responsibility to municipalities a relatively high-risk strategy, with the possibility that municipalities will be unable to sustain service provision. Some provincial departments have not done much to empower local authorities, and some have taken a lot of effort to reduce local government competencies.

- Those municipalities that have been confronted with viability problems during the transitional phase have not received adequate support and assistance from provincial Departments of Local Government and Housing. This has been a weakness in inter-governmental relations, where provincial government is required by the Constitution to provide assistance to the municipal sphere.

The local government sphere in the Northern Cape has survived a difficult time. New and inexperienced local authorities had to deal with their problems virtually on their own, with almost no support from the provincial government. In fact, some District Councils feel quite besieged by a perceived wall of hostility from the Department of Local Government and Housing. Strong party-political rivalries between the African National Congress and the National Party, and between the new officials in the provincial government and the "old guard" officials at local level, have worsened the situation.

The vacuum has come to be filled by District Councils, as well as occasional interventions by the Department of Water Affairs and Forestry, SIDA, the provincial legislature, the Auditor-General's Office and recently, NOCLOGA. These institutions are all growing stronger in their supportive role vis-à-vis local government. Recently, fairly positive signs have emerged from the Department of Local Government and Housing, which has turned to SIDA for assistance. Whether the department will be able to build up an effective system of local government support is still uncertain. This is the greatest challenge facing intergovernmental relations in the Northern Cape.

Notes

[1] This chapter was completed in March 1999, and as such does not take into consideration developments after that date. (Editor's note.)

[2] There were six District Councils, 64 Transitional Local Councils and 42 Transitional Representative Councils in the Northern Cape prior to the demarcation of new municipalities by the Municipal Demarcation Board.

[3] Doreen Atkinson, "Institutional Aspects of Development at Local Level: Problems and Prospects", report for Department of Economic Affairs, Northern Cape Government, 15 April 1997; Doreen Atkinson & Mark Ingle, research conducted for White Paper process, Northern Cape, June 1997.

[4] Interview, Bo-Karoo District Council CEO, 3 February 1999. The Bo-Karoo District Council is responsible for the Local Development Objectives (LDOs) of Brandboom, Masizakhe and similar settlements.

[5] Report to Council, District Council Director of Finance, 15 July 1998.

[6] Letter to Diamantveld District Council, dated 24 March 1995.

[7] Letter from Diamantveld District Council to DLGH, 28 December 1998.

[8] Meeting in Pretoria, 18 November 1998. Drawn from District Council letter to the DLGH, 28 December 1998. (The letter was copied to a Mr S. Louw, Department of Constitutional Development.)

[9] This issue is dealt with more fully below. District Councils and the national Department of Finance are in an ongoing dispute about the appropriateness of rural administration as a function of District Councils.

[10] Letter, DLGH to Diamantveld District Council, 9 June 1998.

[11] Letter, Diamantveld District Council to DLGH, 28 December 1998.

[12] The CEO also came under pressure from his councillors on other issues, notably the insistence by the District Council to spend R150 000 on an official car for the chairman.

[13] Doreen Atkinson, *Institutional Aspects of Development at Local Level: Problems and Prospects*, for Department of Economic Affairs, Northern Cape, April 1997, p. 22.

[14] Interview, Diamantveld District Council CEO, 1 February 1999.

[15] Interview, Bo-Karoo District Council CEO, 3 February 1999.

[16] Diamantveld District Council, Department of Finance, report to Council, 19 November 1997.

[17] Department of Finance, letter to Diamantveld District Council, 10 September 1998.

[18] Letter to Department of Finance, 2 October 1998.

[19] It appears, therefore, that the Department of Finance's prescriptions ran counter to the evolving policy of the DPLG, which called for the rationalisation of municipal services.

[20] Letter from Diamantveld District Council to Department of Finance, 8 October 1998.

[21] Once again, there was a tension between the philosophy of the Department of Finance and that of the DPLG. The latter believed (in terms of the White Paper) that local authorities (including District Councils) had to play a prominent role in economic development.

[22] In the Northern Cape, the Diamantveld District Council's experience was similar to that of other District Councils, including the Bo-Karoo District Council. The relationship between District Councils elsewhere, and the Department of Finance, should be investigated. Do District Councils in other provinces have similar problems with the Department of Finance?

[23] Interview, Bo-Karoo District Council CEO, 3 February 1999.

[24] Dr V. Mafungo, "Provincialisation of ambulance and emergency services", Department of Environmental Affairs, Developmental Social Welfare and Health, Northern Cape, 20 August 1998.

[25] Preamble, Agreement of Secondment of Personnel, Department of Environmental Affairs, Developmental Social Welfare and Health, Northern Cape.

[26] Dr V. Mafungo, Ibid., p. 2.

27   Diamantveld District Council, Department of Health report to Council, 8 May 1998.

28   Dr V. Mafungo, Ibid., p. 3.

29   Letter from IMATU to Diamantveld District Council, 8 December 1998.

30   NOCLOGA letter to District Councils, 11 August 1998.

31   Diamantveld District Council, report by Department of Health to Council, 29 July 1998.

32   Interview, Diamantveld CEO, 1 February 1999.

33   Interview, Bo-Karoo District Council CEO, 3 February 1999.

34   Minutes, Public Accounts Committee, 16 July 1998.

35   Doreen Atkinson, *Institutional Aspects*, Ibid., p. 24.

36   Based on NOCLOGA documentation.

37   Bo-Karoo District Council Executive Committee minutes, 23 October 1998.

38   These arguments were made before the nature of the new demarcation process became evident.

39   Interview, Diamantveld District Council CEO, 1 February 1999.

40   District Council, Department of Finance, report to Council, 27 January 1999.

41   Interview, Bo-Karoo District Council CEO, 2 February 1999.

42   Bo-Karoo District Council Executive Committee minutes, 7 September 1998.

43   Bo-Karoo District Council Executive Committee minutes, 7 September 1998.

Chapter 8

Resisting Ethnicity from Above: Social Identities and Democracy in South Africa[*]

Abebe Zegeye, Ian Liebenberg and Gregory Houston

Introduction

The relationship between social identity and ethnicity is a thorny issue. The commitment to democracy in South African society requires every sector of society to claim authority, rights and responsibilities. The new South African Constitution enacted in 1996 further underpins these claims. These claims should, however, not be vested in ethnic antagonism, cultural supremacy or any other form of social exclusivity.

Given that ethnicity, language and colour have determined membership of state and society in the recently abolished apartheid system,[1] how can formerly excluded communities be recognised without perpetuating apartheid categorisations? This chapter addresses this question by focusing on South Africa's transition to democracy.

After being on the brink of a full-scale civil war for several years, South Africa has experienced relative stability in the last years of the 20th century as a consequence of almost ten years of transition-directed negotiations, ounding elections, compromises and reforms on various levels. Even contemporary "urban terrorism" (such as in the Western Cape) is

---

[*] A version of this chapter has appeared earlier (May, 2000) as an HSRC monograph with limited distribution inside South Africa. Permission by the HSRC to publish it here is greatfully acknowledged by the authors.

expected to be contained by an appropriate crime prevention policy and its implementation.[2]

However, South Africa remains a deeply divided society. Culture, race, historical background, language and religion have all served to reinforce this segmentation (Bekker, 1996, p. 8).[3] Furthermore, ethnic, cultural, racial and religious differences often coincide with class differences.[4]

In addition, South African society still suffers from the legacy of colonialism and racial segregation imposed by continual minority governments.[5] The apartheid government, in particular, was a powerful allocator of identity (Singh, 1997). According to Pieterse (1992, p. 106), apartheid was a matter of "ethnicity from above" as the government used legislation and other sanctions to enforce acceptance of the most impoverished definitions of identity. It also suppressed and distorted identity to the extent that it excluded and suppressed all constituents of identity except race and ethnicity.

The struggle against apartheid—which resulted in nearly two decades of low-profile war and later mass mobilisation—served to facilitate identity formation by unifying opponents to apartheid in a common assertion of non-racialism and anti-racism. To an extent it also unified South Africans around anti-colonialism and perhaps a common "Africanness". The varied social and political movements that participated in the anti-apartheid struggle created a new identity by jointly and actively undermining apartheid notions of whiteness as representing political superiority and non-whiteness as representing political inferiority. *Thus anti-apartheid organisations and movements were important agents of identity construction*—and to an extent this legacy remains.

The radical inclusive definition of identity created by these movements formed the basis for many citizen-based checks on governmental authority in the new democratic dispensation. In short, some anti-apartheid movements fostered links between groups in civil society and legitimised citizens' expectations to the extent that the prevailing citizen identity became quite complex.

There were, on the other hand, anti-apartheid organisations that continued to base identity on race and ethnicity. Such exclusionist notions of identity are still operative in the relative stability of the new democratic dispensation.

Parameters of Identity Formation in South Africa

This chapter explores the ramifications of social identity for South African society. Fundamentally, we are interested in definitions of identity that do not openly set "self" against "other".[6] One such definition describes identity as being open-ended, fluid and constantly in a process of being constructed and reconstructed as the subject moves from one social situation to another, resulting in a self that is highly fragmented and context-dependent.

The notion of fluidity and context-dependence is particularly apt. After all, conflicting racial, ethnic, gender, class, sexual, religious and national identities are a reality. Hence members of a particular group do not all have the same concerns and viewpoints. The policies that have emerged from the "rainbow nation" philosophy must have taken cognisance of this fluidity as they embrace the multiplicity and dynamism of groups and discard the notion of the "natural", static and unchanging "group" or groups as expounded by apartheid.

Lipton (1985, pp. 14-15) summarises this contrast by listing the following defining characteristics of apartheid:

- The hierarchical ordering of the economic, political and social structures on the basis of race, identified by physical characteristics such as skin colour, hair texture and so on.

- Exclusion of "non-Europeans" from many of the civil, political and economic rights enjoyed by "Europeans", such as the right to vote, to move freely, to be full citizens of South Africa, and to own property and work anywhere in South Africa.

- Confining "non-Europeans" to inferior housing, schools, universities, hospitals and transport; and prohibiting sexual relations and inter-marriage across the colour bar. This discrimination insinuated that "non-European" cultures were inferior to that of the Europeans.

- Institutionalising this hierarchical, discriminatory and segregated system in law, enabling the government to enforce it through various measures.[7]

Moreover, the above characteristics came to be underpinned by a *civil religion* that conferred "Christianity" on apartheid and "apartheid" on Christianity (Bosch, 1984; De Klerk, 1975; Du Preez, 1983).

The policy of apartheid then became pervasive in that it aimed at the "separate development" of different race and ethnic groups to the extent that some were defined out of South African national politics altogether. Each group would exercise the right to develop, in its own area, its own culture, heritage, language and concept of "nationhood". Thus, apartheid involved the institutionalisation of categorisations emanating from colonial anthropology. Socialisation was structured by the separation of people along racial as well as, in many cases, ethnic lines. Racial and ethnic segregation emphasised cultural "differences", often translated into stereotypes (Malan, 1995).

The most significant piece of legislation underlying the apartheid policy was the Population Registration Act of 1950[8] that classified the South African population into four racial groups—white, black, Indian and coloured. A white person was defined as someone who "in appearance obviously is a white person and who is not generally accepted as a coloured person; or is generally accepted as a white person and is not in appearance obviously not a white person". A black was seen as any person who "is, or is generally accepted as a member of any aboriginal race or tribe". A coloured person was defined as any person "who is not a white person or a black" sub-classified under the Malay, Griqua (*Griekwa*), Chinese (*Sjinese*) and Indian groups and two residual groups, the "other Asiatic group" and the "other coloured group".

These categories were distinguished from one another on the basis of descent, that is, classification of the natural father, and/or social acceptance as members of a particular sub-group (Du Toit & Theron, 1988, pp. 136-137; Horrel, 1982).

Apartheid, and the material interest and prejudice which informed it, generated privilege and status for Europeans and displaced and disadvantaged "non-Europeans". The best evidence of this is the pattern of population movement. Blacks were forced to live in "homelands", which were generally rural areas with scant opportunities for employment. The homelands acted as labour reserves for a migratory black South African workforce, allowing the enforcement of low wages and the neglect of working conditions.

Ever since the discovery of major mineral deposits in the 19th century, white entrepreneurs had entered into exploitative labour contracts with "non-whites" to maximise capital gains from the mineral resources of the country. "Non-whites" could enter into such contracts only if they relocated to the urbanising and industrialising regions of the country. However, they were prohibited from bringing their families to the economic cores with them.[9]

The political construction of "communities" through residential and social segregation was perhaps the most significant factor in creating collective racialised identities. This was complemented by the homeland policy which aimed to divide the African population by entrenching ethno-regional identities. The government proclaimed that "South Africa was not a multiracial society, but consisted of many 'nations', each of which should have the right to control its destiny and preserve its identity" (Lipton, 1985, p. 30).

Before the colonial penetration of the region, South Africa, like many other parts of Africa, had what Ake (1993, p. 1) terms 'ethnic politics—political societies with governmental institutions in a local space where territoriality and ethnic identity roughly coincided'. In an attempt to reinforce ethnic identity, the apartheid government, following colonial tradition, identified eight African tribes or "nations", each of which would eventually be given "independence" in its own "homeland". All Africans were to be linked politically with their homeland, which would have as its citizens "its *de facto* population, plus members of its tribe in 'white' South Africa, its *de jure* citizens" (Lipton, 1985, pp. 23 and 30).

Ethnic mobilisation played a significant role in the development of apartheid and its programmes. In the process, Afrikaner social identity, the National Party (NP) and the state became inextricably intertwined (Adam

& Giliomee, 1978; O'Meara, 1983; Moodie, 1975). Afrikaner nationalism went beyond culture to include a close emotional attachment with the state and national symbols and values (Giliomee & Schlemmer, 1989). Indeed, because Afrikaner leaders used their political power to underwrite Afrikaner culture, state politics became infused with Afrikaner cultural considerations, including national symbols and values (Munro, 1995).

The Afrikaner image was forged by ideologues. To be an Afrikaner entailed having a sense of belonging to that group, and birth into the *Volk* (i.e. a group of racially similar people) superseded identification with the state. Thus, race, as opposed to the symbols and icons of cultural inclusiveness, remained the ultimate test of membership of the group (Adam, 1994; Bosch, 1984; Munro, 1995). The systematic repetition of certain key notions—such as that whites were superior and blacks inferior; South Africa belonged to the Afrikaner; the Afrikaner had a special relationship with God; Afrikaners constituted the *(Boere)volk*;[10] the Afrikaner was threatened; and the Afrikaner had a God-given task in Africa—reinforced Afrikaner identity. The Afrikaans language also became a cornerstone of Afrikaner identity (Cloete, 1992; Bosch, 1984). *But there were other identities calling for space in South Africa.*

The first Indians arrived in Natal in the 1860s as indentured labourers, followed by traders in the 1870s. Because their village, city or caste served as the basis for identification, a common group identity did not exist at the time (Ericksen, 1993; Desai & Maharaj, 1996). However, throughout the 19th century, "the construction of a broader collective Indian identity was fostered by the South African state", a process which became more pronounced during the apartheid era (Desai & Maharaj, 1996, p. 121).[11]

According to Minter (1986, p. 95), the antagonism of Afrikaners was first directed against Indian South Africans who, with their retail chains, were their closest economic competitors. Other processes also encouraged a collective Indian group identity. For the Indian community, "religion, music, customs, traditions and distinctive food tastes formed part of a womblike structure to act as a bulwark against a hostile environment" (Moodley, 1986, p. 234). The antagonism of the white minority and the hostility of the Zulu majority fostered a collective identity based on these common cultural traits. The brand of Zulu nationalism under the Inkatha Freedom Party (IFP) and its anti-Indian sentiments consolidated this identity (Maré & Hamilton, 1987; Desai & Maharaj, 1996).

A conscious effort was also made by progressive Indian organisations to draw the Indian community as a coherent bloc into the anti-apartheid struggle. Thus, the Natal Indian Congress (NIC) acknowledged the differences—heritage, culture, language, customs and traditions—between the four "national groups" (Desai & Maharaj, 1996, p. 121). Earlier on, the Transvaal Indian Congress (TIC) had moulded itself very much along the same lines.

Perhaps the most significant political construction of "community" and a collective identity is evident in the case of the coloureds. As a result of the systematic separation induced by apartheid, the coloured community was forged from heterogeneous elements (or at least understood themselves to be "coloureds" by historical coincidence). Slaves originating from Indonesia, Malaysia, India, Madagascar, East Africa and West Africa formed the early core of the coloured population in South Africa. By 1838, this heterogeneous group had one common feature—they were of mixed parentage, that is, descendants of European pioneers and Khoi-San women, settlers and slaves, and former "free blacks" (i.e. political prisoners deported from the East Indies or African slaves who had bought their freedom from Cape colonial masters). They constituted all those people who could be considered neither as whites nor as indigenous Africans (Martin, 1998). Crudely put, they were seen to be neither European nor "*Abantu*" or "native Africans".[12]

Despite being subject to discriminatory measures, coloureds at the beginning of this century could vote, were elected into political office and formed political organisations. The coloured elite struggled to demonstrate their level of civilisation by internalising the very codes and values used by the white elite to classify them. Class differentiation in the course of the century generated differences in attitudes and political strategies, and a political rift between collaborationists and anti-apartheid activists developed. Many of them were also subject to political fatalism and alienation from black South Africans as a result of National Party propaganda which instilled a fear of black South Africans (Martin, 1998, p. 533).

The Inkatha Freedom Party was the most notable black organisation in South Africa to use ethnicity and regionalism as mobilising factors. Inkatha Freedom Party, a cultural movement with political undertones—much like the Afrikaner Broederbond—was established in 1922. It fell into inactivity during the depression years of the 1920s and 1930s along with other political organisations such as the Industrial and Commercial Union (ICU). When the organisation was reactivated in 1975, membership was determined through acceptance of the notion of a Zulu cultural solidarity and linked to a common territory, namely the KwaZulu homeland (Maré, 1995).

This "national cultural movement" declared its aims to be the liberation of Africans from cultural domination by whites; eradication of socialism, neocolonialism and imperialism; eradication of all forms of racial discrimination and segregation; and upholding the "inalienable rights" of Zulus to self-determination and national independence (Davies et al., 1988). Being a black Zulu speaker and a resident of KwaZulu was no longer enough for people to "qualify" as Zulu. People had to show allegiance to the KwaZulu "state", the Zulu monarchy and the Inkatha Freedom Party. This entailed participating in Inkatha Freedom Party's political and cultural activities such as Shaka Day (Dlamini, 1998, p. 482).

While portraying itself to Africans as a political organisation following the tradition of the ANC, Inkatha Freedom Party was thus also a Zulu nationalist movement, often displaying extreme Zulu chauvinism. The organisation solicited adherents on the basis of two themes. On the one hand, it exhibited aggressive anti-apartheid reformism (initially), maintained a critical distance from the state, appealed to the traditions of the ANC and the liberation struggle and asserted a broad African nationalism. On the other hand, it appealed to traditionalism, ethnic loyalties, patriarchal and hierarchical values, discipline and a Zulu nationalism (McCaul, 1988).

Inkatha Freedom Party was entrenched in the power structures of the KwaZulu homeland, with all members of the KwaZulu Legislative

Assembly being Inkatha Freedom Party members. Thus, Inkatha Freedom Party wielded power in a regional appendage of the South African state as a one-party administration. It tended to portray the Zulu nation and itself as synonymous and mobilised ethnicity by means of the proclaimed distinctiveness of the Zulu nation and its history. The extent to which this history was distorted by colonial ethnography has largely been overlooked. By virtue of its primary cultural orientation and non-boycott approach, Inkatha Freedom Party later became an easy target for partial co-option by the apartheid and tricameral regime (see Maré, 1992; Liebenberg & Duvenage, 1996; Liebenberg et al., 1994, Introduction).

Segregation came to play a significant role in the formation of collective racial identities in South Africa and in a strong out-group aversion. Residential segregation was firmly entrenched by the 1980s, and by the early 1990s very few urban dwellers lived in racially and ethnically integrated areas (Christopher, 1994; Desai & Maharaj, 1996). This led to the development of politically constructed "communities", in which people defined as members of the same race group lived together, worshipped together and went to school together. Social segregation allowed very little social interaction between people of the different race groups. Besides, coloureds, Indians and poor whites were misrepresented as being beneficiaries of apartheid.

The economic differentiation emerging from residential and social segregation resulted in separate schools and universities and separate newspapers, television and radio stations; and these in turn facilitated the reification of group identities (Desai & Maharaj, 1996).[13]

Nevertheless, common interests were shaped in the struggle against white domination and, in particular, apartheid. For instance, opposition to the policies of various white governments from the last decade of the 19th century generated a sense of unity among the various (ethnic) groups in the African population. Pixley ka Isaka Seme, in calling for the formation of the South African Native National Congress (SANNC)—renamed the African National Congress in 1925—argued that the lack of unity among the indigenous people was the greatest obstacle to progress (Karis & Carter, 1972, VI, p. 72. Cited in Greenstein, 1995, p. 9).

It is clear that a common African identity did not exist at the time but had to be constructed to develop the unity so necessary for success. The SANNC focused on African unity and regarded fragmentation on the basis of clan and tribe as a serious danger (Greenstein, 1995).

At the same time as Afrikaner nationalists were building their nation through sentimental calls for devotion to their national cause and the *Volk*, "non-Europeans" were also experimenting with nation building. Nationalism seemed to be the preferred political option of the time. Ethnic identification was not simply a danger in itself. It was part and parcel of an imperialist tendency that seriously debilitated many African groups and contributed to the carnage of the liberation struggle. Pixley ka Isaka Seme praised the leaders of the many African communities in the hope of engendering unity among them. But ethnicity did not necessarily obstruct the development of a broad African identity. Instead, when not constructed as a force opposing African nationalism, ethnicity strengthened the African identity by promoting pride in African history. Seme often invoked the images of Shaka Zulu, Sobhuza of Swaziland and the Xhosa prophet Ntsikane when appealing for African national unity (Greenstein, 1995).

In the late 1960s a new movement emerged in South Africa as a result of disenchantment among African intellectuals with liberal and multiracial resistance against apartheid. This was to be referred to as the "Black Consciousness Movement" (BCM),[14] which can partially be traced back to dissatisfaction among students with the white-led, multiracial National Union of South African Students (NUSAS). The dissatisfied BCM students felt that the predominantly white leadership was unable to reflect the concerns of African students (Lodge, 1983) and therefore sought the psychological liberation of blacks (including coloureds and Indians) in an attempt to eradicate dependency on white leadership in the liberation struggle and to shape the post-apartheid society. Underlying this was a group response to oppression and a reliance on indigenous cultural traditions. Psychological liberation would lead to solidarity among black people, thus paving the way for their mobilisation towards liberation.[15]

During the early 1980s black opposition in South Africa underwent a radical transformation. This was informed by the replacement of the exclusionist black nationalism of some members of the BCM and the Pan-Africanist Congress (PAC) by a commitment to non-racialism. This was justified by the need to "isolate the regime" and to draw the widest possible number of people into the anti-apartheid struggle, that is, *strategic populism.* All South Africans who shared a commitment to the ideals of a non-racial, democratic country were encouraged to join the "national democratic struggle" against apartheid (Marx, 1992, p. 126). The United Democratic Front (UDF), a multiclass, multiracial organisation formed in August 1983 to oppose the apartheid system, included among its principles "an adherence to the need for unity in struggle through which all democrats, regardless of race, religion or colour, shall take part together".[16]

The UDF (later to become the Mass Democratic Movement or MDM) called for the unity of all oppressed groups (Africans, Indians and coloureds) but also for participation by individual white democrats. It argued that in order to elicit immediate and long-term advantages, whites had to be included in the liberation struggle (Marx, 1992).

The experience of political domination and economic exploitation among blacks and the commitment to a non-racial democracy among whites resulted in the formation of an umbrella organisation for members from every race and ethnic group and virtually every class in the country and moved beyond religious affiliation. The UDF drew together close to 700 organisations, the most important being youth and student organisations, women's organisations, civic associations and trade unions. Many of these organisations drew their membership from the different race, religious and ethnic groups in South Africa, leading to the construction of a collective identity across racial and ethnic lines.

The tricameral Constitution introduced in 1984 included coloureds and Indians in the highest decision-making organs. This created divisions within both the coloured and the Indian communities. Some members of these communities opted to support group politics by participating in elections for the racial assemblies. Others were strongly opposed to the tricameral Parliament. Indeed, voter turnout in the coloured election was 30% and in the Indian election 20% of registered voters.

Coloured ethnic politics underwent another dramatic change in the late 1980s and early 1990s when the majority of MPs in the House of Representatives crossed the floor to join the NP. This led to the ultimate dissolution of the political party which had led "institutionalised" coloured politics for much of the preceding two decades, namely the Labour Party.

Although the leading Indian political party in the tricameral Parliament, Amichand Rajbansi's Minority Front, continued to exist after the 1994 election, defections to the NP, Democratic Party (DP) and Inkatha Freedom Party (IFP) (and to a lesser extent the ANC) from then dramatically reduced its support in this community.

All these events coincided with the technocratic "reforms" initiated by P.W. Botha in the early 1980s. Though the boundaries of inclusion and exclusion within the polity shifted under the tricameral Parliament, continued segregation and a top-down approach marked the reforms. Selective "co-optation" combined with repression and top-down restructuring led some critics to refer to this as an era of an imperial presidency or "domination through reform" (Van Vuuren, 1985).

At the same time that a shared identity was being created among anti-apartheid activists, Afrikanerdom became divided. The first significant break followed the emergence of ideological differences between two camps in Afrikaner politics, the *verligte* (enlightened/liberal) and *verkrampte* (conservative) groups, in the 1970s. The two groups clashed on the question of introducing certain reforms to apartheid, including the recognition of African trade unions and the permanence of the urban African population, as well as the introduction of a new constitutional dispensation which would extend political rights to coloureds and Indians. This led to the establishment of the Herstigte Nasionale Party (HNP) that chose to maintain Verwoerdian principles. The Broederbond as an "ethnic vanguard" drove the HNP, led by Dr Albert Hertzog and later Jaap Marais, out of Afrikaner politics during John Vorster's rule.

A second break occurred when P.W. Botha mooted the idea of parliamentary representation for Indian and coloured South Africans (see Giliomee, 1982 for more detail). The ascendancy of the "verligte" camp led to the breakaway of another group in 1982 and the formation of the right-wing Conservative Party (CP) under Andries Treurnicht. The CP based its political appeal on the language of ethnic solidarity, group identity and cultural cohesion, invoking Afrikaner "tradition" as the wellspring of identity politics. It claimed that the NP regime had betrayed the Afrikaner culturally, politically and materially (Munro, 1995). The fragmentation of Afrikaner unity that followed led to a plethora of right-wing fringe groups.[17]

Afrikaner self-concepts thus moved from a "constructed Afrikaner homogeneity" to "pieces of broken images" (Cloete, 1992, p. 42). As Serfontein (1990, p. 19) points out:

> Afrikanerdom or the *Afrikanervolk* or the Afrikaners simply do not exist as a separate, identifiable group any longer. There are, however, different groups or fragments of Afrikaners, or Afrikaans-speaking whites. Some regard themselves as the *Afrikanervolk*, others simply as Boere, others as South Africans and others again as Afrikaans-speaking Africans (cited in Cloete, 1992, pp. 42-43).[18]

Similarly, individual self-perceptions among coloureds and Indians indicated a variety of identities. Some regarded themselves as belonging to a distinct "racial group", separate from other apartheid-defined racial groups, while others saw themselves as "blacks", a collective identity which included all non-whites. Still others embraced the non-racialism of the ANC by defining themselves as South Africans.

Indeed, broad collective practices and historical circumstances made some members of these groups more receptive to ethnocentrism and others more receptive to an all-inclusive and non-racial identity.

In late 1996, a survey of primary social identities carried out by Gibson and Gouws (1998) found that nearly one-third (32%) of those interviewed identified most strongly with the label "African", while 19% of the respondents identified themselves as "South African", 14% as "black", and the rest in terms of the various ethnic (33%) or religious (3%) groups. Most of the whites (28%), coloureds (30%) and Indians (31%) thought of themselves as just "South Africans", and only a few whites thought of themselves as "white" (5%). "Afrikaner" still formed a significant (24%) term of self-identification among whites. Among the coloureds interviewed, almost 29% identified themselves as "coloured" and 3% as "brown", while 16% of Indians identified themselves as "Indian" (in addition to 17% and 12% who gave their primary social identity as Hindu and Asian respectively). Only 3% and 0,4% of coloureds and Indians respectively gave "black" as their primary identity. This can be compared with 4% of coloureds, 2% of Indians and 0,8% of whites that identified strongly with the label "African".

But, as Adam (1994, p. 25) puts it:

> Apartheid ideology had institutionalised group differences. They were imposed and therefore rejected. Hence, the ground was laid for democratic inclusivism rather than counter-racism. At the same time, the historical racial and ethnic perceptions of difference—partially invented, reinforced and entrenched by Apartheid, but, above all, underscored by material inequality— did not psychologically homogenise the population, the ideology of colour-blind non-racialism notwithstanding. This legacy of Apartheid lives on in everyday racial and ethnic consciousness. Even if blacks as political rulers have modified ethnic hierarchy, racism as the everyday false consciousness of socially constructed difference has not disappeared with the repeal of racial legislation.

As the Gibson and Gouws study (1998) shows, most South Africans use racial or ethnic terms to describe themselves, with nearly 40% of the respondents selecting a general racial term and another 30% using a more specific sub-racial or ethnic term as their primary identity. Only slightly more than 20% of the respondents claim a national identity as their primary means of describing themselves. The study shows a strong sense of group identification in South Africa, with the overwhelming majority of respondents attaching great political significance to their primary group.[19]

To deny this is to repeat the common mistake, especially on the part of the "left", to underestimate ontological commitments[20] to racial and ethnic identities and their role in shaping historical struggles (Robinson, 1982, pp. 23, 243-245 and 447-451).

South African researchers thus far have tended in most cases to investigate shifting identities without taking cognisance of identity markers such as gender, age, family, religion, economic position (class) and physical environment, despite the greater acknowledgement of these markers in the democratic South Africa. Therefore, ontological commitments to race or ethnicity, far from being denied, should be placed in the richer context of these identity markers. Moreover, "ethnicity cannot be divorced from other changes of the twentieth century: urbanisation, communication networks, new relationships of production ..., the increase in migratory and commercial movements" (Maxted & Zegeye, 1997b, p. 66). Despite its apparent fixedness, ethnicity in Africa is constantly changing in response to changes in the form of the state (and notions of civil society, one might add).

Accommodating Identity and a Deepening of Democratic Processes—the Civil Community

According to Calhoun (1994), a major problem facing heterogeneous states is identification with distinct sub-cultures, groups or regions. Hence, many governments in diverse societies regard nation building as an essential strategy to develop a common culture and patriotism towards the state. However, strategies of nation building differ in the extent to which they recognise sub-groups. In some cases, loyalty to the state is regarded as much more important than loyalty to sub-groups. In other cases, ethnic, racial and other groupings are regarded as important building blocks of the state.

The current wave of democratisation across Africa has provoked a defence of the authoritarian state among certain African leaders. This defence has been built on the Huntingtonian ideal of "order amid change". This notion of "order" has been carried into para-ideological discourses such as "democratic order". Following Huntington's endorsement of the authoritarian state in Africa, President Daniel Arap Moi of Kenya argued that the liberties of democracy would unleash ethnic rivalry and destroy the fragile unity of his country. Zambia's head of state, Kenneth Kaunda, argued that the adoption of a multiparty system would bring "chaos, bloodshed and death".[21] President Paul Biya of Cameroon defended the power monopoly of his political party by arguing that it ensured a "united Cameroon devoid of ethnic, linguistic and religious cleavages" (Ake, 1993, p. 5). In Namibia, the party-dominant system under President Sam Nujoma seems to be moving towards greater centralisation and intolerance towards the Lozi-speaking people in Caprivi after nearly a decade of peace and tolerance.

The majority of states emerging from colonialism dealt with diversity by subordinating diversity to "nation building". Diversity was vilified on account of its relatedness to colonial divisions of regions, leaders, groups and communities, which divisions were aimed at delineating spheres of influence. Post-colonial leaders, in order to justify the one-party state, used these very divisions in doing so. These one-party states created a comprehensive apparatus of hegemony, co-opting within their structures all the important organs of civil society, including amongst others trade unions, student and youth organisations.

In 1965-66 a wave of military interventions—in Algeria, Nigeria, Zaire, Central African Republic, Burkina Faso (Upper-Volta), Benin and Ghana—led to the spread of the one-party system on the continent. This system was justified by asserting that opening the political system to competition and opposition would inevitably lead to ethnic mobilisation and political conflict (Young, 1997). Thus in these multi-ethnic societies public expression of ethnic or tribal claims was banished and ethnic associations were prohibited.

Yet the first step towards accommodating diversity in multicultural constitutional democracies (or even non-racial polities?) would be to acknowledge the heterogeneity of the society. This must be coupled with an assurance that different groups (and individuals) will not be harassed, discriminated against or persecuted on account of their sub-group membership. The highest priority must be the outlawing of discrimination. State officials and citizens must be prevented from and penalised for discriminating against their fellow citizens. The political framework should include constitutional guarantees, a Bill of Rights or laws that safeguard language, cultural, religious, gender and individual rights. *These prescriptions are a tall order but, if successfully instituted, will contribute significantly to the maintenance of a working democracy.*

Possible Impediments to Democratic Consolidation

Some scholars argue that the most significant aspect of identity politics in the late 20th century is ethnic struggle. They point out that "conflict between language, religion, physical appearance, beliefs, and customs of people from different ethnic groups has been—and probably will continue to be—a primary source of unrest in the world" (Landis & Boucher, 1987, p. 18; Ismagilova, 1997a, pp. 298-299). With the exception of class struggles, such as the rise of Nazism and Fascism (the latter two attempting to "indigenise" class power bases), the majority of 20th century social conflicts have been either "ethnic" or "religious". Ethnic conflicts occur when political struggles become ethnicised or when various cultural traditions become racialised and mobilised for political ends (Adam, 1994).

The essential problem in heterogeneous societies is the potential for sub-groups based on ethnic, cultural, linguistic, racial, religious, regional, class or caste identities to feel excluded. For example, they feel that they do not participate fully in the political system and/or that the government constantly acts in opposition to their preferences. Therefore many scholars are sceptical about the prospect of creating a common democratic culture or consolidating a democracy in a heterogeneous society. Some scholars even suggest the maintenance of separate groups within a polity through pillar-like structures, one example being the consociational theory advanced by Lijphart (1977). However, accommodating sub-groups—and especially ethnic consciousness, ethnocultural claims, and ethnic political behaviour—is widely considered to obstruct democratic consolidation as well as modernisation, industrial development, nation building, institutional and socio-economic pluralism and the promotion of individual liberties (Safran, 1991).

Conflicts over language in heterogeneous societies represent a fundamental threat to democracy for these theorists. They conclude that simply being multilingual, for example, makes people eschew democracy. They repeat the appalling reductiveness of the ideology of nation-statism, as Maxted and Zegeye (1997a, p. 390) point out, by asserting that "the wealth of cultures [is] really an impoverishment". Language policies may spark conflict because language represents culture, recognition, legitimacy and autonomy. In a like manner, ethnicity and religion, too, often give rise to enmity. Thus they should be neutralised before they become justifications for nationalism.

This perspective contends that when an ethnic group struggles to achieve political power, freedom and self-determination in an autonomous region or nation-state, the group pulls apart the fabric of multicultural societies. However, this argument is unhelpful in South Africa. There is a danger in understanding all conflicts engaged in by states during the 20th century as fundamentally *ethnic*. The danger is that struggles against undemocratic regimes—military-ruled or rule by ethnic (class?) majorities or minorities—that fundamentally sought to undermine the "nation-state" are equated with the struggles to build the state (i.e. in South Africa) even though they are not the same kind of struggle. This is because the "nation-state" underminers did not have the kind of material, military or capital base that the nation-state builders had, which makes them categorically different. So the problem is not simply that ethnicity, in the broadest possible sense, can be mobilised by the regime, but more importantly that ethnicity can be mobilised by groups of people seeking to undo the state and its priorities. The legacy of such a cycle of "ultimate" rule and resistance to the ruler may last for many years to come.

So far we have discussed the ways in which the state can utilise identity. We have yet to discuss the ways in which identities formerly excluded by the state can create a different kind of state.

The position of the newly enfranchised is quite problematic. They must ensure a number of crucially important things: that the new laws and policies protect them; that administrators at all levels of government are responsive to their interests; that their organisations become lobbying instruments with as much clout as other groups. They must also secure their ability to constantly develop social capital and to plug into the existing networks in civil society, as well as create new ones. While they have much to gain by supporting their government, they also have much to lose.

Unlike those who may be able to invest offshore or live the "good life", the newly enfranchised must prove to their fellow citizens that their acknowledgement as full members of the society will promote democracy. More important, in joining institutions in formal politics they may have to loosen their former ties and focus on social and political mass movements. Thus, during democratic consolidation, the newly enfranchised face particular disadvantages. They must reconstitute constituencies and establish organisations based on different principles. Critically put: To conclude that the newly enfranchised will threaten democracy smacks of the same sort of justifications used to deny them the franchise.

We concede that sharp differences may prevent a society from sustaining democracy because such differences may be used to justify non-conciliation, non-reparation or the outright punishment of members in the society. *But we take umbrage at the insistence in the debate on democratic consolidation that the newly enfranchised are more likely to use their social identities as a basis for oppressing their fellow citizens than others.* Rather, we submit that a consolidated democracy will be characterised by the absence of fear about difference. This does not mean that differences can be resolved by pretending that they do not exist, nor that we promote the liberal view of equality wherein personal habits and customs are confined to the private sphere. We suggest that the hysteria surrounding what the newly enfranchised may do with identity, culture or civil society be diffused. And perhaps the most effective way to reveal the baselessness of this fear of difference is to reveal how societies cope with difference.

Perhaps we can begin with the indigenous understanding that the landscape of democracy is already known and can be mapped. Identification with subgroups is not at all dysfunctional, since people can (and do) have multiple identities. In fact, if people are not forced to rank their identities they can bring more of themselves and more crosscutting cleavages into democracy (Spivak & Lorde, 1992). If democratic political systems cannot accommodate identification with sub-groups then something else will be necessary to guarantee participation in electoral and constitutional politics for excluded groups.

We contend that forcing people to rank their identities resembles the hegemony created by apartheid. The people who fought against apartheid achieved their identity by varied identity entry points. They mobilised distinctly as socialists, democrats, women's rights activists, artists, traditional leaders, cultural nationalists, anarchists, farmers or rural dwellers, and so on. And yet the overarching ideology of anti-apartheid did not eradicate their local identities. In fact, they were encouraged to see their local identities as resources that could enhance the anti-apartheid movement.

A politics of erasure underlies some of the debate on the dysfunctional nature of ethnicity. Moreover, a level of confusion has crept into the debate on democratic consolidation. The fear that ethnicity will rip societies apart is not grounded on the historical reality that nation-sized communities are ethnically, linguistically or religiously heterogeneous. *We claim that the debate on democratic consolidation by means of the denial of ethnicity is in fact based on the authoritarian and not the democratic approach to identity.*

A democratic political system consists, then, of any variety of measures which ensure, firstly, that citizens with their various identities participate fully in the political system in their country and, secondly, that the government acts in accordance with the preferences of its citizens.

The Process of Democratic Consolidation in South Africa

A number of issues relating to social identity became prominent during the negotiations for a democratic South Africa.[22] The first was the ruling National Party's constitutional proposals which emphasised group rights and protection for minorities. The second was the issue of federalism and regional autonomy for KwaZulu-Natal. And the third issue was the right-wing demand for a "homeland" (*Volkstaat*) for the Afrikaner nation.

During the late 1980s and early 1990s the NP through its prominent spokespersons shifted away from its emphasis on statutory group rights. This was clearly stated in 1991 by the former NP leader, F.W. de Klerk, in the following statement: "We commit ourselves to the creation of a free and democratic political system ... in which ... the rights of all individuals and minorities defined on a non-racial basis shall be adequately protected in the Constitution and in a constitutionally guaranteed and justifiable Bill of Rights" (cited in Kotze, 1994, p. 61).

The NP's Charter of Fundamental Rights (1993), however, set out to protect certain rights of apartheid-defined groups. In particular, it stipulated that every state-aided educational institution (as well as the parent community of every state or state-aided school) should have the right to determine the medium of instruction (read: Afrikaans) and the religious and general character (read: Christian and white) of such an educational institution or school. The Charter also called for the protection of the right to free association, which, in the absence of the application of a non-discrimination clause, would enable walls of privilege to be built around nearly all social institutions (Asmal, 1993).

The NP's proposals in its *Constitutional rule in a participatory democracy* (1991) as well as its submissions to the Convention for a Democratic South Africa (CODESA) at the end of 1991 called for a system of power sharing which would guarantee minority participation in government. The NP argued that "the political party is the most effective means of furthering the interests" of groups and therefore proposed a form of "participatory democracy" at national and regional levels in which "a number of parties effectively participate and in which power-sharing therefore takes place, as contrasted to the Westminster model in which one party exclusively enjoys power". Such a system was necessary because it "takes into account the diversity of South African society and the reality of the existence of a multiplicity of socio-economic and cultural interest groups" (cited in Asmal, 1993, p. 56).

For the NP government, minority participation was to be ensured through the participation of minority political parties in both the executive and the legislative organs of the state. Executive authority was to rest in a presidency constituted on a multiparty basis, with the leaders of the three to five leading parties sharing the chairmanship of the presidency on a rotational basis. All decisions of the presidency were to be taken by consensus, thus effectively providing a veto on all executive functions. The leading political parties were to be allocated an equal number of seats in a second house with the same powers as a first house, elected by proportional representation. The principles of "participatory democracy" and power sharing for the leading political parties and "effective measures for minority protection" were also to be extended to the regions (Asmal, 1993, pp. 56-57).

KwaZulu-Natal was the first provincial government to draft a provincial Constitution. Underlying this eagerness was the Inkatha Freedom Party's (IFP's) quest for a federal system with strong regional powers. The party identified a strong central government in a unitary system as an obstacle to democratisation because it would inevitably lead to an authoritarian system. A federal Constitution which conferred on the regions their own legislative, administrative, judicial and executive powers within a broad unifying framework would be intrinsically more democratic. As the IFP's power base was in the province of KwaZulu-Natal, it was important for the party to strengthen provincial autonomy. However, the IFP notion was declined by the Multiparty Negotiating Party (MPNP)[23] which drew up the interim Constitution in late 1993. After 1994, the Western Cape followed suit in writing a provincial Constitution.

The IFP only agreed to participate in South Africa's first election after the ANC and the NP signed the Agreement for Reconciliation and Peace on 19 April 1994. The ANC and NP consented to international mediation on provincial powers, the role of traditional leaders, and the constitutional role of the Zulu king. The IFP contended that these issues were not dealt with adequately in the interim Constitution. Above all else, the IFP was concerned with constitutional issues relating to the powers of the provinces (Smith, 1995), and since then has consistently pointed out that the new Constitution, adopted in 1996, does not deal adequately with these issues. Part of this relates to—apart from identity issues—the fact that the IFP adhered to a rather classical (obsolete?) notion of federalism at the time.

The Afrikaner right wing, organised into the Afrikaner Volksfront (AVF) under the leadership of General Constand Viljoen, demanded that freedom for the Afrikaner be accommodated through the formation of a *volkstaat*. The AVF consisted of 21 right-wing parties and organisations, including the Afrikaner Weerstandsbeweging (AWB) and the Conservative Party (CP). The AVF rejected a unitary state and said that Afrikaners wanted a *volkstaat*, which would be part of a future confederation of states. It aimed to unite all Afrikaners behind this ideal and to embark on a three-phase programme to achieve the *Volkstaat*: political pressure; popular resistance, including mass action, boycotts and strikes; and, as a last resort, secession from South Africa by an Afrikaner state.

This ethno-nationalist ideal was temporarily accommodated in the negotiation process by amendments to the interim Constitution which made constitutional provision for the right to self-determination by any community sharing a common cultural and language heritage, whether in a territorial entity within the Republic or in any other recognised way. It also provided for the establishment of a *volkstaat* council (*Volkstaatsraad*) to enable the proponents of the idea of a *volkstaat* to constitutionally pursue its establishment.

These issues reflected a concern for minority group rights, a resurgence of ethnic separateness, and the manifestation of cultural exclusivity.[24]

The results of the first democratic election in April 1994 were another demonstration of the salience of group identity in South African politics. The election results reflected a racial census although considerable cross-racial voting took place with all major parties drawing support from every race group. The NP was supported by 65% of the coloured and Indian voters nationally, with 60% to 70% of coloured voters in the Western Cape voting for the party (Reynolds, 1994). Apartheid-indoctrinated fears of African domination and distrust of African administrative competence, loss of relative status in the racial hierarchy, and competition for jobs and housing were in large part responsible for this support (Finnegan, 1994; Adam, 1994). The IFP was supported by over 50% of the voters of KwaZulu-Natal in the provincial election, while almost 85% of the IFP's national total came from this region. The Freedom Front achieved 2,17% (400 000 white votes) of the national voters. The ANC gained 94% of its support from the African community, and predominantly from speakers of Xhosa, Sotho, Venda, Ndebele, Tswana and Tsonga, although one-third of its supporters were Zulu speaking (Reynolds, 1994).

After its victory in 1994, the ANC adopted the approach followed by most post-colonial governments, namely emphasising nation building in non-ethnic and non-racial terms. The ANC is overtly non-racial in terms of its core ideology and seeks to decrease the barriers between different identities, language groups and cultures. In this regard Adam (1994, p. 17) observes:

> The ideology of non-racialism rejects an ethnic nation in favour of a civic nation, based on equal individual rights, regardless of origin, and equal recognition of all cultural traditions in the public sphere. The civic nation is based on consent rather than descent. Citizenry in ethnic nationalism on the other hand is based on blood and ancestry.

The ANC's *Constitutional guidelines for a democratic South Africa* (1989) advocated a unitary, democratic and non-racial state in which sovereignty was to be exercised through a central legislature, executive, judiciary and administration. Provision was made, however, for delegation of the powers of the central authority to subordinate administrative units (Welsh, 1989). The guidelines posited the need for a national identity in the following terms:

> It shall be state policy to promote the growth of a single national identity and loyalty binding on all South Africans. At the same time, the state shall recognise the linguistic and cultural diversity of the people and provide material for free linguistic and cultural development.[25]

The ANC identified a Bill of Rights as the means of guaranteeing the fundamental rights of all citizens. The legal right of parties to exist was based on a prohibition on the advocacy or practice of racism, Fascism, Nazism or the incitement of ethnic or regional exclusiveness or hatred (Welsh, 1989). The ANC's major policy document, *Ready to govern* (presented in 1992), provided further references to the nature of the constitutional order. The ANC rejected the association of political power with race or ethnicity as well as the protection of group rights or the representation of racial interests through political parties. It was argued that this approach would promote racial conflict rather than harmony and was not in the ultimate interest of minorities. Asmal (1993) pointed out that minority protection became necessary when the minority was in a position of sub-ordination to a majority, which would clearly not be the case in a democratic South Africa.

Basic citizenship rights and constitutionalism were thus presented as an antidote to authoritarian ethnic and racial group rights.[26] The nation was to be constituted on the basis of a "community of equal, rights-bearing citizens, united in patriotic attachment to a shared set of political practices and values" (Ignatieff, 1993, pp. 3-4).

The ANC's Revised Draft Bill of Rights (1992), which stated that language, cultural and religious rights should be protected in a new Constitution, was in line with the internationally recognised method of protecting minority rights contained in Article 27 of the International Convention on Civil and Political Rights. This convention provides that, "in those states in which ethnic, religious or linguistic minorities exist, persons belonging to such minorities shall not be denied the right, in community with the other members of their group, to enjoy their own culture, to profess and practice their own religion, or to use their own language" (cited in Asmal, 1993, p. 56).[27]

There was, however, according to Asmal (1993), a difference in emphasis as to the extent to which the equality principle, especially that prohibiting discrimination on the grounds of race, should apply to the exercise of these rights. Putting it another way, the right to associate should not allow persons the right to exclude others from participation in activities associated with schooling, sports, hospitals, etc.

One way of exploring minority rights vis-à-vis equality in the new South Africa is to examine the ANC's conception of culture and its place in the country. The ANC's driving policy, the RDP, pointed to the depoliticisation of ethnicity by affirming cultural unity at the national level and cultural diversity at the personal but not the community level (Venter, 1996). Furthermore, culture is conceived of as art, not as lifestyle-of-an-ethnic-group, and as such must be incorporated into the national culture. Thus, ethnic association and exclusion, particularly in schools, sports, etc., are counteracted by the demand for non-discrimination, which underpins the ideology of non-racialism as espoused by the ANC until 1997. This seemingly paradoxical notion may well imply some social tensions—but more about this later.

The new South African Constitution made provision for the establishment of a Commission for the Promotion and Protection of the Rights of Cultural, Religious and Linguistic Communities (Chapter 9, sections 185 and 186). Its primary objectives were to promote respect for the rights of these communities; to foster and develop peace, friendship, humanity, tolerance and national unity among cultural, religious and linguistic communities on the basis of equality, non-discrimination and free association; and to recommend the establishment or recognition of cultural or other councils for any communities in South Africa (see Chapter 9 in this book). The commission was potentially empowered to monitor, investigate, research, educate, lobby, advise and report on issues concerning the rights of cultural, religious and linguistic communities (Dlamini, 1998).

The four-year negotiation process in South Africa culminated in the acceptance of a consensus-based Government of National Unity (GNU), a cabinet staffed on a proportional basis by members of the majority party and the two leading opposition parties, the NP and IFP. Proportional representation ensured the participation of smaller parties in the legislature, while the GNU was extended to the provinces whose executive committees were also staffed on a proportional basis. Minority participation in government was also guaranteed by the so-called "sunset clause", which guaranteed the jobs of civil servants and members of the security forces (both comprising largely white Afrikaner males, but including civil servants of the former homeland and tricameral administrations) for five years. Nine African languages were added to the list of official languages (in the previous era Afrikaans and English were the only official languages), thus demonstrating a commitment to equal recognition of the rights of the different language communities.

The negotiating parties also agreed to entrench the powers of the regions in a new Constitution, and that a special majority would be required for any change in the powers, structure and competence of regional government. At the centre of the debate around the nature and functions of the provinces was the question of federalism.

Support for federalism in South Africa at the time came largely from the Democratic Party (DP) and the IFP, while the NP called for regionalism with strong federal elements. The ANC's regional policy of 1993, on the other hand, opposed the formation of political groupings on racial, ethnic or linguistic bases. The ANC aimed to discourage "political mobilisation on the basis of race, ethnicity or language and to prevent state power at any level from being used for purposes of ethnic domination, intolerance and forced removals of population" (cited in Venter, 1996, p. 13).

De Haas (1993) outlines three preconditions for the establishment of a federal system. First, a federal Constitution should be predicated upon specific communal identities or building blocks; second, communal identities should operate within a definable geographic base; and third, either the said geographical base is economically viable, or the central political organ is willing to subsidise the federal constituents through fiscal transfers. However, the conglomerations of subgroups sharing the same living space in South Africa made it virtually impossible to demarcate ethnically homogeneous or economically viable units (Hislop, 1998, p. 83).

In July 1997 the ANC released a discussion document entitled *National formation and nation building* which dealt with the national question and the nature of the nation. The document reaffirmed the ANC's non-racial stance and commitment to deracialising South African society. However, the ANC emphasised that the liberation of Black people in general and Africans in particular should be the main content of the national democratic revolution. The document acknowledged the reality of diversity and the persistence of cultural, religious and other identities in South Africa (Filatova, 1997).

Over the years the ANC has repeatedly reaffirmed its commitment to the Charterist ideal of the South African nation as a union built on cultural diversity and equality while seeking to promote the growth of a single national identity (Filatova, 1997, p. 49).[28]

Another ANC discussion policy document entitled *Building the foundation for a better life* released simultaneously with the *National formation and nation building* document, mentions an "African nation" and "the affirmation of our Africanness as a nation" but also stresses "equality among the racial, ethnic, language, cultural and religious communities" within "a united nation", "multiple identities" in "the melting pot of broad South Africanism", and the importance of "an over-arching identity of being South African" (cited in Filatova, 1997, p. 55). The central thrust of ANC policy has been to encourage the development of a *national identity based on unity-in-diversity*.[29]

It is also important to note here two contrasting ways in which the ANC government responded to the apartheid-constructed group identities. On the one hand it retained certain apartheid identities as a means of addressing imbalances of the past, for instance through affirmative action and black empowerment. On the other hand, overarching identities which cut across race and ethnicity were encouraged in a variety of ways. For example, group identification across racial and ethnic boundaries was promoted in labour, business, sport, youth, rural and women's affairs and the affairs of the disabled. This was done in order to make group identification as inclusive as possible and to make participation in institutions and processes, including consultative bodies, parliamentary public hearings, and consultative conferences and workshops, as representative as possible.

However, as Grobbelaar (1998) points out, there are dangers in both strategies. Strategies that aim at equitable and affirming outcomes for all groups could reinforce racial identification in certain ways and be used to solicit group support for political parties. On the one hand, addressing racial imbalances implies a drastic reduction of white and in particular Afrikaner access to the socio-political system, wealth and opportunities. The danger then exists that "people will not only fall back into the organic or laager-like comfort of group-mobilising identities like Afrikaner nationalism, but also that the loss of self-esteem and dignity experienced would contribute radically towards undermining a vision and strategy of equity across the board" (Grobbelaar, 1998).

On the other hand, affirming strategies could reinforce racial identities within the black population if they are seen to apply only (or largely) to the African segment of this group. For instance, coloured people may experience relative deprivation vis-à-vis the African population because the black majority government is seen to adopt policies which reaffirm the former "second class" status that coloureds held under apartheid. Indeed, such a perception recently led to the formation of coloured political and cultural movements in the Western Cape and Gauteng. Within the Indian communities the same problem has surfaced.[30]

Group identity as a driving force in South African politics can be seen in the efforts of some coloureds to use the term "coloured" as a symbol of collective identity against other groups, in particular whites and Africans (Maré, 1995). The appeal to this sense of identity lies in their perception of marginalisation, which, it could be argued, has continued into the democratic South Africa.

Affirmative action has also brought claims of new forms of racial discrimination from whites as well as Indians and coloureds—although these complaints must be scrutinised since in most parts of the country "black" empowerment is understood by many policy implementers as "non-Europeans" empowerment. The new non-racial democracy has been criticised for undermining the contingent "benefits" of the tricameral Parliament (in terms of jobs, houses and education) during the 1980s (Maré, 1995, p. 7). It is perhaps here that the role of civil society as pointed out by Liebenberg and Zegeye (1998) could be nurturing a culture of democracy, human rights and (communal) tolerance.

Attempts to include stakeholders take many forms. The new government embarked on various strategies to attempt inclusion. The National Economic Development and Labour Council (Nedlac), a statutory consultative body, for example, was formed in 1995 to consider all matters relating to economic and social issues before they are placed before Parliament or implemented. Nedlac includes representatives of organised labour and business, as well as women's organisations, rural dwellers, young people and the disabled. These constituencies are organised on a non-racial basis, and participate in Nedlac as units in their respective categories.

This national institution has contributed to a growth in the organisation and co-operation of these categories across racial and ethnic barriers. It is here that the democratic government is moving towards establishing overarching identities—for workers, youth, women, rural dwellers, disabled people, and businessmen—which are not based on racial or ethnic identities.[31]

The South African case has the potential to inform our understanding of diversity and democracy. The politicised nature of communities and individuals in this country under apartheid has set the stage for democracy and thus a choice in terms of the kind of society communities wanted for themselves. The African majority was not to be satisfied with simple autonomy for their group. Rather, they insisted that the economic inequalities of the past be remedied for everybody disadvantaged by apartheid.

Conclusion

Shortly after the transformation process towards the new South Africa started in all seriousness, Taylor (1992, Foreword) posed the question: "Can a democratic society treat all its members as equals and also recognise their specific cultural identities?" The answer is yes if culture is defined as the "common core of humanity" and "practices that all human beings engage in" (Alexander, 1989). When culture includes the tangible beliefs and philosophies that are reflected in how we recreate our humanity, culture can play a decisive role in democracy.

The South African Constitution seeks to foster a single political community while respecting the existence and worth of cultural communities. The resolution of the language question offered by the Constitution and the incorporation of traditional leaders and customary law are the outgrowths of respect for culture. We suggest that the art of "complex mapping" be applied in order to understand the role of culture in consolidating the South African democratic polity. Thereafter the lessons learned from this "mapping" of identity in South Africa can be used to enrich democratic theory elsewhere.

The prospect of creating a common democratic culture or consolidating working democracy is realisable in heterogeneous communities (Liebenberg & Duvenage, 1996). In South Africa, the very existence of multiracial, multilingual, multicultural and multiclass communities reveals the major flaw in theories of democracy that presume that homogeneity of society or community is a prerequisite for a working democracy.

Some democratic theorists further presuppose that diverse communities make social identity less of a contest and more of an amicable necessity. While not following exactly the same route as the multiculturalists, we assert that heterogeneity is not necessarily a threat to political order. We utilise the metaphor of mapping to illustrate that the cultural, linguistic, racial, religious and ethnic groups in the new South Africa indeed know how to sustain a heterogeneous community without resorting to the rigid measures of the previous minority regime. They provide evidence for the fact that heterogeneity does not preclude harmony, sympathy for others or commiseration, which are the bases for sustaining a community. In fact, the assumption that communities are automatically uniform has proven to be the Achilles heel of authoritarian schemes time and again.

We concede that societies attempting to consolidate democracy usually politicise some social category so that people can become citizens or non-citizens. However, we disagree that stable democracies use this overarching category in ways that exclude other crosscutting and overlapping identities that residents may claim or create. Hence the metaphor of mapping gives credence to our assertion that the South African society can avail itself of knowledge of how to achieve equity despite its multiracial, multiclass and multilingual composition.

Civil society—*societé civile* in Francophone literature—is no new concept in the analysis of democratic systems (Gorus, 1996). Camerer (1992 and 1996) sees civil society as an inherently pluralistic realm, distinct from yet interacting with the state, and consisting of numerous associations organised around specific issues and seeking to form links with other interest groups without seeking to become an alternative to the institutionalised state. Using the social capital generated through association and organisation around policy concerns and interests, civil society sustains negotiations and bargaining with the state.

However, lately civil society is claimed to be the invention of theorists in favour of multiparty democracy. As a matter of course, these theorists accept that civil society should be distinct from the state, and if possible exercise its activities peacefully. The debate on civil society and its role today in South Africa can contribute to establishing rules about who governs and under what conditions—and may turn out to develop differently from manifestations of civil society elsewhere.

Bekker (1996: 32) argues that "in civil society South Africans are free to choose from a menu of identities ... at many levels". To put this into practice may be more problematic given our historic legacy. We argue here that civil society need not be strictly a liberal or "one-community" construct. It embodies both the potential and reality of a flux of identities within the broader community of self-chosen citizens.[32]

Civil society (or the civil community) is the arena in which democratic attitudes, including tolerance, have to be developed. Civil society can be fostered by government but it is, in turn, part of its cultural basis (Maxted, 1999). The following are some important questions to help evaluate the role of civil society in an emerging democracy: How does civil society contribute to good governance, accountability and sound opposition politics amid balanced reconstruction? How can civil society maintain such a role during the growth of the state? What lasting role can it have and under what conditions? Can (or should) it counteract tendencies towards one-party dominance? What should its role be—strengthening government or opposing it, strengthening the state or weakening it, strengthening elite pacts and/or political parties or weakening them?

We are concerned with how interpretations of and allegiance to the concept of identity will influence civil societies because these determine the nature of checks on the state. Identity creates the requisite social capital to mobilise interest groups. We want to know how identity and identity issues (as reflected by civil society) impact on local government, regional/provincial government, national government, intergovernmental relations/management, civil-military relations, foreign affairs and international economic integration/globalisation (or resistance to it), democratic opposition and one-party dominance. Civil society organisations participate in debates at each level of government. Such organisations provide critical security against the over-extension of governmental powers (Foley & Edwards, 1996).

The very fact that group identities are associated with volatile social issues and concerns about redistribution should not be seen as an automatic threat to the consolidation of democracy. As new players are brought into government, parastatals, education and the public service in South Africa today, the right to freedom of speech and assembly allows civil society to actively investigate and change government policy. For example, the 1999 ISCOR case against affirmative action policies, the replacement of the RDP by the Growth, Employment and Redistribution strategy (GEAR), and nationwide criticism of the unemployment crisis and the prevalence of anti-crime strategies reflect that civil society is rather effective at challenging government. Moreover, these challenges did not come from homogeneous groups of people but from conglomerates of citizens "agglutinated" by their common concerns.

Within the new democracy, heterogeneity and unity have to be negotiated and reconciled more or less continually. South Africans furthermore have to reflect on the extent to which they want cultural, religious, ethnic, linguistic and racial identities to shape the reconstruction of national, community and individual identity (Singh, 1997). In addition, identity is complicated by the fact that the new government has embarked on reconciliation and nation building simultaneously (see Liebenberg & Zegeye, 1998).

The apartheid system cemented a division of labour and citizenship on a racial and ethnic basis, which resulted in the development of ontological commitments to racialised and ethnic identities. The current government aims at de-emphasising the apartheid-constructed divisions through its policy of non-racialism and the construction of a national identity. This should not be done in a way that subordinates the immediate interests of subgroups to a given national undifferentiated interest. It should begin from the point of departure that *people are what they are by virtue of how they actually live, produce and reproduce themselves; how they actually shape and reshape their everyday world.* The theoretical and practical issue is whether there is sufficient commonality in our sufferings and our hopes, in the modes and sources of our oppressions and expressions, and in the creation of a social order to eliminate destructive divisions and forge a concrete unity in diversity.

The continuous excursion through a "rainbow" of differences involves more than a concern on the part of people to tell their own stories and in so doing reaffirm themselves. It involves a thorough consideration of why their histories and culture—the modalities of being in the life-world—are meaningful and important, and of why they have an integrity worth preserving while subjecting it to progressive refinement. It involves commitment to the ideal of maintaining our own integrity without encroaching upon the integrity and well-being of others.

Notes

[1] This was a system inherited from earlier colonialist rule, pragmatically maintained by colonial white political entrepreneurs and later refined by apartheid rulers. One may, or may not, venture to refer to it as colonialism of a special type.

[2] The deteriorating crime situation in South Africa led to community-driven anti-crime activities. One such strategy led to the establishment of People Against Gangsterism and Drugs (PAGAD) mainly based in the Western Cape province. The actions taken by PAGAD and anti-PAGAD members and sympathisers over the past three years are bordering on "urban terrorism" that includes car-bomb attacks, attacks on people representing pro- or anti-factions, assassinations, intimidation and so on. While some see anti-crime sentiments in PAGAD activities, other see some tendencies towards Muslim fundamen-

talism or a struggle about control over syndicate (and drug) territory. But this is a topic for another article.

3 Religion played an important part in South Africa's history by providing justification for colonisation and apartheid as well as for resistance to colonial and apartheid oppression. See *inter alia* Boesak (1977), De Gruchy (1979), Hope and Young (1981), Mosala and Tlhagale (1986), Villa-Vicencio (1994) and Nel (1989 and 1997).

4 Bekker (1996) argues that a theory of identity should encompass constructivist conceptualisations and primordial elements, and be instrumental. However, South Africa has, apart from past ideological divisions, also been deeply divided on a class basis. For instance, fewer than 1,5 million South Africans earned more than R3 500 per month in 1996. Furthermore, unemployment totalled approximately 49% in the Eastern Cape, 46% in the Northern Province, 39% in KwaZulu-Natal, 38% in North West, 32% in Mpumalanga, 30% in the Free State, 28% in Gauteng, 18% in the Western Cape and 34% in the country as a whole. In addition, those who were employed at less than R500 per month in 1996 totalled approximately 42% in the Northern Cape, 41% in the Northern Province, 38% in the Free State, 36% in Mpumalanga, 32% in the Eastern Cape, 30% in North West and 27% in KwaZulu-Natal. See Statistics South Africa (1998, pp 46-48). The impact of all these figures on current and future class differences is immense.

5 See Kruger (1969: 3ff) on the heritage of the past. See also De Klerk (1975, p 50ff) and Magubane (1996) on the earlier roots of a racist state in South Africa. For some insight into the impact on historiography and collective memory, see Wright (1977).

6 The concept of "identity" has become a primary medium for understanding the relationship between the personal (subjective) and the social, the individual and the group, the cultural and the political, as well as the group and the state. "Identity" can refer to forms of (individual) personhood as well as collectivities or groups (Rousse, 1995). On the individual level, identity as a definition of personhood refers to uniqueness, that is, differentiation from other people or the whole of mankind, as well as sameness or continuity of the self across time and space (Baumeister, 1986; Erikson, 1968; Murgufa, Padilla & Pavel, 1991; Rousse, 1995). In addition, identity also incorporates the emotional attachment that individuals often have to group membership (Tajfel, 1978). Being a member of a group influences the way in which individuals see

themselves, especially if certain social categories are reviled or hated. These definitions of identity are fundamental to understanding the link between the individual and personal experience and large-scale cultural, social and political processes.

[7] Du Preez (1983) had earlier pointed out many of these underlying characteristics identified by Lipton in a study on master symbols in South African school textbooks.

[8] The other contending acts that enforced "apartheid" from earlier times were the Land Act of 1913, the "Native Reserves Act" and pass-carrying (a Dutch-British invention that started in the times of Colonial Rule and became entrenched by the 1800s).

[9] The impact of enforced "internal migration" due to apartheid laws and the use of surplus black labour from rural areas (non-economic core areas) is well described by Davenport (1977), a South African historian. See also Davenport (n.d.), pp. 13-18.

[10] The *Boerevolk* were seen to be descendants of the whites who settled in the interior of the Cape from the 17th century, relocated to areas further north in order to gain political freedom from British control, engaged in the Anglo-Boer Wars against Britain and established themselves anew after their defeat (1910 onwards).

[11] That Indian people, no doubt well meaning, chose to act as members of an Indian medical corps (sometimes referred to as "the Indian stretcher bearers") during the Anglo-Boer War or South African War also played a role in worsening relations. Whether intended or not, the Indian people by sheer "war-geographics" were seen to be mostly assisting the British forces against the Boers and their supporters. This aspect and the effect it had on later relationships have been under-researched and deserve more academic attention.

[12] A South African poet, Breyten Breytenbach (1999, p. 3), provides a description: "Afrikaan (inclusive of whites/Europeans) deur ondertroue en die verkragting van inheems Khoisan-mense, dalk met 'n stroopseltjie swart daarby; Oosters weens die inname van ambagslui en ballinge uit Maleisië en Indonesië en die Indiese kuste …". Ironically this "bastard" image/status applies equally to modern-day "white" South Africans (inclusive of Afrika-

ners), so-called "coloured people" and the majority of "black" South Africans. In a way this deconstructs any argument around South African identities.

[13] On the role of radio and television under apartheid, see Martinis (1996).

[14] The influence on the South African Black Consciousness Movement of similar intellectual streams in the United States has been under-researched. Sono (1993), Alexander (1985), Nel (1989 and 1997) and Motlhabi (1985) were some of the few who dealt with this topic—albeit from different angles.

[15] See Maphai in Liebenberg et al. (1994, pp. 125-137).

[16] Statement by the "Commission on the feasibility of a united front against the constitutional reform proposals", at the Transvaal anti-SAIC conference. Cited in Barrell (1984, p. 10). See also Houston (1999) on the national liberation struggle in South Africa with specific reference to the UDF.

[17]. English-speaking South Africans mostly stayed aloof from these debates. The Afrikaner-dominated state provided enough security for other "whites" to continue their daily lives (i.e. in the economic sphere) without getting embroiled in Afrikaner politics. The state provided the needed social and economic security and stability, which rendered political risks on any side unnecessary. The gradual militarisation of politics was a major contributor to this security and stability. Under the State Security Council (again dominated by Afrikaners and some carefully selected entrepreneurs) praetorian tendencies developed. The military, however, did not step in of their own accord. Rather, they were invited into politics on a piecemeal basis, as the government became ever more vulnerable due to international isolation and internal resistance. Ironically, the co-option of the military to maintain state hegemony neutralised the threat of a right-wing coup and delayed profound reforms.

[18] For some reason Serfontein does not refer to Afrikaans-speaking Pan-Africans.

[19] A similar finding is reached by Roefs and Liebenberg (1999), though they are tentatively more optimistic about non-racialism.

[20] Ontological commitments or ontological identities point to how an individual or group is structured in terms of practical historical being. Moreover, ontological consciousness is not a shadowy feature of consciousness juxtaposed with the "real" world. In contrast, ontological commitments inform day-to-day norms and perceptions of what it is to belong to a community, nation or

racialised group. Indeed, according to Hall and Held (1990, p. 175), "from the ancient world to the present day, citizenship has entailed a discussion, and a struggle, over the meaning and scope of membership of the community in which one lives". Consider the Aztec, Egyptian, later Phoenician, Judaeo-Christian, Muslim and other empires during the past few millennia.

[21] Kaunda's successor, Frederick Chiluba, asserted that the end of the Kaunda regime would bring about a "new" Zambia. However, the "new" Zambia did not materialise.

[22] For background on the negotiations, see Rantete (1998), Sisk (1995, pp. 88ff, 166ff and 249ff) and Tjonneland (1990).

[23] See, among others, Liebenberg (1996, p. 43). Note that the IFP's notion to write a "provincial" Constitution started earlier, between 1986 and 1988, with the "Indaba" experiment.

[24] The "Far Right" later split into many minor groups, with the AVF becoming the Freedom Front (Vryheidsfront).

[25] For a more detailed discussion of the ANC's Harare Declaration and subsequent release of the Constitutional guidelines, see Liebenberg (1990).

[26] For an earlier argument along these lines see Liebenberg and Duvenage (1996, pp. 48-64).

[27] This idea found itself eventually espoused in the South African Constitution (Act No. 108 of 1996), Chapter 9, sections 185 and 186 on the protection and promotion of the rights of cultural, religious and linguistic communities.

[28] The national democratic revolution and the Reconstruction and Development Programme (RDP) have been jettisoned in favour of "state-building" and GEAR.

[29] Interesting to note that in the month of Ramadan, South Africa's vice-president, Jacob Zuma, chose in his national address not to mention the terms "non-racialism" and "non-sexism" (SABC News, 9 December 1999). The terms "nation building", "peace" and "ubuntu", "reconciliation" and "self-sacrifice" came up, however.

³⁰ A Hindu leader quoted by Singh (1999, p. 45) for example stated: "To the Indians in this country the struggle goes on, as democracy unveiled new trends such as affirmative action."

³¹ On the counterside it remains to be said that Nedlac has succeeded in various agreements but failed in solving the tensions between the current government and worker-oriented organisations/trade unions and labourers (Marais, 1998, pp. 234 and 266-267).

³² In an earlier article Liebenberg (1990) has pointed out that civil society or what he terms the "civil community" need not be restricted to type-specific polities such as multiparty systems or societies with liberal economies.

References

Adam, H. (1994), "Ethnic Versus Civic Nationalism: South Africa's Non-racialism in Comparative Perspective", *South African Sociological Review*, vol. 2, no. 2.

Adam, H. & Giliomee, H. (1978), *Ethnic Power Mobilised*, Yale University Press, New Haven.

Ake, C. (1993), "What is the Problem of Ethnicity in Africa?", *Transformation*, vol. 22.

Alexander, N. (1985), *Sow the Wind: Contemporary Speeches*, Skotaville Publishers, Johannesburg.

Alexander, N. (1989), *Language Policy and National Unity in South Africa/Azania*, Buchu Books, Cape Town.

Asmal, K. (1993). "Neighbourhood Laager: The Devolution of White Power", *Indicator SA*, vol. 10, no. 3.

Barrell, H. (1984), "The United Democratic Front and National Forum: Their Emergence, Composition and Trends", *South African Review*, vol. 2.

Baumeister, A. (1986), *Identity: Cultural Change and the Struggle for the Self*, Oxford University Press.

Bekker, S. (1996), "Conflict Ethnicity and Democratisation in Contemporary South Africa", in Bekker, S. & Carlton, D. (eds), *Racism, Xenophobia and Ethnic Conflict*, Indicator Press, Durban.

Boesak, A.A. (1977), *Farewell to Innocence: A Socio-ethical Study on Black Theology and Black Power*, Orbis Books, New York.

Bosch, D.J. (1984), "The Roots and Fruits of Afrikaner Civil Religion", in Hofmeyer, W.G. & Vorster, W.S. (eds), *New Faces of Africa*, UNISA Printers, Pretoria.

Breytenbach, B. (1999), "Gedagtes van 'n Kulturele Baster: Andersheid en Andersmaak—Oftewel Afrikaner as Afrikaan", *Rapport (Aktueel)*, 28 November.

Calhoun, C. (ed.) (1994), *Social Theory and the Politics of Identity*, Blackwell, Cambridge, Massachusetts.

Camerer, L. (1992), *Civil Society and Democracy: The South African Debate*, Paper read at the bi-annual South African Political Science Association Colloquium, Broederstroom, South Africa, 16 October.

Camerer, L. (1996), "Party Politics, Grassroots Politics and Civil Society", *Orientation*, pp. 79-82, December.

Christopher, A.J. (1994), *The Atlas of Apartheid*, Routledge, London.

Cloete, E. (1992), "Afrikaner Identity: Culture, Tradition and Gender", *Agenda*, vol. 13.

Davenport, T.R.H. (n.d.), "The 1913 Land Act", *Sash Magazine*, vol. 26, no. 2.

Davenport, T.R.H. (1977), *South Africa: A Modern History* (Second edition), Macmillan, Johannesburg.

Davies, R. et al. (1988), *The Struggle for South Africa: A Reference Guide to Movements, Organisations and Institutions*, Zed Books, London.

De Gruchy, J.W. (1979), *The Church Struggle in South Africa*, David Philip, Cape Town.

De Gruchy, J.W. & Villa-Vicencio, C. (eds) (1999), *Doing Theology in Context: South African Perspectives*, Orbis Books, New York.

De Haas, M. (1993), "Ethnic Mobilisation: KwaZulu's Politics of Secession", *Indicator SA*, vol. 10, no. 3.

De Klerk, W.A. (1975), *The Puritans in Africa: A Story of Afrikanerdom*, Penguin Books, Middlesex.

Desai, A. & Maharaj, B. (1996), "Minorities in the Rainbow Nation: The Indian Vote in 1994", *South Afrcan Journal of Sociology*, vol. 27, no. 4.

Dlamini, C. (1998), "The Protection of Individual Rights and Minority Rights", in De Villiers, B., Delmartino, F. & Alén, A. (eds), *Institutional Development in Divided Societies*, Human Sciences Research Council, Pretoria.

Du Preez, J.M. (1983), *Afrikana Afrikaner: Master Symbols in South African School Textbooks*, Librarius, Alberton.

Du Toit, P. & Theron, F. (1988), "Ethnic and Minority Groups and Constitutional Change in South Africa", *Journal of Contemporary African Studies*, vol. 7, vol. 1 and 2.

Elphick, R. & Davenport, R. (eds) (1998), *Christianity in South Africa: A Political, Social and Cultural History*, David Philip, Cape Town.

Ericksen, T. (1993), *Ethnicity and Nationalism*, Pluto Press, London.

Erikson, E.H. (1968), *Identity: Youth and Crisis*, Norton, New York.

Filatova, I. (1997), "The Rainbow Against the African Sky or African Hegemony in a Multi-cultural Context"?, *Transformation*, vol. 34.

Finnegan, W. (1994), "The Election Mandela Lost", *New York Review of Books*, 20 October.

Foley, M.W. & Edwards, B. (1996), "The Paradox of Civil Society", *Journal of Democracy*, vol. 7, no. 3.

Gibson, J.L. & Gouws, A. (1998), *Social Identity Theory and Political Intolerance in South Africa*, Paper read at a meeting of the Midwest Political Science Association, Chicago, Illinois, 23-26 April.

Giliomee, H. (1982), *The Parting of the Ways: South African Politics, 1976-1982*, David Philip Publishers, Cape Town.

Giliomee, H. & Schlemmer, L. (eds) (1989), *Negotiating South Africa's Future*, Southern Books, Johannesburg.

Gorus, J.F.J. (1996), "Grijpt Afrika Zijn Kans? De Rol van Societe Civile in Transitieprocessen in Centraal Afrika", *Noord-Zuid Cahier*, vol. 211.

Greenstein, R. (1995), "Identity, Democracy and Political Rights: South Africa in Comparative Perspective", *Transformation*, vol. 26.

Grobbelaar, J. (1998), "Afrikaner Nationalism: The End of a Dream?", *Social Identities: Journal for the Study of Race, Nationality and Culture*, vol. 4, no. 3.

Hall, S. & Held, D. (1990), "Citizens and Citizenship", in Hall, S. & Jacques, M. (eds), *New Times: The Changing Face of Politics in the 1990s*, Verso, London.

Hislop, R. (1998), "The Generosity Moment: Ethnic Politics, Democratic Consolidation and the State in Yugoslavia (Croatia), South Africa and Czechoslovakia, *Democratization*, vol. 5, no. 1.

Hope, M. & Young, J. (1981), *The South African Churches in a Revolutionary Situation*, Orbis Books, New York.

Horrel, M. (1982), *Race Regulations as Regulated by Law in South Africa, 1948-1979*, Natal Witness Press, Pietermaritzburg.

Houston, G. (1999), *The National Liberation Struggle in South Africa: A Case Study of the United Democratic Front, 1983-1987*, Ashgate, Aldershot.

Idasa (1989), *Constitutional Guidelines for a Democratic South Africa: African National Congress Proposals, 1955 and 1988*, Cape Town, Idasa.

Ignatieff, M. (1993), *Blood and Belonging*, Vintage, London.

Ismagilova, R. (1997a), *Africa: Ethnicity and Cultural Pluralism*, Paper read at a joint conference of the International Sociological Association and IDASA, Cape Town, 15-17 December.

Ismagilova, R. (1997b), *Ethnicity and Politics and Self-determination in Africa*, Paper read at the Seventh All Russia Conference of Africanists, Moscow, 1-3 October (Abstract).

Karis, T. & Carter, G. (1972), *From Protest to Challenge: A Documentary History of African Politics in South Africa, 1882-1964*, Volume 1, Hoover Press, Stanford.

Kotze, H. (1994), "Federalism in South Africa: An Overview", in Kotze, H. (ed.), *The Political Economy of Federalism in South Africa: Policy Opportunities and Constraints of the Interim Constitution*, University of Stellenbosch and Konrad Adenauer Stiftung, Johannesburg.

Kruger, D.W. (1969), The Making of a Nation: A History of the Union of South Africa, 1910-1961, Macmillan, London.

Landis, D. & Boucher, J. (1987), "Theories and Models of Conflict", in Boucher, J., Landis, D. & Clark, K.A. (eds), *Ethnic Conflict: International Perspectives*, Sage, London.

Liebenberg, I. (1992), *Kultuur en Konteks*, Paper delivered at Unisa, Department of Religious Studies, Pretoria, May.

Liebenberg, I. (1996), "The Long Haul to Democracy: The Story of Constitutional Development and Transition in South Africa", *Journal for Contemporary History*, vol. 21, no. 2.

Liebenberg, I. (1990), *Responses to the ANC Constitutional Guidelines*, IDASA, Mowbray.

Liebenberg, I. et al. (eds) (1994), *The Long March: The Story of the Struggle for Liberation in South Africa*, Kagiso-Haum Publishers, Pretoria.

Liebenberg, I. & Duvenage, P. (1996), "Can the Deep Political Divisions of South African Society be Healed? A Philosophical and Political Perspective", *Politeia*, vol. 15, no. 1.

Liebenberg, I. & Zegeye, A. (1998), Pathway to Democracy? The Case of the South African Truth and Reconciliation Process", *Social Identities: Journal for the Study of Race, Nationality and Culture*, vol. 4, no. 3.

Lijphart, A. (1977), *Democracy in Plural Societies*, Yale University Press, New Haven.

Lipton, M. (1985), *Capitalism and Apartheid: South Africa, 1910-1986*, Wildwood House, Aldershot.

Lodge, T. (1983), *Black Politics in South Africa since 1945*, Ravan Press, Johannesburg.

Magubane, B.M. (1996), *The Making of a Racist State: British Imperialism and the Union of South Africa, 1875-1910*, Africa World Press, Asmara.

Mahali, V.P. (1996), *Contradiction, Conflict and Convergence of Class and Nation in Black South African Politics, 1925-1985*, Unpublished D.Phil. thesis, University of Illinois, Urbana, Illinois.

Malan, L. (1995), *Cultural Identity and Needs in Bellville South and Newtown: An Ethnographic Investigation*, Human Sciences Research Council, Pretoria.

Marais, H. (1998), *South Africa: Limits to Change,* Zed Books/UCT Press, London/Cape Town.

Maré, G. & Hamilton, G. (1987), *An Appetite for Power: Buthelezi's Inkatha and South Africa*, Ravan Press, Johannesburg.

Maré, G. (1992), *Brothers Born of Warrior Blood: Politics and Ethnicity in South Africa*, Ravan Press, Johannesburg.

Maré, G. (1995), "Ethnicity, Regionalism and Conflict in a Democratic South Africa", *South African Journal of International Affairs*, vol. 3, no. 1.

Martin, D.-C. (1998), "What's in the Name Coloured?", *Social Identities: Journal for the Study of Race, Nationality and Culture*, vol. 4, no. 3.

Martinis, D. (1996), *Democracy and the Media: From Policy to Practice in Public and Community Broadcasting*, Paper read at the Culture, Communication and Development International Conference, Human Sciences Research Council, 29-31 August.

Marx, A. (1992), *Lessons of the Struggle: South African Internal Opposition, 1960-1990*, Oxford University Press, Cape Town.

Maxted, J. (1999), *Globalisation, Spatial Restructuring and Social Exclusion in South Africa*, Position paper, Human Sciences Research Council, Pretoria.

Maxted, J. & Zegeye, A. (1997a), "Regional Introduction: North, West and the Horn of Africa", in *World Directory of Minorities*, Minority Rights Group International, London.

Maxted, J. & Zegeye, A. (1997b), "State Disintegration and Human Rights in Africa", in Lauderdale, P. & Amster, R. (eds), *Lives in the Balance: Perspectives on Global Injustices and Inequality*, Koninklijke Brill, Leiden.

McCaul, C. (1988), The Wild Card: Inkatha and Contemporary Black Politics", in Frankel, P., Pines, N. & Swilling, M. (eds), *State, Resistance and Change in South Africa*, Croom Helm, Kent.

Minter, W. (1986), *King Solomon's Mines Revisited: Western Interests and the Burden of History of Southern Africa*, Basic Books, New York.

Moodie, T.D. (1975), *The Rise of Afrikanerdom: Power, Apartheid and the Afrikaner Civil Religion*, University Press, Berkeley.

Moodley, K. (1986), "The Legitimation Crises of the South African State", *Journal of Modern African Studies*, vol. 24, no. 6.

Mosala, I.J. & Tlhagale, B. (eds) (1986), *The Unquestionable Right to be Free: Essays in Black Theology*, Skotaville Publishers, Johannesburg.

Motlhabi, M. (1985), *The Theory and Practice of Black Resistance to Apartheid: A Socio-ethical Analysis*, Skotaville Publishers, Johannesburg.

Munro, W.A. (1995), "Revisiting Tradition, Reconstructing Identity? Afrikaner Nationalism and Political Transition in South Africa", *Politikon*, vol. 22, no. 2.

Murgufa, E., Padilla, R. & Pavel, M. (1991), "Ethnicity and the Concept of Social Integration in Tinto's Model of Institutional Departure", *Journal of College Student Development*, vol. 32.

Nel, F.B.O. (1989), *Om Mens te Wees: Die Storie van Swart Teologie in Suid-Afrika*, M.A. thesis, University of the Western Cape, Bellville.

Nel, F.B.O. (1997), *The Role of Christian Fundamentalism in Apartheid South Africa*, Unpublished paper, London.

O'Meara, D. (1983), *Volkskapitalisme. Class, Capital and Ideology in the Development of Afrikaner Nationalism, 1934-1948*, Ravan Press, Johannesburg.

Pampallis, J. (1991), *Foundations of the New South Africa*, Maskew Miller Longman, Cape Town.

Pieterse, J.N. (1992), *White on Black: Images of Africa and Blacks in Western Popular Culture*, Yale University Press, New Haven.

Rantete, J. (1998), *The African National Congress and the Negotiated Settlement in South Africa*, J.L. van Schaik (Academic) Publishers, Pretoria.

Reynolds, A. (ed.) (1994), *Elections '94 South Africa*. James Curry, London.

Robinson, C. (1982), *Black Marxism: The Making of the Black Radical Tradition*, Zed Press, London.

Roefs, M. & Liebenberg, I. (1999), *Non-racialism in South Africa on the Eve of 2000: Eyeing South African Survey Data and Notes on Policy Making*, HSRC Website: http://www.hsrc.ac.za/delivered/nonracial.html.

Rousse, R. (1995), "Questions of Identity: Personhood and Collectivity in Trans-national Migration to the United States", *Critique of Anthropology*, vol. 15, no. 4.

Safran, W. (1991), "Ethnicity and Pluralism: Comparative and Theoretical Perspectives", *Canadian Review of Studies in Nationalism*, vol. 18, no. 1 and 2.

Serfontein, H. (1990), "Die Afrikanervolk Bestaan nie ... en Breyten is A rebel without a cause", *Vrye Weekblad*, 24 August.

Singh, M. (1997), "Identity in the Making", *South African Journal of Philosophy*, vol. 16, no. 3.

Singh, P. (1999), "Our 139 Years of History", *Indigo*, November.

Sisk, T.D. (1995), *Democratization in South Africa: The Elusive Social Contract*, Princeton University Press, Princeton.

Smith, P. (1995), "Playing with Fire: Inkatha's Fight for Federalism", *Indicator SA*, vol. 12, no. 2.

Sono, T. (1993), *Reflections on the Origins of Black Consciousness in South Africa*, HSRC Publishers, Pretoria.

Spivak, G.C. & Lorde, A. (1992), "French Feminism Revisited", in Butler, J. & Scott, L. (eds), *Feminists Theorise the Political*, Routledge, New York.

Statistics South Africa (1998), *Census in Brief, 1996*, Pretoria.

Tajfel, H. (1978), "Social Categorization, Social Identity and Social Comparison", in Tajfel, H. (ed.), *Differentiation Between Social Groups: Studies in the Social Psychology of Intergroup Relations*, Academic Press, New York.

Taylor, R. (1992), "South Africa: A Consociational Path to Peace?", *Transformation*, vol. 17.

Tjonneland, E.N. (1990), *Negotiating Apartheid Away?*, PRIO (Report No. 2), Oslo, Sweden.

Van Vuuren, W. (1985), "Domination Through Reform: The Functional Adaptation of Legitimising Strategies", *Politikon*, vol. 12, no. 2.

Venter, D. (1996), "It May be Art, But is it Culture? The ANC's Conceptions of Culture and Orientation Towards Ethnicity in the 1994 RDP Booklet", *Politikon*, vol. 23, no. 1.

Villa-Vicencio, C. (1994), *Civil Disobedience, Resistance and Religion in South Africa*, David Philip, Cape Town.

Villa-Vicencio, C. (1988), *Trapped in Apartheid: A Socio-theological History of the English-speaking Churches*, Orbis Books, New York.

Welsh, D. (1989), "The Governing of Divided Societies: A South African Perspective", *Africanus*, vol. 19, no. 1.

Wilson, R.A. (1996), "The Sizwe will not Go Away: The Truth and Reconciliation Commission—Human Rights and Nation-building in South Africa", *African Affairs*, vol. 55, no. 2.

Wright, H.M. (1977), *The Burden of the Present: Liberal-radical Controversy over South African History*, David Philip, Cape Town.

Young, C. (1997), "Democracy and the Ethnic Question in Africa", *Africa Insight*, vol. 27, no. 1.

Chapter 9

Challenges of Promoting and Protecting the Rights of Cultural, Religious and Linguistic Communities

Meshack Khosa[1]

Introduction

One of the key features of the South African Constitution is its explicit commitment to the creation of independent institutions to support democracy. One such institution which has generated heated debate over the past five years is the Commission for the Promotion and Protection of the Rights of Cultural, Religious and Linguistic Communities. This chapter presents an overview and analysis of debates leading up to the second national consultative conference (1999) on the Commission for the Promotion and Protection of the Rights of Cultural, Religious and Linguistic Communities.

The chapter comprises the following sections:

- A summary and analysis of debates in the national and provincial legislatures on the proposed establishment of the commission. This brief section sketches the broad political context in which the formation of the commission was debated. Among the issues raised are the imperatives of the Constitution, the relationship between the needs of the majority and those of minorities and the relationship between the various statutory bodies.

- An analysis of the constitutional framework in which the commission is to function. This section offers a detailed analysis of ss 185 and 186 of the Constitution and locates such analysis within the context of other provisions supporting, in varying degrees, a range of minority rights. An attempt is made to highlight the specific role of the commission under s 185 through reference to its wording and the broader requirements of the protection of minority rights. In addition, this part of the chapter briefly refers to examples from foreign juris-dictions (Canada, India and Namibia) which might be of interpretive assistance in detailing the functions of the commission.

- A consideration of the issues relating to the specific demarcation of functions of the commissions outlined in Chapter 9 of the Constitu-tion. A brief outline is sketched of the relationship between the s 185 commission, the South African Human Rights Commission, the Commission for Gender Equality and the Pan South African Language Board.

- A summary of all submissions received by the Department of Provincial and Local Government (DPLG) by the closing date of 11 September 1998. This section provides a short overview of recommendations in the submissions with regard to the composition and powers of the proposed commission. It highlights areas of consensus and difference as they are articulated in the submissions.

- Finally, eight themes or issues derived from the second consultation conference (1999) are presented with a view to raising critical issues for consideration prior to the establishment of the commission.

The process of implementing s 185 of the Constitution—the formation of the Commission for the Promotion and Protection of the Rights of Cultu-ral, Religious and Linguistic Communities—was initially outlined by the Deputy President in Parliament on 4 August 1998 and largely endorsed by the majority of parliamentarians.

The implementation of s 185 consists of several phases:

The first phase involves debates in the national and provincial legislatures.

The second phase involves public participation in the policy process initiated through a call for submissions and public hearings on the func-tions and composition of the commission.

The third phase comprises a national consultative conference where representatives from cultural, religious and linguistic communities will gather to map out key areas of consensus and difference which will inform the establishment of the commission.

In the final phase, a consolidated discussion document will be submitted by the Minister of Constitutional Development to cabinet for approval and possible implementation in 2000.

This chapter also draws on the debates held and submissions made in the period preceding the national consultative conferences held on Heritage Day, 24 September 1998 and 1999.

Table 9.1:   Land marks of the consultation process

Task	Date	Milestone
Sections 185 and 186 of the Constitution of the Republic of South Africa	1996	Consensus reached during the constitutional negotiations for the inclusion of Sections 185 and 186. The Constitutional assembly adopts the Constitution in May 1996 with final amendments in October 1996.
National and Provincial Parliamentary debates	August 1998	Special debates took place in the National Parliament and also at all Provincial Legislatures. Consensus was reached to speed the process for the establishment of the Commission for the Promotion and Protection of the Rights of Cultural, Religious and Linguistic Communities.
Call for submissions on functions and structure of the Commission for the	September – August 1998	38 submissions were received from a wide range of stakeholders. Summaries of the submissions were

Task	Date	Milestone
Promotion and Protection of the Rights of Cultural, Religious and Linguistic Communities		distributed at the first National Consultative Conference, which took place on 24 September 1998.
First National Consultative Conference	24 September 1998	The Ministry of Provincial and Local Government and that of Arts, Culture, and Technology hosted the conference. In attendance were the ministers of the two ministries, the then Deputy President, Mr Thabo Mbeki, and several other ministers, and government officials. The HSRC presented a position paper which teased out the key themes emerging from the submissions and research undertaken in association with the Department of Provincial and Local Government
Additional submissions received	October – December 1998	Five additional submissions were received and inputs considered in the writing of the final report of the conference by the HSRC and submitted to the DPLG.
Stakeholder interviews	August – September 1999	Major stakeholders were interviewed prior to the conference. Further interviews were scheduled for completion in December with a

Task	Date	Milestone
		possibility of a workshop to be arranged under the auspices of the Department of Provincial and Local Government.
Stakeholder and expert workshop to discuss the draft bill and four theme papers drafted by the HSRC in collaboration with the Department of Provincial and Local Government.	23 September 1999	Four draft papers and the draft bill were circulated to the delegates for the purpose of discussion, comment and debate. The four working papers were as follows: • Model and structures • Cultural councils • Mandate • Relationship between the commission and other institutions.
Second National Consultative Conference	24 September 1999	Keynote speech by Deputy President, Mr J. Zuma, underscored the importance government attached to the commission. The Minister of Provincial and Local Government also affirmed this. Rapporteurs presented reports of the working group theme papers. The workshop on 23 September 1999 was not mandated to make recommendations but to flag important issues for consideration by delegates at the conference.

Task	Date	Milestone
Way forward		Taking on board views and inputs at the Second National Consultative Conference, the four theme papers were revised and a final report submitted to the Department of Provincial and Local Government.

Political Debates

Implementing the new Constitution has been one of the most important yet challenging tasks facing both legislators and civil society. The aim in this section is to reflect on the origins of the Commission for the Promotion and Protection of the Rights of Cultural, Religious and Linguistic Communities, and to outline themes emerging from the legislative debates on the commission from both the National Assembly and provincial legislatures.

The political debates should be understood in the context of the priority given by the negotiating parties to the creation of a stable and sustainable democracy in South Africa. South Africa's history of deep socio-economic inequalities bolstered by divisive state intervention has left a legacy of fragmentation. These divisions threaten to undermine the fragile democracy that was crafted in 1994. For this reason, the constitutional framers have attempted to secure the stability of the new order through the creation of a range of institutional mechanisms to support democracy. These institutions are cited in Chapter 9 of the Constitution. The institutions are to function independently and impartially, subject only to the Constitution and the law. All organs of state are compelled to assist and protect these institutions to ensure their independence, impartiality, dignity and effectiveness. The commission under s 185 is therefore a critical element of our constitutional democracy.

Origins of the Commission

During the constitutional negotiations, fears were raised by some political parties that majoritarian democracy would undermine the rights and interests of minority groups. When the Constitution was drafted, major political parties accepted ss 185 and 186 of the Constitution to accommodate concerns that the rights of cultural, religious and linguistic communities should be directly addressed. These sections provided for the establishment of the Commission for the Protection and Promotion of the Rights of Cultural, Religious and Linguistic Communities as one of the key institutions supporting democracy. Section 185 was agreed to in the Constitution on account of its being a pillar for nation building, a catalyst for the "African Renaissance" and a way to promote and protect the rights of cultural, religious and linguistic communities as enshrined in the Constitution.

As outlined in the Constitution, the functions of the commission are as follows:

- To promote respect for the rights of cultural, religious and linguistic communities.

- To promote and develop peace, friendship, humanity, tolerance and national unity among cultural, religious and linguistic communities on the basis of equality, non-discrimination and free association.

- To recommend the establishment or recognition, in accordance with national legislation, of a cultural or other council or councils for a community or communities in South Africa.

Section 185(4) stipulates that additional powers and functions of the commission should be prescribed by national legislation. To give effect to this sub-section, the Minister of Constitutional Development requested all provinces to debate this constitutional requirement in order to enhance and enrich legislation.

As part of facilitating the implementation of the Constitution, a resolution was passed by the African National Congress in December 1997 to expedite the process towards the establishment of the commission.

Impetus was further added in February 1998, at the opening of Parliament, when the President committed Parliament to passing the necessary legislation to implement ss 185 and 186 before the end of 1998.

On 4 August 1998, a debate on the implementation of s 185 took place in Parliament, and all nine provincial legislatures had similar debates. The aim in this section of the chapter is to elaborate upon common themes emerging from the National Assembly and the provincial legislatures.

Political Dimensions

An analysis of parliamentary debates in national and provincial legislatures suggests that there is overwhelming support from political parties for the establishment of the commission. This is primarily because differences had already been aired and resolved during the constitutional negotiations. Opposition to the number and scale of statutory bodies was raised by some political parties in 1997.[2] However, there appears to be an acceptance among the majority of political parties that amendments to the Constitution should be considered only under exceptional circumstances. Parliamentary debates therefore focused on the possible functions and composition of the commission.

In the National Assembly, on 4 August 1998, former Deputy President Mbeki viewed the debate on s 185 as "one of the most important in the life of Parliament since the birth of democracy in South Africa". Mbeki further endorsed President Mandela's call for setting in place "practical steps to create the Commission for the Promotion and Protection of the Rights of Cultural, Religious and Linguistic Communities". This was further supported by the Minister of Constitutional Development who asserted that the process of setting up the commission is an "opportunity to lay the foundation for nation building". The lively debates in Parliament signified the importance attached to s 185 of the Constitution. In the words of one parliamentarian, this clause has "forced" South Africans to engage in the "great national debate" on what it means to be South African and what it means to assert "one nation, many cultures".

With one exception, all those who spoke in the National Assembly accepted ss 185 and 186 of the Constitution and argued for a speedy implementation of this constitutional provision. The majority of those who addressed the National Assembly conceived the commission as playing several roles: inter alia nation building, the instilling of patriotism, and reconciliation. Others went so far as to suggest that the commission could "create common patriotism", be a "unifying factor in national life" and "weld a deeper sense of South African nationhood". However, one party rejected the commission as "meddlesome bureaucracy, police monitoring" and indicated that it "loathes the creation of such body".

Among those supporting the commission, divergent views were expressed on its functions and roles. There was some clarity that the commission was not intended to replace the Volkstaat Council or duplicate the work being done by the Pan South African Language Board or the Human Rights Commission. Emphasis in most debates in national and provincial legislatures focused largely on the social and political dimension of the commission. Others saw the commission as an instrument of "empowerment", as a means to "sustainable reconciliation" or as "one means of resolving the national question". For some speakers the commission was defined more narrowly as a monitoring body providing research and advisory services to Parliament. Some political parties argued that ss 185 and 186 were not properly drafted and required constitutional amendment to focus on governance issues—in particular, the devolution of power to the provinces.

Although some saw the commission as a vehicle for reconciliation, others perceived the commission as a platform for cultural, religious and linguistic minorities to address issues of common concern. In debates in the provincial legislatures, the concern about the twin difficulties of protecting minorities while at the same time ensuring stability was most evident. There is emerging recognition that whereas the commission has significant potential to advance nation building, it also has the potential to stimulate division and undermine the nation-building project. Two broad arguments are relevant in this context. The first argument is that the commission should be established as a mechanism for addressing the "national question". Proponents of this view suggest that the commission should be linked to other approaches as part of a comprehensive strategy of nation building. Advocates of this view argue that the challenge is to manage the national question and address it in a way which advances the "democratic transition". From this perspective, the commission's task is to allow people to express their multiple identities in a way that advances the building of a united South African nation.

A second argument takes as its point of departure the need to protect the interests of cultural, linguistic and religious minority communities. Those who hold this opinion are of the view that the present political, economic and social landscape does not necessarily take into account these "minority" needs and aspirations and that special mechanisms are necessary to articulate and protect these needs and aspirations. It was suggested that the commission should take on board s 30 of the Bill of Rights, which states:

> Everyone has the right to use the language and to participate in the cultural life of their choice, but no one exercising these rights may do so in a manner inconsistent with any provision of the Bill of Rights.

While accepting the need for the commission, some parliamentarians argued that it should be acknowledged that past economic and political systems created divisions and inequality in society. It was further argued that, under the new Constitution, the commission should not be seen as protecting narrow interests of "minorities" at the expense of the majority. There was some concern that commissions in general have not contributed much in resolving key problems facing South Africa. A note of caution was sounded against seeing the commission as a purely mechanistic and inflexible body. It was suggested that in the process of implementing s 185, emphasis should be placed on nation building, and the structural form of implementation should be determined by the exigency of fulfilling this task.

Some parties argued that the commission should have the power to introduce legislative proposals at both the national and the provincial level. However, fears that the commission could be made a talk shop with little power were rebutted by arguments that the Constitution creates a legislative framework to safeguard against any form of discrimination.

What emerged as a common concern to all supporting the commission was whether sufficient resources would be allocated to the work of such a commission. Concern was also raised that due to lack of resources, national priority may not be given to the work of the commission.

A central concern raised in the debates was the need to ensure that there is proper co-ordination between the work of the commission and other statutory bodies. In particular, the overlapping roles of the proposed commission and the Pan South African Language Board need to be addressed (see the section entitled "Demarcation of Commission Functions").

Critical Areas for Discussion

Support for the commission is not unqualified. Qualifications have been debated outside Parliament during the past five years. There are two areas of disagreement between major political actors as to the scope of the statutory bodies. The first relates to the cost implications of commissions in the context of a fiscally constrained budget. While this has been a major point of criticism of commissions from opposition parties, it is also a matter of concern for the majority party in government. In 1996, the Deputy Minister of Finance warned that

> the Constitution has created various bodies, commissions and obligations all of which require additional expenditure. We urgently recommend that this be costed and an approach taken that fits what we can afford.

This consideration, while not denying the necessity of such institutions and obligations on the state, nevertheless flags a key concern which has to be addressed in implementing s 185. These fiscal considerations will have to be accommodated in the final shape of the commission.

A second area of difference between key actors centres on the composition and functions of the proposed commission. The divergent views, while broadly expressed in parliamentary debates, are fleshed out in some detail in the public submissions outlined in the section entitled "Analysis of Submissions" and in the table outlining the key recommendations derived from the submissions.

An area of debate not addressed explicitly in parliamentary debates relates to the notion of community. Communities are not homogeneous entities. Linguistic commonalities often cut across religious and cultural differences and vice versa. Determination of what constitutes a community in the context of the Constitution, as well as of how community representatives will be selected, will be a matter of enormous political debate. This debate is likely to be stronger where the commission itself is most empowered; in other words, the deeper the scope of the commission and the broader its powers and access to resources, the more likely it is that competing interests claiming representivity will emerge. This would suggest that Parliament will need to pay special attention to the implications of the criteria for the composition of the body.

Constitutional Dimension

The very notion of constitutionalism, that is, the elevation of certain values and rights above the vicissitudes of political processes, is founded on the need to protect interests that would otherwise be neglected or subordinated through such processes.[3] So, while our constitutional order is expressed through a single, sovereign, democratic state, whose people are governed by freely elected representatives, it is simultaneously a mechanism for conserving interests deemed inviolable, certain intrinsic features of the constitutional landscape that are to subsist regardless of electoral outcomes. This is the general principle which underscores the need to protect the more vulnerable and the more marginalised sectors of our society. But, added to this general principle, our Constitution also places considerable value on the principle of diversity itself. While national symbols and other forms of national expression remain vitally important to social well-being, the Constitution also recognises the right of communities to be different, to engage in unique cultural, linguistic and religious forms of expression. It contains specific features that provide targeted protection of these rights.

The quality of difference is highly prized by our Constitution. These principles and features are, in a sense, brought together in the provisions of s 185.

It is the functioning and composition of the commission which are the issues for discussion here. It is the aim of this section of the chapter to ground the discussion within the broader constitutional context, to explore the nexus between the commission and other constitutional provisions, particularly s 31, intended to advance the cultural, linguistic, religious and related interests of minority communities.[4] The debate will be informed by judicial pronouncements on these and related issues, and to a lesser extent by comparative foreign law, particularly the jurisprudence of comparable constitutional democracies such as Canada, India and Namibia. It is felt that a detailed exposition of the relevant principles of international law (and there are only a few of direct relevance) is beyond the scope of this chapter. These principles will, however, be referred to in this chapter.[5]

Interim Constitution

The interim Constitution, characterised as a document of significant negotiated compromise, had, in reality, little institutional protection for minority cultural, linguistic and religious interests. Chapter 11A and Constitutional Principle XXXIV were inserted into the interim Constitution to placate right-wing elements. Chapter 11A provided for the establishment of a Volkstaat Council to enable proponents of a Volkstaat to constitutionally pursue its fulfilment. But beyond this extremely narrow and obscurely framed political interest, the broader rights of minorities were not secured institutionally. Principle XXXIV offered a vague recognition of an even vaguer notion of self-determination. As a constitutional principle it did not, in any event, have immediate effect. "Minority" rights fell to be protected under s 31 of the interim Constitution which afforded "every person the right to use the language and to participate in the cultural life of his or her choice".

The right to common culture, language and religious educational institutions, in s 32(c), was made conditional on practicability and the absence of racial discrimination. Of all minority interests, it was apparent that language rights were entrenched most significantly. Section 3, one of the four constituent provisions of the interim Constitution, established eleven official languages. It allowed for the right of own language usage, regional differentiation and the power of Parliament and the provinces to make provision for the use of official languages for government functioning.[6] Certain principles were established as a framework guide to legislatures and policy makers: the creation of conditions for the development and promotion of equal use and enjoyment of official languages; the extension of language rights and status beyond restricted regions; the prevention of use of language as a means of exploitation; domination and division; the promotion of multilingualism; the fostering of respect for the non-official languages; and the non-diminution of language rights as were extant at the commencement of the interim Constitution. The interim Constitution, in addition, made provision for an Act of Parliament to establish the Pan South African Language Board, which was to function as an independent body to advance the above principles, to further the development of the official languages, to make recommendations regarding any legislation contemplated by the section and to promote respect for and development of certain named languages used by cultural and religious communities. The board was eventually established under the Pan South African Language Board Act 59 of 1995. The objectives of the board, determined constitutionally, are restated in s 3. Section 4, thereafter, emphasises the board's independence and impartiality. Section 8 sets out the recommendatory, advisory, monitoring, investigatory, research and general promotional powers and functions of the board.

The constitutional principles, the collection of broadly-stated foundational attributes which were to be the yardstick against which the final Constitution had to be measured, contained significant references to minority rights. Principle XI compelled the final Constitution to acknowledge and protect the diversity of language and culture and to encourage conditions for their promotion.[7] Principle XII safeguarded the collective rights of self-determination in forming, joining and maintaining organs of civil society, including linguistic, cultural and religious associations, provided they were based on principles of non-discrimination and free association.[8]

Sections 185 and 186 of the Final Constitution

The significance of these provisions lies in the degree to which they provide an institutional framework for protecting the rights to expression of community identity through culture, language and religion. It is also significant that they are situated in Chapter 9, which details a number of other institutions, all said to be essential to supporting constitutional democracy.[9] That the commission is of such importance as to warrant inclusion here, forges a very powerful link between minority cultural, linguistic and religious rights and constitutional basics.

Section 185 deals with the functioning of the commission. Section 185(1) sets out three primary objectives of the commission. First, it is to promote respect for the rights of cultural, religious and linguistic communities. This role is primarily an educative one. It calls for the commission to instill in South Africans an awareness of the cultural, linguistic and religious rights of communities, what these rights entail, who can be said to be bearers and how such rights fit into the pattern of rights that distinguishes our constitutional order. The aim of such efforts must be to inculcate the principle of equality of status and value of all cultures, religions and languages. Such equality entails equivalent respect for all such cultures, religions and languages, and thus for the composite cultural, linguistic and religious diversity that characterises South African society.[10] This educative function, "the promotion of respect for", coincides with that of the Human Rights Commission under s 184, whose promotion of respect brief encompasses human rights and a culture of human rights more generally. Nevertheless, the overlap will require a measure of jurisdictional demarcation or, indeed, co-operation between these institutions. This is a theme which will be revisited later.

Second, the commission is to promote and develop peace, friendship, humanity, tolerance and national unity among cultural, religious and linguistic communities on the basis of equality, non-discrimination and free association. This objective captures the duality inherent in the recognition of minority cultural and like rights, namely that between differentiation and equality. Our Constitution will never unduly compromise the equality principle. It is firmly entrenched, indeed has been described as the very "focus and ordering principle" of the Constitution.[11] Apartheid South Africa was characterised by brutal racial differentiation and discrimination. Race and ethnic distinctions were the means of determining the allocation of resources. A whole armoury of laws enforced a system of rigid separation and controlled movement. This history and its lessons were very vivid for the drafters of the final Constitution.[12] Thus, we have not only an established equality right which places the principles of redress and equity at its centre, but equality as a value frames the whole limitation of rights exercise.[13] Indeed, the Constitution unequivocally states in s 185 that, while recognition of cultural, linguistic and religious difference is socially relevant, it is only relevant to the extent that it is disassociated from racism and political domination.[14] Of importance in this regard is the reality of the relative material and cultural advantage of many of South Africa's communities. To sanction, indeed encourage, the expression of their unique identities is not to perpetuate this advantage. Indeed, it may well be so that the cultural, religious and linguistic expression that has been historically disadvantaged, will have to be preferentially advanced in accordance with the equality principle.[15] The protection of minority/ community rights is further not to detract from the principle of free association, the right of every person to organise and act in the collectivity of choice.

While the first objective is directed at the population at large, the second of the commission's objectives is directed at cultural, religious and linguistic communities themselves. What signifies here is the principle that while diversity is valued, it is recognised that it can, in addition, be the source of immense social conflict where detached from a conception of national unity. The commission therefore has a special role to play in promoting and developing harmonious relationships between diverse communities so as to achieve a state of national oneness. In a sense this is also an educative process of promoting respect among such communities for each other. But the role of the commission extends beyond the educational role, important as that role doubtlessly is. The section implies that the commission plays a role as facilitator of a process of nation building, a process of strengthening the bonds of nationhood through the celebration of national diversity. Indeed, it is significant that the phrase "national unity" is utilised in the section. The phrase underlines the intention that the commission operate as, or at least create the conditions for the establishment of, a forum for the articulation of the interests of diverse cultural, religious and linguistic groups. Such a forum will serve as a means of bringing such groups together, encouraging them to interact and debate with one another. And in so doing, the commission is to showcase the richness of our diversity, the congeniality of such diversity and the capacity of differences to be transcended and to work towards national goals.

The third objective of the commission is of a more prosaic nature: to recommend the establishment or recognition of cultural or other councils for cultural, religious and linguistic communities. As merely recommendatory, and subject to national legislation, this objective is the most open-ended. It certainly offers no guarantee of the establishment of institutional mechanisms to express particular community interests. The objective also encompasses the possibility that the commission might only play an overarching role, leaving the real institutional focus of s 185 to subsidiary councils.

Section 185(2)-(4) deals with the powers of the commission. Subsection (2) offers a somewhat cursory list of powers but emphasises that the scope of such powers is a matter for Parliament. The powers listed are similar in nature (although here merely sketched) to those of the Pan South African Language Board, already discussed. They include any power necessary to achieve its primary objectives, including the power to monitor, investigate, research, educate, lobby, advise and report on issues pertaining to the rights of cultural, religious and linguistic communities. These powers are clearly connected to the aforementioned objectives. To promote respect for minority rights and to create the necessary forum for community interaction, the commission will be required to research the operational efficacy of equivalent mechanisms utilised abroad, and generally the requirements of s 185; to educate communities and South

Africans at large; to investigate complaints; to monitor group adherence to constitutional dictates, those of legislation and the commission's own procedures; and to lobby, advise and make recommendations to organs of state, particularly Parliament, regarding policy and legislation impacting on cultural, religious and linguistic rights. Subsection (3) brings home the interconnectedness of the operation of several of the Chapter 9 institutions, by allowing the commission to report any matter within its powers to the Human Rights Commission for investigation. The provision conceives the possibility of a close working relationship between these commissions. Subsection (4) merely states that the commission will possess such additional powers and functions prescribed by national legislation. What is emphasised both here and within s 185 as a whole, is that while that section establishes a framework for the operation of the commission, Parliament has to fill in most of the detail.

The most important of such detail is the composition of the commission. Per s 186, the number of members, their appointment and terms of office must be prescribed by Parliament provided that the composition is broadly representative of the main cultural, religious and linguistic communities and is reflective of the gender composition of South Africa. These principles will serve to ensure that the commission does not function as a means of exclusion. It also serves to indicate the relevance of the principle of representivity, particularly in matters of complexity and potential divisiveness.

Constitutional Context

Sections 185 and 186 do not exist in a vacuum. They are grounded in other constitutional features which, while self-standing, collectively reveal something of the role of the commission which is constitutionally ordained. The Constitution cannot be read in a fragmented fashion. Many of the rights contained in the Bill of Rights evince a concern with the interests of minorities, particularly in relation to the expression of their identity through culture, religion, language and education. Some do so indirectly. Section 18, which deals with the right of freedom of association, does not refer to minorities or communities but is indispensable for the collective expression of identity. As too, of course, is s 16, which deals with the right to freedom of expression, and s 15, which deals with the right to freedom of religion and the possibility of legislative recognition of religious or traditional law.

However, certain rights are of direct relevance. They do not only implicate issues of community identity, but also seek to capture in various terms the right to such an identity. They can be described as provisions containing minority rights.[16] The most obvious of these is s 31. In terms of this section:

(1) Persons belonging to a cultural, religious or linguistic community may not be denied the right, with other members of that community

   (a) to enjoy their culture, practise their religion and use their language; and

   (b) to form, join and maintain cultural, religious and linguistic associations and other organs of civil society.

(2) The right in subsection (1) may not be exercised in a manner inconsistent with any provision of the Bill of Rights.

The use of the three categories of community—cultural, religious and linguistic—marks this section as the rights component of s 185. Without such a provision, the relevance of any commission to secure or, at least, provide the means for articulating such rights, would be meaningless. The right sources the commission's functioning. But this does not mean that the commission is to give effect to the totality of the right. It is patently not envisaged that the commission will be the only means for claiming the protection of the right. On the contrary, the right will be accessible to all persons within communities defined in cultural, religious or linguistic terms. Section 185 serves to bolster these rights, providing a recognition of the salient truth that a right, particularly carried by minority groups, can often be rendered meaningless without an institutional mechanism to effect it. In addition, and as should have become apparent through the repeated reference to "community" both in ss 185 and 31, the right of cultural, religious and linguistic identity and expression, in this context, attaches to a collective.[17] While many of the rights in the Bill of Rights, particularly the class of civil and political rights, are individual in nature, s 31 rights are claimed by persons only as members of a wider collective entity. While this might seem obvious inasmuch as culture, religion and language are "communal objects", there are instances where the individual expression of a collective right might differ from the collective expression.[18]

The collective rights' feature marks s 31 as unique, not only in character but in the manner in which it will be enforced. Important in this regard, too, is the casting of the right in negative terms—"persons ... may not be denied the right". This would seem to indicate that the right is primarily defended in a negative manner, that is, by preventing its interference by the state or other persons. But this is not to argue that the state is absolved from taking positive measures to promote and develop minority cultures, religions and languages. Indeed, it is highly arguable that s 185 is a clear indication of one such measure. The wording of s 31 is taken largely from art 27 of the International Covenant on Civil and Political Rights, and the import of the wording will be taken from the interpretations of special rapporteurs,[19] supplementary international law instruments[20] and academic treatises.[21] In terms of s 39(1)(b) of the final Constitution, a court, when interpreting the Constitution, must consider international law. So the apparent vagueness of the language used in s 31 will be sharpened by prior interpretation. Clearly, these words will be generously interpreted to mean activities engaged in by cultural, religious and linguistic communities which are integral to those communities' identity. This interpretation dovetails well with the role of the commission envisaged in s 185. But an important distinction should be drawn between ss 31 and 185 and art 27 of the international covenant. In the latter the right adheres to the individual and is not a collective right (although its exercise depends on the collective ability of the minority to maintain its identity). But it is this collective dimension that really signifies in ss 31 and 185. In addition, as indicated, ss 31 and 185 studiously avoid any reference to the term "minority", signifying the constitutional need to transcend the divisive connotation of that term under apartheid.[22]

The collective dimension of the right is enhanced by the right afforded communities to form, join and develop associations and other civil organs to give expression to cultural, religious and linguistic interests. While communities are the principal bearers of these rights, further collective organisation might be required to give fuller expression to them. By implication, s 185 will compel the commission to interface not with amorphous communities but with community interests represented in specific associations. The specific wording of this portion of the provision was an attempt to satisfy Constitutional Principle XII, which, as we have seen, sought to guarantee the right of collective self-determination in forming, joining and maintaining organs of civil society, including cultural, religious and linguistic associations. It is the cultural, religious and linguistic dimension of self-determination that receives expression here, the internal dimension of self-determination. A political, external component of self-determination is quite clearly not connoted by Principle XII.[23] The internal limitation provided by s 31(2) is suggestive of a concern with the effect of collective rights on individual rights more generally and with the more immediate possibility of tension between such rights to collective identity and expression and the right to equality.

Section 30 of the final Constitution is a recapitulation of the old s 31 of the interim Constitution. Many would question its relevance in the light of s 31. It emphasises the individual assertion of what appear to be collective rights. The rights in s 31 are not held or mediated by communities. And as such the right does not connect directly to s 185, under which the commission will function to facilitate the interaction of community interests. Nevertheless, the right emphasises the constitutional value of the rights to language and culture, at least at the level of individual choice. It will function in circumstances where individuals are prevented from participating in the cultural life of a community where that community rejects such participation. It is arguable that the freedom of religion provision in s 15 is the "religious" equivalent of the cultural and language rights protected under s 30. Perhaps it was to complete this trinity that s 30 was retained. It is submitted that this right does not have particular significance for the commission's work under s 185.

The right to education contained in s 29 has direct relevance to community cultural, religious and linguistic rights. Education is the primary mechanism for perpetuating and advancing cultural, religious and linguistic tradition. Decisions around language of instruction, and the content of instruction with it, are forcefully contested. Under s 29 (2) everyone has the right to receive education in the language of their choice in public educational institutions where that education is reasonably practicable. However, s 29(3) will be of more immediate concern to cultural, religious and linguistic communities. It affords the right to establish and maintain, at own expense, independent educational institutions that do not discriminate on the basis of race, and are registered and maintain standards comparable to public educational institutions.[24] The education right provides the starkest counterplay between cultural, religious and linguistic rights and the right to equality. The Constitution, recognising the extent to which apartheid skewed educational opportunities, has reached into the private domain to ensure that even where funded entirely privately, no educational institution can turn a pupil away on grounds of race. This is a very powerful endorsement of the principle of non-discrimination which runs like a thread throughout the constitutional text. Also significant for our purposes will be the ancillary requirement that the commission at least establish the relationship between private cultural, religious or linguistic schools and the communities they serve.

As in the interim Constitution, language is dealt with as an issue antecedent to the Bill of Rights, in what is now termed a "founding provision". Section 6 is a shorter but no less substantial version of s 3 of the interim Constitution, already discussed.[25] The official languages are stated, but the state is called upon to redress linguistic imbalances by taking practical and positive measures to elevate the status and advance the use of indigenous languages. National and provincial spheres of government are permitted to use any particular official language, taking into account a variety of listed criteria. Both spheres enjoy the power to regulate and monitor use of official languages, all of which are to have parity of esteem and are to be treated equitably.[26] Municipalities are now compelled to take into account the language usage and preferences of their residents. This marks a significant addition to the text.[27] The Pan South African Language Board under subsec (5) continues to be the main institutional means of fulfilling the broad conditions of s 6. However, this does not detract from the relevance of the section for the commission under s 185. The question of the relationship between commission and board will be deliberated later but it is a relationship of acute importance. Their difference lies really in the subject matter of their respective foci. The board is concerned with language development and promotion. The commission is concerned with the place of linguistic communities within South African society and the interplay of their distinct interests with those of other cultural and religious communities.

Foreign Jurisdictions

It is good to remember that although our courts have repeatedly shown a willingness to invoke the lessons of foreign jurisprudence in construing the meaning of rights contained in our Bill of Rights or extra-Bill of Rights provisions, they have also issued a caveat that these lessons should not be imported uncritically. The basis of interpretation must remain rooted in our specific "legal system, our history and circumstances, and the structure and language of our own Constitution".[28]

Canada *The Canadian Constitution Act, 1982 evinces a particular concern with language use and language of instruction. These are issues of specific historical resonance and should not detain us here.[29] Of interest, but also of little utility, are the provisions detailing the rights of aboriginal peoples under s 35. Of some significance though is the interpretation provision contained in s 27 of the Canadian charter. The section provides that the charter shall be interpreted in a manner consistent with the preservation and enhancement of the multicultural heritage of Canadians. The interpretation provision of South Africa's final Constitution, s 39, does not refer specifically to multiculturalism, but more generally to an open and democratic society based on human dignity, equality and freedom. Respect for the diversity of cultural, religious and linguistic communities is nevertheless central to this conception.*

India *Articles 29 and 30 of the Indian Constitution have an indirect bearing on the interpretation of our s 31 and, as a corollary, on an assessment of the role of the s 185 commission. Article 29(1) provides that any section of citizens residing in the territory of India or any part thereof having a distinct language, script or culture shall have the right to conserve it. Article 30 is analogous to our s 29(3). It stipulates that all minorities whether based on language or religion shall have the right to establish and administer educational institutions of their choice. Both art 29 and 30 contain anti-discriminatory provisions. Indian courts have given these provisions a broad interpretation. It has been stated that their function is to ensure that the rights of minorities are respected and that minorities feel as much a part of India as do majorities. The provisions function thus both to ensure equality and strengthen the perception of equality.[30] Many Indian cases have emphasised that the right under art 30 is subject to the regulatory power of the state.[31] However, the absence of any constitutionally ordained institutional mechanism to forward such rights renders Indian examples merely of interpretive assistance.*

Namibia *The relevant provisions of the Namibian Constitution are arts 3 and 19. The former, in a manner not dissimilar to s 6, positions the issue of language before that of the Bill of Fundamental Human Rights and Freedoms. The provision accentuates the right to use a language of choice as the medium of instruction in public and private schools subject to requirements as may be imposed by law. The core minority rights features, though, are located in art 19, in terms of which every person is entitled to enjoy, practise, profess, maintain and promote any culture, language, tradition or religion subject to the Constitution and further subject to a non-violation of the rights of others or the national interest. The right, in many ways, is better structured than our ss 30 and 31. It de-emphasises the collective dimension of the right, preferring to treat a claim to the right in individual terms. But it is surely implicit that for a cultural right to have any meaning whatsoever, it must have an associative dimension. As it stands, the omission of any reference to community or like collective entity does not so much denature the right, but makes it less capable of being translated into an institutional form. The existence of our s 185* *commission is assured by the collective dimension expressly given the right in s 31. The commission will serve to bring together interests which are collectively articulated through communities.*

Demarcation of Commission Functions

As indicated in the section dealing with parliamentary debates, a key concern in the definition of the structure and roles of the commission is the extent to which the commission will be distinct from other statutory bodies. The central consideration is to define the tasks of the commission so as to ensure minimal duplication between commissions. This considera-tion is motivated by the need for efficiency as well as cost-effectiveness of the commissions.

We have attempted to spell out the various functions of the commis-sion as defined by the Constitution as well as by the contours of the political debate. However, this does not resolve the question as to how the commission's functions are to be sharply demarcated in respect of other commissions, particularly the Human Rights Commission (HRC) and the Commission for Gender Equality (CGE) as well as the Pan South African Language Board (PanSALB).

The Constitution has given all the commissions wide-ranging powers. Even though it appears that functions overlap, it needs to be recognised that in view of the specialised orientation of each institution such overlap does not necessarily imply duplication. For example, the Human Rights Commission, the Commission for Gender Equality and the Commission for the Promotion and Protection of the Rights of Cultural, Religious and Linguistic Communities are all concerned with the promotion of respect for human rights. The Commission for Gender Equality primarily pro-motes the right to gender equality, the s 185 commission promotes the rights of cultural, religious and linguistic communities and the Human Rights Commission promotes the totality of rights and a human rights culture. The HRC and the CGE further have an express role in the protection of human rights, which role is only implicitly afforded the s 185 commission, although it is significant that an investigatory power is granted the commission where necessary to achieve its primary objectives.

It seems apparent that the commission is to promote broader reconciliatory values and is, under s 185(3), empowered to report matters falling within its powers and functions to the HRC for investigation. This suggests that the commission is more properly a forum for debate than a complaints directorate. This is not to say, however, that the commission does not protect the rights of communities in the broader sense.

The HRC and CGE are also afforded powers of development and attainment of rights. Such powers are not explicitly given under s 185. Again, this seems to indicate that the core promotional functions of the commission lie in respect of building a democratic culture and national unity founded on the mutual respect for diversity.

In summary, it should be noted that the rights functions of the commission under s 185 are narrower in scope than those of the HRC and CGE, but in respect of cultural, religious and linguistic rights the commission is afforded wide powers including those specifically mentioned under s 185(2).

The role of the commission in regard to language rights brings the issue of its relationship with PanSALB into question. However, there appears to be a clear distinction between their respective roles. PanSALB has as specific objectives the promotion of equal use and enjoyment of official languages, the promotion of multilingualism more generally and the fostering of respect for all languages. It is concerned, in addition, with extending language rights and status and developing South African languages. Although it is impossible to distinguish language from a linguistic community, the commission under s 185 will play a role in facilitating the promotion of language and linguistic communities through a process of interaction with other communities. The broad function of the commission to promote respect for the rights of linguistic communities does dovetail with PanSALB functions, and co-ordination in this respect will be required.

A further area of concern in the public debates has been the pressure exerted on the fiscus by the creation of the statutory bodies. There has been a range of meetings between the Department of State Expenditure and the Department of Finance and the existing commissions to consider appropriate levels of funding, and disagreements have arisen as to the level of funding necessary to ensure the commissions' ability to perform their constitutional obligations. In general, the commissions have been requested to trim their budgets.

The existing statutory commissions have already recognised the need for co-operation in defining their work plans. In 1996, a co-ordinating forum was set up. This, in many ways, will be the mechanism through which unwarranted duplication can be obviated. One of the ways in which cost-cutting can be effected is through the rationalisation of administrative expenses through sharing of offices, personnel and equipment. In addition, working together on defining programmes will ensure that statutory commissions are maximally effective.

Analysis of Submissions

In August 1998, following a directive from the Minister for Provincial and Local Government and debates in the national and provincial legislatures, the Department of Provincial and Local Government called for public submissions on the establishment of a commission in terms of ss 185 and 186 of the Constitution.

A total of 37 submissions was received by the Department of Provincial and Local Government by the closing date of 11 September 1998. These submissions came from a wide range of organisations and individuals in civil society. By far the majority were from cultural and religious organisations. In addition, one of the statutory commissions—the South African Human Rights Commission—made a separate submission. While most submissions presented carefully considered organisational and legal positions, there were a number of submissions from individuals, some of which were handwritten and all of which displayed a passionate commitment to the need for the recognition of minority rights.

The submissions were analysed according to the following categories:

- Basis of the argument: in other words, the underlying rationale for support or opposition to the proposed commission.

- Recommendations with respect to the composition of the proposed commission.
- Recommendations with respect to the functions of the proposed commission.

A summary of these categories is appended in the form of a table. In this section of the report, we present a brief analysis of the submissions as a guide to reading the table. As was to be expected from the Parliamentary debates outlined earlier in this chapter, there were no submissions which opposed the formation of a commission. However, there were some differences with regard to the structures and powers of the commission which require consideration.

Basis of Argument

There is a high degree of consensus as to the rationale for the establish-ment of a commission. The central and most common argument is based on the constitutional requirement as set out in s 185. Some submissions further cite the United Nations Declaration on the Protection of National, Ethnic, Religious and Linguistic Minorities as providing an international guideline for the establishment of such a body. Some submissions further referred to the need to promote equality, itself a constitutional imperative as previously outlined. It was argued, for example, that

> we are all equal and have to live with and accept one another as people who are destined to live side by side.

A second common set of arguments focused on the broader political dimensions of the proposed commission. The usefulness of the commis-sion for promoting nation building and reconciliation was highly regarded. Associated with this was the perceived need to promote respect for diversity through active efforts in educational and advocacy programmes.

A single submission was based on the argument that the commission was necessary to protect minorities from political manipulation:

All institutions to be established must be isolated effectively from being influenced unduly by the policies and pressures of political parties, organisations and governments.

Composition

There were significant differences in the ways in which the structure of the proposed commission was envisaged. Some submissions favoured an expansive and deep structure. In this option, a national structure would be bolstered by provincial bodies with extensive links to civil society and would be representative of the full scope of diverse cultural, religious and linguistic communities. At the other end of the spectrum was proposed a single national body with representatives from religious, cultural and linguistic communities.

On the whole, the need for representivity was strongly supported. However, there were differences on how this should be interpreted. On the one hand, some organisations recommended that the principle of proportionality should apply (i.e. numerically dominant groupings should have greater representation), while on the other hand it was argued that the full diversity of communities of interest, as well as of government and gender, should apply. Yet others argued that the selection of commissioners should be based primarily on merit rather than representivity:

> Gender should not be the basis of election of the commission—only merit should be the criteria.

Although the number of commissioners suggested ranges from 15 to 30, some submissions, if accepted, would result in a larger commission. If the full range of constituencies requiring representation on the commission and the number of substructures which some of the submissions advocated were realised, the number of commissioners and staff would in all probability exceed 30.

Powers

Powers were very broadly defined in the submissions. They included a combination of all or some of the following:

- Representation of various groupings
- Mediation in cultural conflicts
- Acting as watchdog, monitoring against discrimination
- Promoting cultural respect, tolerance and understanding
- Conducting research and publishing reports
- Acting as non-political liaison body between government and civil society
- Advising Parliament on legislative changes

The issue of overlapping powers between different statutory bodies was not directly addressed, although clearly the list above would result in duplication of certain tasks. A singular aspect of the recommendations which suggested a power different from the powers of other statutory bodies, was that which related to the commission acting as manager of and conduit for funding from government to various cultural organisations. The perceived value of this task is to ensure the equitable distribution of resources to poorly organised groupings. Related submissions included, according to the commission, the authority to determine the criteria by which group representatives would be officially recognised.

One submission fell somewhat outside the general recommendations as to the powers of the commission. This submission viewed the role of the commission as including the protection of intellectual property rights and the establishment of a blood-testing laboratory to detect diseases.

A significant number of submissions urged a link between the commission and the educational arena, either in terms of developing teaching materials and methods or in creating special cultural and linguistic awareness programmes.

Emerging Policy Considerations

From the extensive discussion over the two days of the Conference on 22–23 September 1999, it is clear that debate among delegates, while wide ranging, touched on eight key themes or issues. These issues will have to be dealt with during the further consultation process.

Issue One: Urgency Over the Establishment of the Commission

Many delegates and keynote speakers referred to the need to proceed quickly towards the establishment of the proposed commission. For example, this point was illustrated by a speaker representing the Khoisan community who said he was eagerly awaiting the establishment of the commission as a means of preventing continued marginalisation of his community, particularly their linguistic rights. The publication of the draft bill will help this process considerably in that it will allow members of the public and cultural, language and religious organisations to respond to a range of concrete suggestion over the form and function of the proposed commission. This task falls to both the Department of Provincial and Local Government and the interim working committee that was formed at the end of the conference.

Issue Two: Identifying the "Main" Cultural, Religious and Linguistic Communities

Some contributions—either from the floor or from comments made at the four workshops held on 23 September 1999 and reflected through the rapporteur's reports—noted some intrinsic difficulties in the notion of "main" communities. For example, it was pointed out that it would be very difficult to define such an approach satisfactorily through legislation. Delegates did not directly address how the difficulties could be avoided except, by implication, to suggest that the difficulties might be reduced through reconceptualising the roles of the commissioners. The dilemma with the use of the notion of "main" is that it might be taken to be largely synonymous with size or population; thus smaller cultural, religious or linguistic groups could feel excluded from the ambit of the Commission's work. It was clear from the conference that a number of what might be regarded as smaller cultural communities were also looking towards the commission as a means to protect or advance their interests.

Issue Three: Promotion and/or Protection?

The proposed commission has the constitutionally defined task of both protecting and promoting cultural, religious and linguistic communities and their associated interests. But it was clear from the debate that some participants saw the main function of the proposed commission as falling more towards the role of promoting various rights while others saw it as falling towards that of protection. Proponents of the first view pointed out, for example, that other Chapter 9 organisations could be seen to fulfill the protective function. While a measure of overlap does occur between these organisations, the proposed commission does nonetheless have a task of both promoting and protecting cultural and other rights.

Issue Four: What Role for Commissioners?

Much debate took place over an appropriate role for persons appointed as commissioners. Many participants pointed out that commissioners had to be persons of status and enjoy public trust. This issue had two elements. The first was that consideration should be given to appointing some commissioners on the basis of their expert knowledge of cultural, linguistic or religious issues, rather than all commissioners being appointed to represent specific communities. The second element was that commissioners should not necessarily be seen to have a representative role linked to a particular cultural, religious or linguistic community. Rather, as one participant conceptualised it, they should be seen as "listeners" capable of straddling divides between communities.

Issue Five: The Commission versus the Annual Consultative Conference

Some participants noted aspects in the draft bill that referred to the link, specifically issues around mandates, between the proposed commission and the annual consultative conference; insofar as this issue was raised as a critical issue there were concerns that the proposed commission would become an administrative agent of the proposed annual consultitive conference. These participants argued that a greater degree of autonomy would be needed for the proposed commission vis-à-vis the annual conferences. A related concern was that the annual conference should not "become a national assembly in disguise" but that it be more a reflection of civil society interests.

Issue Six: The Commission and Traditional Leaders

Many participants and some keynote speakers, especially those drawn from the ranks of traditional leaders, pointed to the necessity for the proposed commission to establish a good relationship with traditional leaders. They argued that the commission would need to work with and consult such persons; by implication they also argued that some commissioners would need to be traditional leaders.

Issue Seven: The Commission and Cultural Councils

The provisions of the draft bill concerning the relationship between the commission and the envisaged cultural councils were explored in depth by one of the working groups; the rapporteur from that group reported back to the full conference. During discussion from the plenary session, similar concerns were raised from the floor. Many of these participants saw the introduction of cultural councils as an integral part of the processes around the introduction of the proposed commission. But other delegates did appear somewhat reluctant to draw as close a linkage; this suggests that the relationship between the functions of the cultural councils and the functions of the commission needs to be carefully considered.

Issue Eight: The Commission and the Youth

Another specific sector identified by some participants during debate was that of the youth; they argued that the proposed commission needed to facilitate and encourage participation by the youth in the activities of the commission. The commission needed to do this, so it was argued, to prevent the marginalisation of cultural, linguistic or religious interests.

Delegates who made this plea did not however offer any concrete suggestions as to how the commission might do so.

The conference in 1999, as in the previous year, was marked by a remarkable degree of good spirit and open debate over the key issues surrounding the introduction and establishment of the proposed Commission for the Promotion and Protection of the Rights of Cultural, Religious and Linguistic Communities.

The circulation of the draft bill allowed the delegates to grapple with fundamental aspects surrounding the proposed commission; it thereby focused debate on the proposed commission. A number of key policy issues—largely but not exclusively dealt with in the preceeding section—need further debate and possible refinement. This process will require on-going consultation with major interest groups in civil society, government and Parliament in an attempt to reach as wide a consensus as possible over the structure and goals of the proposed commission. The major challenge is to proceed with the establishment of the commission in a way which continues to build on the goodwill created towards the proposed commission.

Conclusion

This chapter has consolidated a range of debates concerning the formation of the s 185 commission. The political debates indicated the high level of respect for constitutionality and in particular for respecting minority rights within a single constitutional state. There were obvious differences as to the commission's functioning and composition. These differences had a party-political flavour, but were largely expressed in constructive terms. There is a high expectation that the commission will act as the focal point for redressing past inequities and cultural disadvantages wrought by apart-heid.

The section on the constitutional dimension sought to ground the functioning and composition issues constitutionally by examining the texts of ss 185 and 186, and other constitutional provisions which would assist both in interpreting and giving effect to these sections.

In relation to demarcating commission functions, two areas were highlighted. The first concerned the overlapping of roles between commissions. It was argued that while there are overlapping functions, this should not be confused with duplication. There were clear differences in specific functions of different commissions. The second area discussed was the need to rationalise costs of administration and programming. It was pointed out that considerable attempts had been made by existing commissions in this regard, and that the s 185 commission should become part of these efforts.

In analysing the submissions and the two national conferences (1998 and 1999) it transpired that while there was considerable divergence there was simultaneously a commitment to giving proper effect to s 185. The tone of the submissions would indicate that there was a high degree of goodwill among diverse communities. The release of the draft bill would mark an important milestone as it would focus the debates and discussion on the way forward. The recommended establishment of a technical committee would no doubt focus the energy of different stakeholders in meeting the proposed milestones of submitting the bill to Parliament in 2000.

Notes

[1] This chapter is based on two original reports prepared for the Department of Provincial and Local Government in 1998 and 1999. Other members of the research team who made contributions during the writing of the original reports are: Shireen Hassim, Sakkie Mpanyane, Ordelia Nkoenyane, Gideon Pimstone, Mandla Seleoane, Gerard Hagg, Richard Humphries, Tony Emmett, Windsor Leroke, Bernard Magubane and Arlene Grossberg.

[2] See Democratic Party Report, September 1997. In particular, the DP recommended that "the Commission on the Promotion and Protection of Cultural, Religious and Linguistic Minorities must be scrapped ... (it) has not yet come into being and so no money has been wasted. Its functions, where they are human rights issues of minority groupings, must be dealt with by the HRC. Where their functions relate to language policy, these can be dealt with by PanSALB."

[3]   See for example *S v Makwanyane and others* 1995 (6) BCLR 665 (CC) at para 87 per Chaskalson P. The court stated there that "(t)he very reason for establishing the new legal order, and for vesting the power of judicial review of all legislation in the courts, was to protect the rights of minorities and others who cannot protect their rights adequately through the democratic process".

[4]   On the meaning of and relationship between culture, language, religion and education, see Dlamini "Culture, Education and Religion" in D. van Wyk et al. (eds) *Rights and Constitutionalism: The New South African Legal Order* (1994).

[5]   In regard to international law the most significant provisions are article 27 of the Universal Declaration of Human Rights, 1948 which affirms the right to freely participate in the cultural life of the community and article 27 of the International Covenant on Civil and Political Rights, 1996. The latter provision provides that in those states where ethnic, religious and linguistic minorities exist, persons belonging to such minorities shall not be denied the right, in community with other members of their group, to enjoy their own culture, to profess and practise their own religion, or to use their own language. This provision undoubtedly confers on minorities the right to protect a distinct identity and establishes same as an international obligation. Article 15 of the International Covenant on Economic, Social and Cultural Rights, 1966 provides that states are to recognise the right of every person to take part in cultural life. These and other provisions are dealt with comprehensively by M. Reddi "Minority Rights in International Law: A Socio-linguistic and Socio-historic Analysis" unpublished and undated submission on file (1998) and P. Lishivha "Commission for the Promotion and Protection of the Rights of Cultural, Religious and Linguistic Communities" unpublished and undated submission on file (1998). These submissions, insofar as they pertain to the functioning and composition of the commission, are summarised below.

[6]   Significantly, the interim Constitution omitted reference to local government in this section. In *Louw v Transitional Local Council of Greater Germiston* 1997 (8) BCLR 1062 (W), the court ruled that it was impermissible for a municipality to determine that a single official language be the written and spoken language of its council. The court found that s 31, the broad right of people to use the language and participate in the cultural life of choice, had no bearing on the question of municipal competence to choose an official language for its functioning. Section 3 limited this competence to the national and provincial spheres of government.

7   The constitutional principles did not require the establishment of the Commission for the Promotion and Protection of the Rights of Cultural, Religious and Linguistic Communities and the question therefore of the independence of such a body was beyond the scope of the Constitutional Court's task in deliberating whether the new constitutional text measured up to the constitutional principles, but the court did note the connection between the provisions of the new text establishing the commission and Principle XI. See *Ex parte Chairperson of the Constitutional Assembly: In re Certification of the Constitution of the Republic of South Africa, 1996* 1996 (10) BCLR 1253 (CC) at para 179.

8   This principle, according to the Constitutional Court, did not indicate how the collective rights of self-determination were to be recognised and protected. "Self-determination did not embody any notion of political separateness, but what may be done by way of the autonomous exercise of ... associational rights in the civil society of one sovereign state". See *Ex parte Chairperson of the Constitutional Assembly: In re Certification of the Amended Text of the Constitution of the Republic of South Africa, 1996* 1997 (1) BCLR 1 (CC) at paras 22-4.

9   See *In re Certification of the Amended Text of the Constitution of the Republic of South Africa* (supra) in which the court described the commission, together with other Chapter 9 institutions, as enhancing civil society's protective framework (at para 25).

10 Such richness and its significance are eloquently captured in the preamble to the final Constitution by the phrase "united in our diversity". See, too, speech of Deputy President Mbeki in Hansard unrevised copy 4 August 1998 at 2 and 14.

11 See Kriegler J in *President of the Republic of South Africa and Another* 1997 (6) BCLR 708 (CC) at para 74. On the constitutional importance of equality see, too, *Prinsloo v Van der Linde and Another* 1997 (6) BCLR 759 (CC), *Harksen v Lane NO and Others* 1997 (11) BCLR 1489 (CC), *Larbi-Odam and Others v Members of the Executive Council for Education and Another (North-West Province)* 1997 (12) BCLR 1655 (CC) and *City Council of Pretoria v Walker* 1998 (3) BCLR 257 (CC).

12 See, for example, Mahomed DP in *Shabalala and others v Attorney-General of the Transvaal and another* 1995 (12) BCLR 1593 (CC) at para 26. The new order marks "a decisive break from the culture of Apartheid and racism to a

constitutionally protected culture of openness and democracy and universal human rights for South Africans of all ages, classes and colours".

[13] Under s 36, rights can be limited only to the extent that the limitation is reasonable and justifiable in an open and democratic society based on human dignity, equality and freedom.

[14] See Sachs J in *Ex parte Gauteng Provincial Legislature: In re Dispute Concerning the Constitutionality of Certain Provisions of the Gauteng School Education Bill of 1995* 1996 (4) BCLR 537 (CC). "Stripped of its association with race and political domination, cultural diversity becomes an enriching force which merits constitutional protection ... the basic problem is to secure equality in a balanced way which shows maximum regard for diversity ... Democracy in a pluralist society should accordingly not mean the end of cultural diversity, but rather its guarantee, accomplished on the secure bases of justice and equity" (at paras 49 and 52).

[15] See s 6(2) of the final Constitution.

[16] As to these provisions see Iain Currie "Minority Rights: Education, Culture and Language" in Matthew Chaskalson et al. (eds) *Constitutional Law of South Africa* (1996) chapter 35. The terms "minority" and "community" have been used somewhat interchangeably in this chapter. This has been so by virtue of the fact that there are, linguistically and culturally at any rate, only minority communities in South Africa. We should not forget though that the word "minority" has been deliberately omitted in the Constitution by reason of its particularly nefarious use under apartheid. But absent this connotation, "minority" refers more specifically to the notion of minority rights developed under international law. The fullest commentary on the nature of minority rights in international law is provided by Sachs J in *Gauteng School Education Bill* (supra). He identifies six interrelated struts of the minority protection doctrine—the right to existence, non-discrimination, equal rights, the right to develop autonomously within civil society, affirmative action and positive support by the state (see para 69 and ff). In essence, a "minority" or "community" should signify a non-dominant group united by a common culture, religion or language which identifies itself and is identified as a group.

[17] See *In re Certification of the Amended Text of the Constitution of the Republic of South Africa* (supra), in which the court spoke of such rights as "associational" rights "which cannot be fully or properly exercised by individuals otherwise than in association with others of like disposition" (at para 24).

[18] The phrase is used by Currie op. cit. at 35-13. And see the case of *Lovelace v Canada* (Comm. no. R6/24), (1985) 68 *ILR* 17, in which the court held that the withdrawal of applicant's right to live on Indian Reserve land denied her the right to access her culture and language "in community with other members", and was violative of art 27 of the International Covenant on Civil and Political Rights. The withdrawal of the residence right followed applicant's marriage to a non-Indian. The case demonstrates the degree to which the collective expression of cultural and like rights can be distinguished from individual expression within the collective. In *Kitok v Sweden* (Comm. no. 197/1985), (1985) 96 *ILR* 637 individual expression was subordinated to that of the collective. Here, the court found that the restrictions on individual membership of a particular village were founded on the objective of preserving the culture of the collective and were reasonable and consistent with art 27. See Currie generally 35-14 to 35-15.

[19] See for example Special Rapporteur Capotori's Report *Study on the Rights of Persons Belonging to Ethnic, Religious and Linguistic Minorities* UN Doc. E/CN.4/Sub.2/384/Rev. 1 (1979).

[20] Such as art 2 of the UNESCO Convention Against Discrimination in Education 429 U.N.T.S. 94 (1962) and the Declaration on the Rights of Persons Belonging to National or Ethnic, Religious or Linguistic Minorities GA Res 47/135 18 December 1992.

[21] For example Y Dinstein and M Tabory (eds) *The Protection of Minorities and Human Rights* (1992) and P Thornberry *International Law and the Rights of Minorities* (1991).

[22] See particularly Currie op. cit. at 35-12—"the term 'community' has warmer associations than 'minority'".

[23] Section 235 of the final Constitution speaks of "the right of self-determination of any community sharing a common cultural and language heritage within a territorial entity in the Republic or in any other way, determined by national legislation". The use of the phrase "territorial entity" seems to import a measure of geographical distinctiveness but leaves the matter open to be determined by national legislation. The focus remains however on the cultural and linguistic, and not political, expression of self-determination. The provision was inserted to give effect to Principle XXXIV, discussed above.

[24] In *Gauteng School Education Bill* (supra), the court rejected an argument that the old s 32(c), the precursor to the current s 29(3), creates a positive obligation on the state to establish, where practicable, educational institutions

based on a common culture, language or religion so as to disallow the prohibition of language competence testing as an admission requirement, the directing of what religious policy should be followed or who should and who should not attend religious classes. The court gave the provision its ordinary meaning, that of a defensive freedom. While every person was given the right of instruction in the language of choice, where practicable, the section afforded persons who wanted to have educational institutions based on a special culture, language or religion that was common, to have the freedom to set up such institutions on the basis of this commonality, where practicable. This was "an important freedom", one which was abased by apartheid's Bantu education, which compelled black schools to be placed under state control (at para 8). Kriegler J noted that this right was of immense significance—"(d)it is en bly egter 'n skans teen verswelging van enige minderheid se gemeenskaplike kultuur, taal of godsdiens". See too *Matukane and Others v Laerskool Potgietersrus* 1996 (3) SA 165 (CC) and Currie op. cit. 35-26 to 35-28.

25 Although the non-diminishment provisions of s 3 were dropped. As to s 6, see generally Currie "Official Languages" in Chaskalson et al. (eds) op. cit. chapter 37.

26 Not equally necessarily, but treatment that is fair and just in the circumstances. See Currie id at 37-5. The Constitutional Court in the certification judgment found no ground under Principle XI for rejecting the provisions of s 6 of the final Constitution, by virtue of the exclusion of certain Indian languages from the list of official languages. The designation of official language status was a matter for the drafters. Nor was it discriminatory for the final Constitution to place special emphasis on the protection of vulnerable indigenous languages. Nor, indeed, did the final text reduce the status of Afrikaans. See *In re Certification of the Constitution of the Republic of South Africa, 1996* (supra) at paras 209-14.

27 Municipalities, then, are not compelled to utilise at least two official languages and their margin of appreciation in language choice is considerably less than that of other spheres of government.

28 See per Chaskalson P in *S v Makwanyane* (supra) at para 39. See, too, *S v Zuma and Others* 1995 (4) BCLR 401 (CC) para 35 at 419, *Qozoleni v Minister of Law and Order and Another* 1994 (1) BCLR 75 (E) at 80—"the danger of unnecessarily importing doctrines associated with those (foreign) constitutions into an inappropriate South African setting", *Park-Ross and Another v The Director, Office for Serious Economic Offences* 1995 (2) BCLR

198 (C) at 208, *Berg v Prokureur-Generaal van Gauteng* 1995 (11) BCLR 1441 (T) at 1445-6 and *Fose v Minister of Safety and Security* 1996 (2) BCLR 232 (W) at 237.

[29] See *Gauteng School Education Bill* (supra) in which Mahomed DP endorsed the notion that the language provisions of the Canadian Constitution were a "unique set of constitutional provisions quite peculiar to Canada" (at para 14).

[30] See for example *State of Bombay v Bombay Education Society and Others* (1954) AIR 561; *In re Kerala Education Bill* (1958) AIR 956; *Shri Krishna Gujarat University* (1962) AIR Guj. 62 and (1963) AIR 703; *Reverend Father W. Proost v State of Bihar* (1969) AIR 465; *DAV College Bhatinda v State of Punjab* 1971 AIR 1731; *Ahmedabad St Xavier College Society and Others v State of Gujarat* (1974) AIR 1389; *Md. Joynal Abudin v State* (1990) AIR Cal. 193. See Dlamini op. cit. 577.

[31] See for example *Frank Anthony Public School Employees' Association v Union of India* (1986) 4 SCC 707; *Christian Medical College Hospital Employees' Union v CMC Vellore Association* (1987) 4 SCC 691 and *Y Theclamma v Union of India* (1987) 2 SCC 516.

Chapter 10

Appraisal of the Culture of Governance in South Africa, 1994-1999

Meshack M. Khosa

Introduction

The 1994 first non-racial democratic election in South Africa ushered the country in among the democratic states in the world. Since then, South Africa has advanced towards meeting the following democratic criteria: wide public participation in policy formulation and decision making, voting equality during national, provincial and local government elections, increased access to government information, and the creation of institutions that promote and protect democracy. The aim of this chapter is to provide an appraisal of the culture and legitimacy of governance in South Africa. The chapter focuses on public perceptions of government performance at national, provincial and local levels by race, province and income. Trust in national, provincial and local government and in civil society institutions is also assessed according to race, province and income. In order to contextualise South Africans' appraisal of the evolving culture of governance, the discussion starts with some theoretical reflections.

Theoretical Reflections on Governance and Democracy

The concept "governance" in western literature used to refer largely to the domain of the state. However, since the rise of neo-liberal universalism, governance as a concept has come to proliferate in development discourse and increasingly also includes the domain of the non-state. The World Bank, for example, has come to support "good governance" programmes. These are programmes designed not only to curtail the power of the state and make it more efficient, but also to shift the balance of power in society away from government and the public sector to private individuals and groups. Neo-liberal advocates suggest that this approach will give individuals and groups more power than if power was concentrated in a central state or the public sector (De Alcantara, 1998; Philip, 1999).

Habermas (1993) and Offe (1985) identified distinctive mechanisms of governance by which institutions operate—rational communication, influence, prestige, authority and money. Each has quite different implications for representation, democracy and accountability, yet they are interrelated. Anchoring institutions such as property rights and bureaucratic rules create money and authority (typically associated with markets and states as institutions). These two institutions are interdependent but stand at some remove from influence and prestige which, as mechanisms of governance, are rooted in networks of limited rather than rational (open and free) communication. The institutions that utilise these mechanisms and the mechanisms themselves are continuously contested and negotiated.

Because governance entails the development of governing styles, boundaries between and within public and private sectors change, although they remain interdependent. According to Stoker (1998), the concept "governance"

- refers to a set of institutions and actors that are drawn from but beyond government;
- implies the blurring of boundaries and responsibilities for tackling social and economic issues;
- relates to relations of power between institutions involved in collective action; and
- refers to the capacity to get things done, which does not rest on the power of government to command or use its authority;
- refers to public-private sector co-operation and partnerships.

Stoker's five propositions provide an organising framework for understanding the changing world of governance and different forms of co-ordination (Stoker, 1998, p. 26). Any discussion of the concept "empowerment" should therefore centre on the concept "governance". As this concept suggests the creation of structures of authority at various levels of society, within and outside the state, it is indispensable in coming to grips with transnational processes such as globalisation that require creative responses such as empowerment for local beneficiaries (De Alcantara, 1998).

The phrase "deepening democratic governance" provides a new perspective on the basic tension between neo-liberal economic ideology and pluralistic democracy. Literature on deepening democracy recognises that the formulation and implementation of neo-liberal economic packages and policies require the concentration of power in an executive authority capable of closing access to policy process, thereby compromising the openness and participation implied in both democracy and political liberalism.

There is also an emerging body of work that suggests that democratic politics tend to be restricted to periodic elections, while pluralistic notions of ongoing access to policy making are abandoned (Von Mettenheim & Malloy, 1998, p. 7). This implies that until economic policy making is linked to competitive party-electoral politics and is made accessible to groups from civil society after elections by means of institutionalised practices, isolated technocrats in executive agencies will truncate democracy but fail to govern effectively (Von Mettenheim & Malloy, 1998, p. 11). In so doing democracy will be expanding around the world but will be attenuated (Anderson, 1994). In such a scenario democracy will not confer full citizenship rights.

Evidence from Latin America suggests that there is profound tension between the technocratic and exclusive policy-making patterns deemed imperative by rational neo-liberal economists on the one hand, and the ideals of broad-based participation of both citizens and civil society groups historically implied by liberal and pluralistic conceptions of democracy on the other hand (Von Mettenheim & Malloy, 1998). After studying Argentina and Uruguay, Vacs (1998, p. 167) concluded that:

> The use of coercion and free markets as weapons to disarticulate the distributionist coalitions and generate the conditions for the establishment of a liberal export-orientated economy as well as a stable semi-authoritarian regime succeeded in changing

some of the economic structures and processes, but failed to attain the ultimate goals of neo-liberalism.

The central message here is that whether and how the neo-liberal economic policy is adopted depends on domestic politics. In the words of Von Mettenheim and Malloy (1998, p. 181), "[e]conomic policy can no longer be developed in isolation from elected representatives and the diverse organizations that seek to represent social groups". However, although the literature on deepening democracy acknowledges the importance of leadership or statecraft in resolving apparent impasses and economic constraints, and in introducing sets of liberal and democratic political contestation, it fails to provide a viable explanation of the relationship between the processes of globalisation and localisation.

Thus, according to De Alcantara (1998), in future, if the discourse on governance is to open new opportunities for resolving the current crisis of livelihood and governability, the following issues should be attended to:

- Encouraging the creativity and originality of people in concrete social settings;
- Broadening dialogue on the needs for change in specific institutions and programmes;
- Strengthening the public sphere and rewarding contributions to the common good, thereby developing the discourse on citizenship;
- Recognising the necessary interrelation between institutional reform and macroeconomic policy;
- Moving away from artificial separation of national governance and international issues (De Alcantara, 1998).

The key question will be: To what extent are the issues arising out of the global literature relevant to South Africa?

Government Performance

Although government performance can be assessed by means of several yardsticks, in this chapter we evaluate government performance by analysing public satisfaction or dissatisfaction with the different spheres of government. (For the purpose of discussing the survey results, the categories "Very satisfied" and "Satisfied" were aggregated to form one category, "Satisfied", and the categories "Dissatisfied" and "Very dissatisfied" were aggregated to form one category, "Dissatisfied". The same applies to "Strong trust" and "Trust", and "Distrust" and "Strong distrust".)

Perceptions of the Way South Africa is Governed

One of the tasks of the first democratic government was to set in place mechanisms for effective governance. These include the establishment of nine provinces within a "united" South Africa, and also the establishment of local governments.

According to the November 1999 survey (2 700 respondents), significantly more people were satisfied than dissatisfied with the way South Africa was governed. Fifty-two per cent (52%) of the respondents indicated that they were satisfied with the way South Africa was governed, compared with 33% who indicated that they were dissatisfied. Although the November 1999 figure is a significant improvement compared with the December 1998 figure, it still falls short of the 64% satisfaction of October 1994. While levels of satisfaction improved from 36% in December 1998 to 52% in November 1999, the levels of dissatisfaction with the way South Africa was governed decreased correspondingly from 50% to 33% in the same period.

Table 10.1: How satisfied or dissatisfied are you with the way South Africa is being governed at present?

Level	December 1998	November 1999
	Percentage	
Very satisfied	11	16
Satisfied	25	36
Neither satisfied nor dissatisfied	12	12
Dissatisfied	32	21
Very dissatisfied	18	12
Don't know	2	3
Total	100	100

Perceptions of the Way South Africa is Governed by Race

The years of racial discrimination in South Africa ensured the exclusion of the majority of South Africans from the governance of the country. This came to an end with the dawn of the democratic era, which enabled effective participation by all in the different spheres of government.

Perceptions of the way South Africa was governed in November 1999 differed by race, with the majority of blacks (64%) being satisfied, followed by coloureds (32%), Asians (13%) and whites (11%) (Table 10.2). The November 1999 figures for the blacks and coloureds improved significantly from the figures of the December 1998 survey (49% and 22% respectively). The increased satisfaction on the part of these two histori-cally disenfranchised groups bides well for the emerging democracy.

Table 10.2: How satisfied or dissatisfied are you with the way South Africa is being governed at present? (November 1999)

Level	Black	Coloured	Asian	White	SA popu-lation
			Percentage		
Very satisfied	22	5	1	0	17
Satisfied	42	27	12	11	36
Neither satisfied nor dissatisfied	11	22	10	14	12
Dissatisfied	14	30	38	46	21
Very dissatisfied	8	11	37	26	12
Don't know	3	6	2	3	3
Total	100	100	100	100	100

Perceptions of the Way South Africa is Governed by Province

Perceptions of the way South Africa was governed by the ANC differed by province. Analysis of satisfaction with the way South Africa was governed suggests that only respondents in the Western Cape were more dissatisfied than satisfied with governance (45% versus 30%). The top three provinces with more satisfied than dissatisfied respondents were Mpumalanga (66% versus 24%), the Northern Province (63% versus 23%) and the Eastern Cape (66% versus 25%).

In general, provinces under ANC rule tended to have a greater proportion of respondents who trusted governance than provinces governed by other parties, that is, the Western Cape and KwaZulu-Natal. Both these provinces were governed by a coalition, which suggests the need for a broader based government in these provinces.

Perceptions of the Way South Africa is Governed by Income

Asked in November 1999 how satisfied or dissatisfied they were with the way South Africa was being governed at that time, 54% of respondents indicated that they were satisfied compared to 33% who indicated otherwise. Analysis of the data by income level suggests that the wealthy respondents were more likely to be dissatisfied than satisfied.

The high-income segment of the population was the most dissatisfied with the way South Africa was governed. This finding is not surprising as government infrastructure and service delivery programmes in the past five years were largely targeted at low-income groups and not the middle and upper classes of society. Higher satisfaction levels on the part of low-income groups point to the relative success of government's attempts at infrastructure and service delivery. However, higher satisfaction levels did not necessarily translate into unconditional support for all policies or programmes. Indeed, there were cases where infrastructure programmes did not provide much-needed jobs, nor were they sustainable.

Perceptions of Provincial Governance

There has been a significant improvement in South Africans' satisfaction with provincial governance when comparing the December 1998 survey and the November 1999 data. Forty-four per cent (44%) of adult South Africans were satisfied and 38% were dissatisfied with the way the provinces were governed in November 1999. The level of satisfaction increased from 32% in December 1998 to 44% in November 1999. On the other hand, the level of dissatisfaction declined by 14% from 52% to 38%. Several reasons may account for the increase in satisfaction. First, provincial government performance may have improved somewhat with the passage of time. Second, the public was gradually accepting provinces as important institutions in South Africa. Third, a radical overhaul of the provinces was deemed unlikely in view of the constitutional amendments it would require.

Table 10.3: How satisfied or dissatisfied are you with the way your province is being governed at present?

Level	December 1998	November 1999
	Percentage	
Very satisfied	7	10
Satisfied	25	34
Neither satisfied nor dissatisfied	12	13
Dissatisfied	34	24
Very dissatisfied	18	14
Don't know	3	5
Total	100	100

Perceptions of Provincial Governance by Race

The various population groups judged provincial governance differently. For example, more than half of the blacks rated provincial governance positively (52%). Of the coloureds, 31% were satisfied. Only 16% whites and 14% Asians indicated that they were satisfied with the way South Africa's provinces were governed (Table 10.4). The November 1999 survey suggests that significantly more blacks were satisfied with the way South Africa was governed than with the way the provinces were governed (64% versus 53%). Dissatisfaction on the part of Asians and whites with the way South Africa was being governed was slightly higher than their dissatisfaction with the way the provinces were being governed. Slightly more whites were satisfied with the way provinces were governed than they were with the way South Africa was governed.

Table 10.4: How satisfied or dissatisfied are you with the way your province is being governed at present? (November 1999)

Level	Black	Coloured	Asian	White	SA population
			Percentage		
Very satisfied	13	3	1	1	10
Satisfied	39	28	13	15	34
Neither satisfied nor dissatisfied	12	17	10	18	13
Dissatisfied	18	34	38	44	24
Very dissatisfied	14	10	33	16	14
Don't know	4	8	4	7	5
Total	100	100	100	100	100

Perceptions of Provincial Governance by Province

Provincial governance was judged differently by the respondents in different provinces. There were proportionally more people satisfied than dissatisfied in the Eastern Cape, North West and the Free State. However, there were significantly more people dissatisfied with provincial governance in the Western Cape than in the other provinces.

Perceptions of Provincial Governance by Income

The HSRC survey of November 1999 also sought to understand the relationship between provincial governance and income. The findings suggest that the higher the income of respondents the less they were likely to show satisfaction with the way their provinces were governed. There were proportionally more respondents satisfied than dissatisfied among the low-income earners than among the other income groups. There are several reasons for the differences in satisfaction. In the past the poor were under-provided and the wealthy over-provided in terms of resources. With the dawn of democracy in South Africa, resources came to be redistributed to those who were historically disenfranchised. The poor appreciate these benefits, and their appreciation appears to translate into high satisfaction levels.

Perceptions of Local Governance

The local government sphere has the constitutional role to promote local economic development and deliver services. However, this sphere of government has taken longer than the other spheres to undergo transformation. The November 1999 survey reveals that slightly more respondents were satisfied (44%) than dissatisfied (42%) with the way their local areas were governed. The survey points to an improvement in the perception of local governance from December 1998. Whereas there was a decline in dissatisfaction from 55% to 42% between the two surveys, satisfaction with local governance increased from 31% to 44% in the same period.

Table 10.5: How satisfied or dissatisfied are you with the way your local area is being governed at present?

Level	December 1998	November 1999
	Percentage	
Very satisfied	6	10
Satisfied	25	34
Neither satisfied nor dissatisfied	12	10
Dissatisfied	36	25
Very dissatisfied	19	17
Don't know	3	4
Total	100	100

Perceptions of Local Governance by Race

Apartheid thrived in local authorities prior to 1994, and continued to affect local governance thereafter. This explains the difference in the perceptions of local governance by race. More blacks (47%) than coloureds (31%), Asians (25%) and whites (32%) were satisfied with the way their local area was governed in November 1999 (Table 10.6). Important trends can be noticed from the survey data. Proportionally more whites than coloureds and Asians were satisfied with the way their local areas were governed, and whites were more satisfied with the way their local area was governed than with the way South Africa was governed. However, dissatisfaction among coloureds, Asians and whites far surpassed that of blacks in terms of local governance. These findings are not surprising as the majority of historically white municipalities have had the capacity and resources to continue to extract benefits for whites.

Table 10.6: How satisfied or dissatisfied are you with the way your local area is being governed at present? (November 1999)

Level	Black	Coloured	Asian	White	SA population
			Percentage		
Very satisfied	12	4	2	1	10
Satisfied	35	27	23	31	34
Neither satisfied nor dissatisfied	10	11	14	11	10
Dissatisfied	22	36	35	36	25
Very dissatisfied	17	14	25	17	17
Don't know	4	9	2	3	4
Total	100	100	100	100	100

Perceptions of Local Governance by Province

Although the overall findings of the November 1999 survey suggest that more people were satisfied than dissatisfied with the way their local areas were governed, there were more people dissatisfied than satisfied in three of the nine provinces, namely the Western Cape, the Northern Province and the Eastern Cape. Satisfaction levels were higher in the Free State, Gauteng, KwaZulu-Natal, Mpumalanga, the Northern Cape and North West (15% to 40%).

Perceptions of Local Governance by Income

The November 1999 survey suggests that the high-income earners were less likely than the low-income earners to be satisfied with the way their local areas were governed. As the beneficiaries of development programmes in local areas were mainly low-income groups, this may explain why they were more satisfied than high-income groups.

Comparing Public Perceptions of National, Provincial and Local Spheres of Government

South Africa's three-sphere government has averted potential political blood letting in 1994. However, the intergovernmental relations established by the new political order are not optimally effective. It is against this background that public satisfaction with the three spheres of government is analysed.

According to the November 1999 survey, the majority of people in South Africa were more satisfied than dissatisfied with the different spheres of government. However, more people were satisfied with the way South Africa was governed at the national level than at provincial and local level. There was also a dramatic improvement in satisfaction from the December 1998 survey. Analysis of the November 1999 data by race suggests that significantly more blacks than coloureds, Asians and whites were satisfied with the way all three spheres of government were governed. However, satisfaction with governance was slightly higher for local government than for provincial and national government.

The November 1999 survey also highlights some correlation between income and perception of governance at local, provincial and national levels. The higher the income, the more likely were people to indicate their dissatisfaction with the way South Africa was governed in the national, provincial and local spheres.

Table 10.7: How satisfied or dissatisfied are you with performance at the national, provincial and local spheres of government? (November 1999)

Level	National government	Provincial government	Local government
		Percentage	
Very satisfied	17	10	10
Satisfied	36	34	34
Neither satisfied nor dissatisfied	12	13	10
Dissatisfied	21	24	25
Very dissatisfied	12	14	17
Don't know	3	5	4
Total	100	100	100

Trust/Distrust in the Spheres of Government

Trust in the different spheres of government can be seen as a measure of the legitimacy of the government in the eyes of citizens. Moreover, such trust may also signify a certain degree of acceptance by the public of those institutions. This section of the chapter compares trust levels in national, provincial and local government disaggregated by race, province and income. Use is made of the December 1998 and November 1999 HSRC surveys to determine whether there were significant shifts in the levels of trust.

Trust in National Government

When asked how much trust they had in the national government, 60% of respondents confirmed their trust in the national government in November 1999 (Table 10.8). This figure is a significant 15% improvement on the December 1998 survey. Correspondingly, public distrust in the national government decreased from 39% in December 1998 to 23% in November 1999. There are several possible explanations for the improvement: the consolidation of our democracy, improvement in delivery mechanisms and better public policy making over the first five years of democratic rule.

Table 10.8: How much trust/distrust do you have in the national government?

Level	December 1998	November 1999
	Percentage	
Strong trust	14	25
Trust	31	35
Neither trust nor distrust	12	13
Distrust	24	16
Strong distrust	15	7
Don't know	3	4
Total	100	100

Trust in National Government by Race

Further analysis of the November 1999 survey suggests that trust in the national government differed by race. A significant majority of blacks (71%) trusted the national government, but of the coloureds, Asians and whites, 43%, 33% and 19% respectively trusted the national government (Table 10.9). Trust levels for blacks and whites indicate significant shifts when compared with the December 1998 survey. Trust levels increased from 60% to 71% for blacks, while for whites they increased from 6% to 19% between December 1998 and November 1999. The increase in trust in the national government bides well for race relations and nation building. However, whites had the highest levels of distrust in the national government.

Table 10.9: How much trust/distrust do you have in the national government? (November 1999)

Level	Black	Coloured	Asian	White	SA population
			Percentage		
Strong trust	32	12	5	2	25
Trust	39	31	28	17	35
Neither trust nor distrust	11	24	11	16	13
Distrust	10	20	41	43	16
Strong distrust	5	8	11	16	7
Don't know	3	6	6	6	4
Total	100	100	100	100	100

Trust in National Government by Province

The HSRC survey suggests that there were proportionately more people who trusted government than those who did not. Trust levels in government were higher in the Eastern Cape, Free State and Mpumalanga and lower in the Western Cape.

Trust in National Government by Income

The HSRC survey of November 1999 suggests that the higher the income, the more likely respondents were to distrust the national government. There are several possible reasons for the differences in trust by income. First, high-income earners, who are likely to be taxed more than low-income earners, apparently feel that their contribution to the national fiscus is not adequately compensated for. Second, high-income earners are mostly (though not exclusively) whites who apparently feel that the new South Africa has eroded some of the exclusive and excessive social benefits which they previously received. Third, the government focuses on national priorities rather than parochial and minority interests.

Trust in Provincial Government

The results of the November 1999 survey suggest that more respondents trusted than distrusted the provincial government. Half (50%) of the respondents indicated trust, compared with 28% who indicated distrust in provincial government. When comparing data from the December 1998 data, it is evident that trust in the provincial government increased while distrust declined. Trust increased from 39% in December 1998 to 50% in November 1999. On the other hand, distrust decreased from 43% to 28% during the same period (Table 10.10).

Table 10.10: How much trust/distrust do you have in your provincial government?

Level	December 1998	November 1999
	Percentage	
Strong trust	9	12
Trust	30	38
Neither trust nor distrust	14	17
Distrust	27	21
Strong distrust	16	7
Don't know	4	6
Total	100	100

Trust in Provincial Government by Race

As with trust in the national government, more blacks than whites, Asians and coloureds trusted the provincial government. Table 10.11 reveals that 56% blacks trusted the provincial government compared to 38% coloureds, 25% Asians and 26% whites. As for distrust in the provincial government, 49% whites and 55% Asians indicated distrust. It is notable that more blacks trusted the national government than the provincial government.

Table 10.11: How much trust/distrust do you have in the provincial government? (November 1999)

Level	Black	Coloured	Asian	White	SA population
			Percentage		
Strong trust	15	4	0	1	13
Trust	41	34	25	25	41
Neither trust nor distrust	16	24	11	18	14
Distrust	16	21	46	40	22
Strong distrust	6	10	9	9	7
Don't know	5	8	9	8	4
Total	100	100	100	100	100

Trust in Provincial Government by Province

Although more people trusted than distrusted the provincial government, there were provincial variations. The highest trust was registered in the Eastern Cape, Free State and Mpumalanga. However, trust levels in the Western Cape, Northern Province and Northern Cape were below the national average.

Trust in Provincial Government by Income

Income levels appear to influence trust in the provincial government. Whereas the wealthy segments of society tended to distrust the provincial government, the poor segments of society tended to trust it.

Local Governance

As with other spheres of government, local government has come to be trusted more in the past five years. In November 1999, significantly more South Africans indicated that they trusted (49%) the local government than those who distrusted it (32%). Levels of trust increased from 36% to 49% between December 1998 and November 1999. Distrust levels decreased from 49% in December 1998 to 32% in November 1999. One possible explanation is the improvement in local governance and service and infrastructure delivery at the local government level.

Table 10.12: How much trust/distrust do you have in your local government?

Level	December 1998	November 1999
	Percentage	
Strong trust	8	13
Trust	28	36
Neither trust nor distrust	13	16
Distrust	29	23
Strong distrust	20	9
Don't know	3	4
Total	100	100

Trust in Local Government by Race

Trust in the local government differed by race, with 55% blacks indicating trust, compared to 38% coloureds, 25% Asians and 21% whites. More Asians (59%) than any other group distrusted the local government. About 50% whites distrusted the local government. The high levels of distrust among the whites may have to do with the termination by the new non-racial local governments of the advantageous access to resources that white local authorities had during the apartheid period.

Table 10.13: How much trust/distrust do you have in your local government? (November 1999)

Level	Black	Coloured	Asian	White	SA population
			Percentage		
Strong trust	16	5	1	1	14
Trust	39	33	24	20	39
Neither trust nor distrust	14	24	12	19	15
Distrust	14	26	47	41	20
Strong distrust	9	8	12	10	10
Don't know	3	4	4	9	4
Total	100	100	100	100	100

Trust in Local Government by Province

Trust in the local government differed by province. With the exception of the Western Cape and Gauteng trust in the local government was high.

Trust in Local Government by Income

Trust in the local government also differed by income. High-income earners distrusted the local government more than low-income earners. Correspondingly, low-income earners trusted the local government more than did the high-income earners. As with both the national and provincial spheres of government, high levels of trust among the low-income groups are probably associated with perceived improvements in service and infra-structure delivery since 1994. Higher trust levels should however not be interpreted as acceptance of lack of service delivery which occurs in some areas, but as an indicator of visible improvement in some respects. The majority of those in the high-income groups are whites who in the past received better services from local authorities. Since 1994, local authorities have been abiding by a new mandate: to deliver services to all irrespective of race, income or location.

Comparing Trust in the Different Spheres of Government

More South Africans trusted the national government than the local and the provincial government. According to the November 1999 data, 60% of the respondents trusted the national government, followed by 50% who trusted the provincial government and 49% who trusted the local government. Although all spheres of government received higher trust than distrust ratings, about a third of the respondents in November 1999 distrusted the local government. However, levels of trust in the provincial and the local government were probably the highest since 1994. Trust in the national government increased, and trust in the provincial government was decidedly positive. Trust in the local government is however cause for concern. The torturous restructuring of local government and the delays in service delivery probably harmed the image of local government.

Table 10.14: Comparing trust/distrust in organs of civil society (November 1999)

Level	National government	Provincial government	Local government
		Percentage	
Strong trust	25	12	13
Trust	35	38	36
Neither trust nor distrust	13	17	16
Distrust	16	21	23
Strong distrust	7	7	9
Don't know	4	6	4
Total	100	100	100

Trust/Distrust in National Institutions

The dawn of democracy in South Africa witnessed the creation of new institutions with the mandate to protect and promote democracy. Hard work was required to transform old institutions that did not enjoy legitimacy. In successive national surveys over the years, the HSRC included a question to determine levels of trust or distrust in national institutions. This section focuses on public trust in the courts, police, defence force and the Independent Electoral Commission (IEC).

Trust in the Courts

The courts are pillars of the criminal justice system. With the adoption of the 1996 constitution, South Africa became a democratic country acknowledging the rule of law. Public trust in the courts and the role courts play in dispensing justice are important to consolidate democracy and create a culture of fair governance.

Fourty-four per cent (44%) of respondents in November 1999 revealed trust in the courts, compared to a third who indicated distrust. The levels of distrust in the courts declined from 44% in December 1998 to 33% in November 1999. The proportion of people indicating their trust in November 1999 increased from that of December 1998 (Table 10.15).

Table 10.15: How much trust/distrust do you have in the courts?

Level	December 1998	November 1999
	Percentage	
Strong trust	10	11
Trust	30	33
Neither trust nor distrust	12	16
Distrust	26	23
Strong distrust	18	10
Don't know	2	6
Total	100	100

Trust in the Courts by Race

Public perceptions of the courts differed by race. Analysis of the November 1999 survey disaggregated by race suggests that more blacks and coloureds trusted the courts than whites and Asians. The majority of whites (58%) and Asians (45%) indicated distrust in the courts. Distrust among whites and Asians was higher than the national average distrust in the courts.

Table 10.16: How much trust/distrust do you have in the courts? (November 1999)

Level	Black	Coloured	Asian	White	SA popu-lation
			Percentage		
Strong trust	14	5	2	2	12
Trust	35	33	28	20	33
Neither trust nor distrust	16	20	16	13	16
Distrust	19	23	38	45	23
Strong distrust	10	10	7	13	10
Don't know	6	9	10	8	6
Total	100	100	100	100	100

Trust in the Courts by Province

Of the nine provinces, only the Western Cape (43% versus 40%) and Gauteng (42% versus 32%) had more respondents who indicated distrust than trust in the courts. The highest trust levels in the courts were registered in Mpumalanga, KwaZulu-Natal, the Free State, Northern Cape, and the Eastern Cape. Distrust in the courts in the Western Cape may be the result of on-going urban violence (and the perceived inability of the courts to punish offenders), while in Gauteng lack of capacity and resources may explain the distrust.

Trust in the Courts by Income

Trust in the courts differed by income. The November 1999 survey reveals that the low-income earners had proportionally more trust in the courts than the high-income earners. This is contrary to the popular view that low-income earners have low trust in and respect for the courts. Nevertheless, the high-income earners had more trust than distrust in the courts.

The findings also point out that the majority of the middle class did not trust the courts, while low-income and high-income earners had relatively more trust in the courts. There are several reasons for the greater trust of the latter two income groups. The low-income earners may have gained improved access to the courts through state legal aid, and probably viewed the courts as credible arbiters of justice. The high-income earners may have had greater access to costly lawyers and attorneys to represent them effectively.

Trust in the Police

During the political upheavals of the 1980s, the police were seen as the extension of the repressive apartheid state apparatus. Public trust in the police significantly improved since the institution of the democratic government. Trust levels increased from 41% in December 1998 to 47% in November 1999. Levels of distrust in the police decreased from 44% in December 1998 to 37% in November 1999. Increasing trust in the police bodes well for the image of the police and the restoration of order in society (Table 10.17).

Table 10.17: How much trust/distrust do you have in the police?

Level	December 1998	November 1999
	Percentage	
Strong trust	9	15
Trust	32	32
Neither trust nor distrust	12	14
Distrust	24	24
Strong distrust	20	13
Don't know	2	3
Total	**100**	**100**

Trust in the Police by Race

Trust in the police differed by race, with coloureds on top of the scale with 51%, followed by blacks with 49%.

Within the white population there was slightly more distrust than trust in the police (43% versus 37%). This may be explained by the perception among whites that the police is not able to protect property in historically whites areas. It is not surprising that whites are therefore turning in large numbers to private security companies for protection.

Table 10.18: How much trust/distrust do you have in the police? (November 1999)

Level	Black	Coloured	Asian	White	SA population
			Percentage		
Strong trust	18	9	7	6	15
Trust	31	42	39	31	32
Neither trust nor distrust	14	15	11	16	14
Distrust	22	23	31	33	24
Strong distrust	14	8	11	10	13
Don't know	2	3	1	5	3
Total	100	100	100	100	100

Trust in the Police by Province

Some 47% of respondents nationally revealed trust in the police in November 1999. Significantly more Gauteng respondents than other respondents distrusted the police. It is in this province where crime syndicates operate in large numbers and police are implicated in the operation of some of these crime syndicates.

Trust in the Police by Income

The low-income earners had more trust than distrust in the police. This finding suggests that low-income groups and components of the middle class are more likely to trust the police than the high-income earners. This is a far cry from a decade ago when the police was seen as an extension of the repressive state apparatus.

Trust in the Defence Force

The former South African Defence Force was seen as a repressive apparatus of the apartheid regime. Because of the transformation that started in 1994, this section of the report seeks to gauge levels of trust or distrust in the defence force. According to the survey data, trust in the defence force increased from 55% in December 1998 to 57% in November 1999. The level of distrust declined from 35% in December 1998 to 21% in November 1999.

The national defence force is a key national institution with the secondary aim of instilling patriotism. The higher trust in the defence force bodes well for nation building and signifies greater acceptance of national symbols, which in the past were seen as white, racist and repressive.

Table 10.19: How much trust/distrust do you have in the defence force?

Level	December 1998	November 1999
	Percentage	
Strong trust	22	15
Trust	33	42
Neither trust nor distrust	8	16
Distrust	20	14
Strong distrust	15	7
Don't know	2	6
Total	100	100

Trust in the Defence Force by Race

More black than other respondents trusted the defence force. In addition, whereas 61% of blacks trusted the defence force, only 18% distrusted it. The majority of blacks (61%), coloureds (57%) and Asians (50%) trusted the defence force, but the majority of whites distrusted it in November 1999.

The higher trust ratings among blacks point to progress (albeit painful) in the integration of the liberation armies into the national defence force.

Trust in the Defence Force by Province

Trust in the defence force was very high nationally and in the provinces.

Table 10.20: How much trust/distrust do you have in the defence force? (November 1999)

Level	Black	Coloured	Asian	White	SA popu-lation
			Percentage		
Strong trust	17	12	5	5	15
Trust	44	45	45	22	42
Neither trust nor distrust	15	20	12	23	16
Distrust	11	10	22	32	14
Strong distrust	7	5	5	9	7
Don't know	5	9	11	9	6
Total	100	100	100	100	100

Trust in the Defence Force by Income

Trust in the defence force strongly correlated with respondents' income. More respondents earning less than R5 830 per month than those earning more trusted the defence force. In the highest income bracket distrust was very high. These findings suggest that the lower the income the more likely were the respondents to place their trust in the defence force. Conversely, the higher the income level, the more likely were they to distrust the defence force. There are several possible reasons for the increase in trust among the majority of respondents. First, the defence force is sometimes used in poor communities to maintain peace, fight crime and assist if and when there are disasters. Second, the transformation within the defence force and the incorporation of the liberation armies may have increased the legitimacy of the defence force in the eyes of the majority.

Trust in the Independent Electoral Commission (IEC)

The Independent Electoral Commission was established by the 1996 Constitution as a body to conduct, oversee and manage elections. The HSRC included a question in its national survey to determine public trust in the IEC. An overwhelming majority of respondents (54%) in the November 1999 survey indicated that they trusted the IEC. Only about 17% indicated that they distrusted the IEC. This finding bodes well for democracy and the electoral process, as the higher the legitimacy of the IEC, the greater the likelihood that the outcome of an election will be accepted.

Table 10.21: How much trust/distrust do you have in the Independent Electoral Commission (IEC)?

Level	November 1999 %
Strong trust	17
Trust	37
Neither trust nor distrust	20
Distrust	11
Strong distrust	6
Don't know	10
Total	100

Trust in the IEC by Race

The majority of blacks (60%) and coloureds (51%) indicated that they had trust in the IEC. A larger proportion of whites (48%) distrusted than trusted (24%) the IEC. These trust patterns are similar to the trust patterns relating to the other institutions tested in the HSRC surveys.

Table 10.22: How much trust/distrust do you have in the Independent Electoral Commission (IEC)? (November 1999)

Level	Black	Coloured	Asian	White	SA population
			Percentage		
Strong trust	22	7	5	1	17
Trust	38	44	41	23	37
Neither trust nor distrust	20	24	15	17	20
Distrust	6	10	24	35	11
Strong distrust	4	3	10	13	6
Don't know	10	11	6	11	10
Total	100	100	100	100	100

Trust in the IEC by Province

A great majority of the respondents nationally indicated trust in the IEC. Trust in the IEC per province was also high. However, the provincial variations were related to the political dynamics of the provinces.

Trust in the IEC by Income

Although the majority of respondents indicated that they trusted the IEC, trust differed by income. The low-income earners had significant proportions of respondents who trusted the IEC. This finding suggests that the lower their income, the more likely were respondents to trust the IEC. However, high trust was also found among the middle-income earners in November 1999.

Comparing Public Trust in the Different National Institutions

According to the November 1999 survey, 43% of the respondents indicated trust in the courts, 47% in the police, 57% in the South African National Defence Force (SANDF) and 54% in the Independent Electoral Commission (Table 10.23). The results suggest that although some political parties were very critical of the IEC, the public generally had trust in the IEC and believed that it was a fair and independent institution.

Table 10.23: How much trust/distrust do you have in national institutions? (November 1999)

Level	Courts	Police	Defence force	IEC
		Percentage		
Strong trust	11	15	15	17
Trust	32	32	42	37
Neither trust nor distrust	16	14	16	20
Distrust	23	24	14	11
Strong distrust	10	13	14	6
Don't know	7	3	6	10
Total	100	100	100	100

A third (33%) of the respondents indicated their distrust in the courts, 37% in the police, 28% in the defence force and 17% in the IEC (Table 10.23).

Although more respondents trusted than distrusted national institutions, the public's perception of key elements of the South African criminal justice system was somewhat negative. This implies that more is required to both restructure the criminal justice system and share information on such restructuring with the public. In general, the levels of trust in national institutions indicate acceptance of the role these institutions play in the consolidation of democracy in South Africa.

Trust/Distrust in Institutions of Civil Society

Trust in institutions of civil society is an important indicator of a flourishing democracy. Five institutions were selected for the purposes of our analysis. These are political parties, labour unions, business, the media and churches. Trust in these institutions was analysed by race, province and income.

Trust in Political Parties

Political parties play an important role in fostering a vibrant democracy. Since 1994 political parties have freely contested elections at national, provincial and national level. The 1996 constitution makes provision for free political activity and the freedom of expression. The November 1999 survey indicates that the majority of South Africans trusted political parties. Trust levels increased from 29% in December 1998 to 39% in November 1999 (Table 10.24).

Table 10.24: How much trust/distrust do you have in political parties?

Level	December 1998	November 1999
	Percentage	
Strong trust	8	11
Trust	21	28
Neither trust nor distrust	17	20
Distrust	33	23
Strong distrust	18	11
Don't know	4	6
Total	100	100

Trust in Political Parties by Race

Public trust in political parties differed by race. In November 1999, nearly half (48%) of the black respondents indicated their trust in political parties. The corresponding trust level for coloureds was 24%, whites 8% and Asians 15%. Asians (69%) and whites (70%) distrusted political parties significantly more than the other two groups in November 1999 (Table 10.25).

Trust in Political Parties by Income

Trust levels differed by income. The low-income earners had more trust in political parties than the middle- and high-income earners.

These findings suggest that the higher their income the more likely were respondents to distrust political parties. Conversely, the lower their income the more likely were respondents to trust political parties. There are several possible explanations for this. First, the low-income groups largely constitute blacks and are more likely to be politically active. Second, the middle-income and high-income groups are gradually withdrawing from active party politics. The majority of those in the middle- and high-income groups are whites, and they have the highest level of distrust in political parties, and the highest level of distrust in national institutions.

Table 10.25: How much trust/distrust do you have in political parties? (November 1999)

Level	Black	Coloured	Asian	White	SA population
			Percentage		
Strong trust	14	5	0	0	11
Trust	34	19	15	8	28
Neither trust nor distrust	21	25	12	14	20
Distrust	16	36	52	53	23
Strong distrust	10	10	17	17	11
Don't know	6	6	4	8	6
Total	100	100	100	100	100

Trust in Labour Unions

Labour unions have played an important role in protecting the rights of workers over the years. With the introduction of the negotiatory approach to industrial relations by the Labour Relations Act, levels of trust in labour unions became an issue of interest. Trust in labour unions remained the same between December 1998 and November 1999 (38%). However, whereas distrust surpassed trust in December 1998 these two variables were on an equal footing in November 1999. These findings suggest that trust in labour unions is not a necessary outcome of labour union involvement in industrial relations.

Table 10.26: How much trust/distrust do you have in the labour unions?

Level	December 1998	November 1999
	Percentage	
Strong trust	8	9
Trust	30	29
Neither trust nor distrust	14	20
Distrust	22	17
Strong distrust	18	11
Don't know	9	15
Total	100	100

Trust in Labour Unions by Race

Public trust in labour unions differed by race. More blacks (42%) than Asians (35%) and whites (10%) trusted the labour unions. Sixty-seven per cent (67%) of whites distrusted labour unions, compared to only 10% who trusted them (Table 10.27). These figures are not surprising, as the majority of unionised workers and sympathisers are blacks, and they join strong unions such as the Congress of South African Trade Unions (COSATU). White tendencies to see unions as surrogates of political parties may explain the high levels of distrust among whites.

Table 10.27: How much trust/distrust do you have in the labour unions? (November 1999)

Level	Black	Coloured	Asian	White	SA population
			Percentage		
Strong trust	11	7	3	1	9
Trust	31	32	32	9	29
Neither trust nor distrust	22	20	10	12	20
Distrust	13	18	35	37	17
Strong distrust	8	8	10	30	11
Don't know	16	16	10	11	15
Total	100	100	100	100	100

Trust in Labour Unions by Income

Public trust in labour unions differed by income level. Trust in labour unions was higher among respondents earning less than R2 500 per month than respondents earning more. This finding can be explained by the fact that labour unions largely represent the interests of workers, especially those at the lower echelons of the work force, and these workers are mostly blacks.

Trust in Business

Trust in the private sector or business was high, and increased from 54% in December 1998 to 55% in November 1999. The proportion of respondents who indicated that they distrusted business decreased from 25% in December 1998 to 17% in November 1999. These figures are quite surprising given the perception that business in the past aided the apartheid regime in its political repression and economic exploitation.

Table 10.28: How much trust/distrust do you have in business?

Level	December 1998	November 1999
	Percentage	
Strong trust	11	12
Trust	43	43
Neither trust nor distrust	17	22
Distrust	16	12
Strong distrust	9	5
Don't know	4	6
Total	100	100

Trust in Business by Race

The November 1999 survey reveals that the majority of South Africans trusted business. This is one of the few variables where the perceptions of whites were more positive than negative. Substantive trust in business among all South Africans may induce business to play a significant role in future transformation. Sadly, business did not play a significant role in transformation between 1994 and 1999. The protracted negotiations around employment equity legislation, and the reluctance of the organised business sector to introduce effective and far-reaching affirmative action and economic empowerment programmes are evidence of this.

Table 10.29: How much trust/distrust do you have in business? (November 1999)

Level	Black	Coloured	Asian	White	SA population
	Percentage				
Strong trust	15	4	3	3	12
Trust	43	38	55	47	43
Neither trust nor distrust	20	32	13	25	22
Distrust	11	13	18	17	12
Strong distrust	6	2	9	3	5
Don't know	6	11	3	6	6
Total	100	100	100	100	100

Trust in Business by Income

Perceptions of trust in business differed by income. The majority of re-spondents in all income groups indicated trust in business. However, trust levels increased with income. Conversely, lower income correlated with less trust in business but more trust in labour unions in November 1999.

Trust in the Media

The electronic and print media play an important role in the dissemination of information, education and entertainment. The challenge for the media is also to present reliable information to assist citizens to make informed choices about day-to-day governance. The majority of respondents (66%) in November 1999 indicated that they trusted the media. The levels of trust in the media increased from 59% in December 1998 to 66% in November 1999. The level of distrust in the media declined from 22% to 16% in the same period.

Table 10.30: How much trust/distrust do you have in the media?

Level	December 1998	November 1999
	Percentage	
Strong trust	20	23
Trust	39	43
Neither trust nor distrust	16	15
Distrust	16	12
Strong distrust	6	4
Don't know	4	4
Total	100	100

Trust in the Media by Race

Trust in the media differed by race. However, the majority (66%) of all the population groups trusted the media (Table 10.31). This is the second variable (after business) where the majority of all population groups trusted a civil society institution. What is of concern is that, apart from the financial and sport sections of the media, the messages of the media are based on half-truths, sensational reporting and racism that do not promote objectivity. Indeed racism in the media was recently confirmed by a Human Rights Commission inquiry.

Table 10.31: How much trust/distrust do you have in the media? (November 1999)

Level	Black	Coloured	Asian	White	SA popu-lation
			Percentage		
Strong trust	29	10	5	3	23
Trust	45	41	44	34	43
Neither trust nor distrust	12	28	14	20	15
Distrust	7	12	26	32	12
Strong distrust	3	5	7	6	4
Don't know	4	4	4	4	4
Total	100	100	100	100	100

Trust in the Media by Income

Public trust in the media slightly differed by income. The high-income (perhaps more analytical) groups distrusted the media more than the other income groups.

Trust in Churches

Successive HSRC surveys confirm that the majority (82%) of South Africans are religious and trust churches. Trust in church institutions increased from a high 80% in December 1998 to an even higher 82% in November 1999. That is probably why current anti-corruption campaigns are based on "moral" considerations.

Table 10.32: How much trust/distrust do you have in churches?

Level	December 1998	November 1999
	Percentage	
Strong trust	39	40
Trust	41	42
Neither trust nor distrust	9	9
Distrust	5	4
Strong distrust	4	2
Don't know	3	3
Total	100	100

Trust in Churches by Race

Trust in churches was very high among all the population groups in South Africa.

Table 10.33: How much trust/distrust do you have in churches? (November 1999)

Level	Black	Coloured	Asian	White	SA population
	Percentage				
Strong trust	41	48	21	30	40
Trust	40	43	45	51	42
Neither trust nor distrust	10	6	8	6	9
Distrust	4	1	9	7	4
Strong distrust	2	1	3	1	2
Don't know	3	1	15	3	3
Total	100	100	100	100	100

Trust in Churches by Income

An overwhelming majority of respondents indicated trust in churches (82%), which was the largest percentage of trust in any institution. The lower the income of a group, the more likely it was to trust churches. However, even high-income earners had more trust in churches than in other institutions.

Comparing Trust in the Different Institutions of Civil Society

Asked about trust or distrust in organs of civil society, 82% of respondents indicated trust in churches, followed by 66% who indicated trust in the media, 55% in business, 39% in political parties, and 38% in labour unions (Table 10.34).

Table 10.34: How much trust/distrust do you have in organs of civil society? (November 1999)

Level	Labour unions	Business	Media	Churches	Political parties
			Percentage		
Strong trust	9	12	23	40	11
Trust	29	43	43	42	28
Neither trust nor distrust	20	22	15	9	20
Distrust	17	12	12	4	23
Strong distrust	11	5	4	2	11
Don't know	15	6	4	3	6
Total	100	100	100	100	100

A Critical Appraisal

The first five years of democratic rule in South Africa (1994-1999) witnessed an extra-ordinary effort to create institutions to consolidate and protect democracy. At the same time the pace of service delivery was accelerated to give effect to new policies (Khosa, 2000). Evidence in this chapter indicate that there is support for the emerging culture of democratic governance and for the national institutions created after the 1994 election. However, this support is not without qualification, as many South Africans are aware of their rights and the non-compliance with these rights.

The coming to power of the Government of National Unity in 1994 led to significant changes in the perceptions of national institutions. Trust among whites decreased dramatically, while trust among blacks increased sharply. However, South Africans are reluctant to unconditionally put their trust in political parties and labour unions. In addition, white trust in public sector institutions has declined. This could be a result of "lost privileges" associated with the apartheid state. Nevertheless, there is overwhelming support for the IEC, undoubtedly one of the most important institutions during the election period.

Analysis of the November 1999 survey by income brings important insights. First, low-income earners are more likely than high-income earners to trust political parties. Second, trust in government institutions declines with higher income. The only institutions that elicit great trust from all income groups are churches, business and the media.

Perhaps one of the most significant findings is that trust among whites is high on only two variables: business and churches. Among blacks, trust in national, provincial and local government is high, as is their trust in the courts, police, defence force, IEC, labour unions, business, political parties, the media and churches. There is no variable where distrust is higher than trust among blacks. Among coloureds, trust is high in national, provincial and local government, the courts, the media, the IEC, the defence force and the police. The only variable in respect of which distrust is high, is political parties. Among Asians, distrust levels are high in respect of the courts, provincial government, local government and political parties. These findings point to different racial perceptions of the various institutions that support democracy.

Evidence in this chapter suggests that there has been a transformation in trust in key institutions that have supported governance and democracy in South Africa since 1994. The past five years have witnessed the creation of a new political order, which is more credible than before. Whereas trust in and satisfaction with government institutions were relatively low among the poor and historically disenfranchised, the past five years have seen trust and satisfaction levels increasing among them. Conversely, those who benefited from the past political and economic order indicated lower trust in and satisfaction with these institutions. The only common ground was trust in churches, the media, business and the IEC.

By analysing a series of government and civil society institutions, this chapter has demonstrated the maturation of democracy in South Africa. The successful second democratic election in June 1999 attested to this maturation. In addition, it fortified the foundation of democratic order and empowering governance in South Africa.

The HSRC surveys suggest that democracy is being consolidated and that the culture of governance is growing. However, large sections of the population in many a democracy suffer poverty and discrimination, which necessarily compromise capabilities and, therefore, effective participation. This is also the case in South Africa.

Patricio Aylwin (1998), Chile's first democratically elected president (1990-1994) after 16 years of military rule, underlined this issue by asking a pertinent question: What use is freedom of the citizen if it does not include the ability to influence important economic decisions? He posed this question against the background of the fact that small but powerful multi-national financial groups make important economic decisions without considering the disempowerment, dislocation and increased poverty that these decisions will bring for marginalised people. Such circumstances greatly diminish the prospects of democracy in poor countries in the South, as they substantively limit participation and the power to influence the polity.

Aylwin (1998) also provided a useful point of departure for considering this issue. He argued that democracy suffers from serious weaknesses, especially in Latin America. First, due to imperfect formal juridical institutions, the administration of justice is inadequate. Second, due to the absence of democratic traditions and public dialogue, consensus on fundamental issues is low. Third, monopolistic and oligopolistic groups control the news media and hence the dissemination of information. Fourth, civic apathy, low voter turnout, the discrediting of political parties, indifference towards and even rejection of the state, and the deterioration of institutions of civil society are characteristic of developing but poor democracies in Latin America. What are required instead is a powerful and diverse civil society and broad organisation of and participation by the whole society in public affairs. These are to be supplemented by adequate opportunities to access formal institutions.

References

Anderson, P. (1994), *A Zone of Engagement*, London, Verso.

Aylwin, P. (1998), "Democracy in the Americas", *Journal of Democracy*, vol. 9, no. 3, pp. 3-6.

Bardhan, P. (1997), *The Role of Governance in Economic Development: A Political Economy Approach*, OECD, Paris.

De Alcantara, C.H. (1998), "Uses and Abuses of the Concept of Governance", *International Social Science Journal,* vol. 155, pp. 106-114.

Habermas, J. (1993), *The Structural Transformation of the Public Sphere*, Cambridge, MIT Press.

Khosa, M. (ed.) (2000), *Empowerment through Service Delivery*, Pretoria, Human Sciences Research Council.

Offe, C. (1985), *Disorganized Capitalism*, Cambridge, MIT Press.

Philip, G. (1999), "The Dilemmas of Good Governance: A Latin American Perspective", *Government and Opposition*, vol. 32, no. 2, 227-242.

Presidential Review Commission (1998), *Report of the Presidential Review Commission prepared for the State President of the Republic of South Africa,* Government Printer, Pretoria.

Sen, A. (1992), *Inequality Reexamined*, Cambridge, Harvard University Press.

Stoker, G. (1998), "Governance as Theory: Five Propositions", *International Social Science Journal*, vol. 155, pp. 17-27.

Vacs, A.C. (1998), "Between Restructuring and Impasse: Liberal Democracy, Exclusionary Policy Making, and Neo-liberal Programmes in Argentina and Uruguay", in Von Mettenheim, K. & Malloy, J. (eds), *Deepening Democracy in Latin America,* University of Pittsburgh Press, Pittsburgh, pp. 137-172.

Varshney, A. (1998), "Why Democracy Survives", *Journal of Democracy,* vol. 9, no. 3, pp. 36-50.

Villas, C.M. (1997), "Participation, Inequality, and the Whereabouts of Democracy", in Charmers, D.A., Hite, K., Martin, S.B., Piester, K. & Segaria, M. (eds), *The Politics of Inequality in Latin America,* Oxford University Press, pp. 1-47.

Von Mettenheim, K. & Malloy, J. (eds) (1998), *Deepening Democracy in Latin America*, University of Pittsburgh Press, Pittsburgh.

Watts, M. (1995), "A New Deal for the Emotions", in Crush, J. (ed.), *The Power of Development*, London, Routledge, pp. 76-94.

Chapter 11

Public Participation in South Africa as we Enter the 21st Century[1]

Marlene Roefs and Ian Liebenberg

Introduction

The "average citizen" (in Milbrath's (1965) words) did what was "expected from him or her" in South Africa's second democratic election on 2 June 1999. More than three-quarters of the voting public cast their votes. The high voter turn-out reflected the hope among South Africans that they and their children would benefit from the democratic system. The deepening of democracy, however, is dependent on the participation of citizens in civil society and the political system (Diamond, 1993). Moreover, such participation must be inclusive of all in society (Lijphart, 1996). Worldwide, theorists and political practitioners who profess democracy take political participation seriously irrespective of their particular political background. Although there is disagreement as to what the optimum level of participation should be to guarantee a functional democracy, the key dictum remains: Participation by citizens at various levels is essential to make democratic societies work.[2] Indeed, participation is a prerequisite to make any society work—be it populist or technocratic. Once participation drops below a certain level, strains emerge within the society and can eventually lead to its disintegration.

In this chapter participation is regarded as wide-ranging civil activity at national, regional and local levels.

Rationale

South Africa, like many other countries in the southern hemisphere, made its transition from authoritarian rule to democracy with a founding election. In the five years following the 1994 founding election, many changes occurred, notably in terms of the formalisation of structures of civilian representation, oversight and participation.

Whatever form of democracy is chosen (representative or proportional systems, or multi-party, non-party or one-party systems), participation by the citizenry strengthens democracy. In the case of South Africa, a choice was made for multi-party politics during the multi-party negotiations, which culminated in the formal acceptance of the Constitution (Act No. 108 of 1996) as well as the Bill of Rights. The formal structures created at national, provincial and local government levels function well in the majority of cases. Examples abound: the National Economic Development and Labour Council (NEDLAC), the National Council of Provinces, parliamentary constituency offices, forums for community-police interaction and the defence review process. Indeed, the central objective behind these institutions was to enhance public participation.

The democratisation process in South Africa, as well as in other young African democracies coincided with the institutionalisation of civil society organisations. Moreover, strong civil leaders joined the formal politics and became policy makers. Others seized the opportunity to move into the more lucrative business sector. Amongst others, these processes contributed to what critics from the South African NGO sector call the "demobilisation" of civil society organisations. Some argue that this will negatively impact on public participation among South African citizens. Various observers have pointed out that public participation in African democracies—including South Africa—is sub-optimum.[3] The rationale for this study is therefore to assist and encourage policy-making bodies, executives, political practitioners, civil society and other relevant stakeholders in adding value to public participation in democratic institutions at all levels of government. The ultimate aim is to optimise the benefits of public participation for the citizenry, democracy, social justice and economic growth in South Africa following the 1999 election.

In order to achieve this aim, existing policy-making structures in South Africa and public participation in them were analysed on the basis of data collected by means of a quantitative survey in March 1999. The focus is on levels of knowledge on policy making among the citizenry and their reported participation at national, provincial and local levels. Their main concerns around policy making were also gauged. For the benefit of the reader, the data given below are supported by brief analyses and policy recommendations.

Methodology

Survey questionnaires were administered to random clustered national probability samples of 2 200 respondents throughout the Republic of South Africa in March 1999. The results based on the national samples had a maximum margin of error of ±4,7 percentage points.

The sample design was based on the census data of 1991. The former Transkei, Bophuthatswana, Venda and Ciskei (TBVC states) were excluded from the 1991 census and statistics from these areas had to be added to the totals of the provinces of which they now form part in order to determine the proportional representation of the nine provinces in the sample. The universe of the sample design was all members of the South African population of 18 years and older, stratified according to nine socio-economic area types and provinces.

The allocation of respondents to socio-economic categories was roughly proportional to the adjusted 1991 population census figures with a few exceptions. Multi-stage cluster (probability) sampling was used to draw the respondents, using the adjusted 1991 census figures as a sampling frame. Census enumerator areas and similar areas were used as the clusters in the penultimate sampling stage, from which an equal number, one or two by four, of households was drawn. All clusters were drawn from the final clusters with equal probability (systematically). Respondents were drawn at random from qualifying household members. The provincial distribution of the realised sample is given in Table 11.1.

The realised sample was weighted according to the 1996 census data on the biographical features of the South African population of 18 years and older, and is thus a broad reflection of the perceptions of the adult population of South Africa.

It should be noted that the data were analysed by means of SPSS, and the data analysis was restricted to the generation of frequency tables, cross tabulations of variables, correlation analysis and multivariate analysis of variance.

Table 11.1: Sample allocation, March 1999

Province	Realisation	African %	Coloured %	Asian %	White %
Western Cape	256	16	54	–	30
Northern Cape	102	31	49	–	20
Eastern Cape	297	87	7	1	5
Free State	208	83	1	–	16
KwaZulu-Natal	344	79	1	12	8
Mpumalanga	198	87	–	1	13
Northern Province	244	93	–	–	7
Gauteng	344	65	4	2	28
North West	217	89	–	–	11
Total	2 210	72,0	10,3	2,4	15,3

* As percentages were rounded off and some respondents did not give a definite answer to all questions, the totals reflected in some cases do not add up to 100%.

Results

The research was aimed at establishing the knowledge of respondents on local councils, parliament and policy formulation including departmental green papers, white papers, bills and the passing of acts by parliament.

Knowledge

Knowledge of Institutions and Policy-making Processes

The findings are both interesting and disconcerting. Generally respondents felt that they did not have enough knowledge or were uncertain about the stages of policy formulation.[4]

In answer to the question, *"Would you say you have enough know-ledge about the green paper/white paper/bill/act"*, more than one-third said they did not have enough knowledge. Most respondents were uncertain as to whether they had enough knowledge about the stages of policy making. For the purposes of this chapter, the uncertain group was merged with those respondents who indicated that they did not know enough.

Table 11.2: Knowledge of stages of policy making

Knowledge	Green paper	White paper	Bill	Act
		Percentage		
Uncertain/not enough	90	89	83	79
Enough	9	10	16	21
Total	99	99	99	100

* As percentages were rounded off and some respondents did not give a definite answer to all questions, the totals reflected in some cases do not add up to 100%.

When broken down, respondents who "did not know enough/were uncertain" about all four stages or did not answer the question (about 1%) amounted to 72%. Those who "knew enough" about one or two of the stages totalled 20%. Only 8% of respondents indicated that they knew enough about three or four of the stages. With less than one out of ten respondents saying he or she felt confident about his or her knowledge concerning crucial aspects of policy formation, it seems that the ability to participate in contemporary democratic South Africa is seriously undermined by lack of knowledge.

This is further confirmed by the answers to questions about understanding of the activities within political institutions, which is another crucial aspect of knowledge about policy-making processes. A large majority of respondents indicated that they did not understand what was happening in their local council and did not consider themselves to be well informed about decisions made in parliament.[5]

Regarding local councils, respondents were asked, *"What would you say about your understanding of what goes on in your local council?"* As the percentages in Table 11.3 show, less than one-fifth (18%) of the respondents indicated that they understood what was happening in their local council.

Table 11.3: Understanding of local council activities

Little (do not understand, understand a bit)	75%
More (understand, understand completely)	18%

* As percentages were rounded off and some respondents did not give a definite answer to all questions, the totals reflected in some cases do not add up to 100%.

The questionnaire item on parliament read: *"I am well-informed about the political decisions in parliament that affect my community."* Respondents had to indicate their level of agreement with the statement.

Table 11.4: Being informed about political decisions in parliament that affect communities

Do not agree (disagree completely/disagree)	66%
Do agree (agree, totally agree)	25%

* As percentages were rounded off and some respondents did not give a definite answer to all questions, the totals reflected in some cases do not add up to 100%.

The above indicators of understanding and knowledge about policy-making processes and institutions are related but not coinciding. People who thought that they knew enough about the stages of policy making might have had little understanding of what happened in their local council and felt ill informed about decisions taken in parliament. In the same vein, people who felt well informed about political decisions in parliament and/or understood what was going on in their local council, might have felt that they did not have enough knowledge about the stages of policy making.

This point is supported by the fact that 70% of respondents who indicated that they knew enough about one or two, and 60% of those who indicated that they knew enough about three or four of the stages in policy formulation, indicated little or no understanding of what happened in their local council. Moreover, respectively 72% and 56% of respondents who knew enough about one or two or about three or four stages felt that they were ill informed about decisions taken in parliament.

These findings imply that knowledge among respondents (and presumably among the citizenry as a whole) about policy making at national level did not necessarily equal their understanding of their local council. The inverse was also true. Knowledge about the functioning of a local council did not necessarily imply knowledge about parliament or policy-making processes such as green papers, white papers, bills and/or acts.

Understanding of what goes on in local councils and being informed about parliamentary decisions seemed to coincide more strongly.

> More than two-thirds of the respondents did not understand the functioning of their own local council and, at the same time, felt ill informed about decisions taken in parliament.

In order to improve understanding of political institutions and their functioning, the citizenry should be better educated, clearly on more aspects than the four stages of policy formulation. Transparency of political bodies, active citizen interest in the affairs of public institutions and insistence on being informed are other factors that play an important role in people's understanding of policy making.

Responses relating to the functioning of local councils and parliament were broken down to reflect rural/urban and provincial data.

There was little difference between rural and urban respondents in terms of the association between understanding the processes and being informed. Provinces differed somewhat more in terms of understanding and being informed about local councils, parliament and policy-making processes. The provincial differences in lack of understanding about these aspects are clear from the first two columns of Table 11.5.

A comparison of provincial levels of understanding showed that respondents from Gauteng, the Free State and the Eastern Cape had the lowest levels of *lack* of understanding of local councils and parliament. These results suggest that in these provinces people have a better under-standing of political decision making than people in the other six provinces. Respondents in the Northern Province, Northern Cape, Western Cape and North West, on the other hand, had the highest level of lack of understanding. The Northern Province and Western Cape samples also reported little knowledge of the stages in policy making, whereas respondents in the Eastern Cape, Gauteng and KwaZulu-Natal showed relatively high levels of knowledge.

The figures in Table 11.5 show a number of trends that may need to be examined to arrive at a better understanding of public participation. (It was not the aim of this survey to examine such trends in detail, though.)

Table 11.5: Lack of understanding of local councils, parliament and policy-making processes in provinces

Province	Lack of understanding of local council	Lack of understanding of parliament	Lack of knowledge of policy-making processes*
		Percentage	
Northern Province	91	86	89
Northern Cape	91	77	76
Western Cape	89	81	82
North West	88	86	73
Mpumalanga	82	81	77
KwaZulu-Natal	79	83	67
Eastern Cape	78	47	63
Free State	75	68	79
Gauteng	73	63	67
Average total	80	73	72

* This column represents the respondents who did not know enough or were uncertain about their knowledge of green and white papers, bills and acts.

- KwaZulu-Natal was the only province where respondents were better informed about their own local councils than about parliament. The province also showed a higher than average knowledge of policy-making processes at national level.

- Five provinces showed a higher than average lack of understanding of local councils and six provinces did so in respect of parliament. Lack of understanding of local councils and of parliament differed between one and 14%, except in the case of the Eastern Cape where the difference totalled 31%.

- Only Gauteng and the Eastern Cape recorded lower than average percentages of lack of understanding as well as knowledge of policy-making processes.

Knowledge and Level of Education

It is generally believed that knowledge about policies strongly correlates with the level of people's formal education. This would imply that people with little education would have little understanding and knowledge of political institutions and policy-making processes compared to people with a high level of education.

The findings of this study refuted such a deterministic relation: Although the relation between level of education and knowledge about policy formulation was strong, understanding of local councils and parliament correlated weakly with formal education.

As Table 11.6 illustrates, lack of understanding was lowest for local councils, followed by parliament and policy making. A better understanding of local councils, parliament and policy making was more likely among respondents who had Standard 10 or higher. Lack of knowledge about these aspects was highest among respondents with Standard 6 or lower.

The results suggest that education about the state structure and ways to influence political decisions should be incorporated in the early phases of formal education.

Further analyses revealed that knowledge about the various stages of policy making differed more significantly between provinces than between levels of education. Thus independently from educational differences in knowledge significant differences exist between provinces. This suggests that information campaigns on local councils, parliament and policy making should particularly concentrate on the provinces with the greatest lack of understanding of these aspects.

Table 11.6: Levels of understanding based on education

Education level	Lack of under-standing of local council	Lack of under-standing of parliament	Lack of knowledge of policy making
		Percentage	
Standard 6 and lower (**49%**)	87	74	83
Standard 7 + 8 (**21%**)	82	72	68
Standard 9 (**21%**)	73	73	62
Standard 10 and higher (**9%**)	60	64	48

* As percentages were rounded off and some respondents did not give a definite answer to all questions, the totals reflected in some cases do not add up to 100%.

> Educational levels explain variations in understanding of local councils and parliament to a much smaller extent than they explain understanding of policy making.

Participation

Participation in policy-making processes was studied in two ways. Respondents were asked about their intention to join public hearings at various levels of government and their actual participation in policy-making processes and community activities. The intention to join public hearings would indicate people's willingness to participate in policy making, whereas reported participation would provide insight into political activities within civil society.

As will be discussed in the next sections, the willingness to participate in public hearings was generally high, and incidences of (reported) actual participation were not disconcertingly low. However, intended participation and reported participation varied significantly between provinces. Respondents with a better understanding and knowledge of policy-making institutions and processes were more likely to participate. Furthermore, respondents who had relatively more trust in the government reported higher levels of participation, whereas disparities in living standards were not related to the intention to participate and were only weakly related to reported participation.

Participation at Local, Provincial and National Level

Willingness to participate in policy making does not always translate into actual participation. This discrepancy partially results from obstacles to participation. Although it was beyond the scope of this survey to investigate the various obstacles that may stand between people's intention to join and their reported actual participation, some reasons for this kind of behaviour will be alluded to.

Respondents were provided with various options for participation in policy making. They were asked whether they *"would participate or ask advice"* in public hearings at government departments *"if they had the opportunity to do so"*. The choices consisted of public hearings at several levels and were aimed at establishing their intention to join in policy-making processes. As with understanding of and knowledge about policy making, substantial proportions of the respondents were uncertain what to answer (varying from 13% to 22%). The majority of the respondents were prepared to join in local and provincial public hearings, however. Participation at national level was less likely among most of the respondents.

In terms of reported participation, provincial differences were substantial. Rural/urban differences were less salient, but nevertheless significant, with slightly higher rates of participation in urban areas.

Respondents in the Eastern Cape and Mpumalanga showed greater willingness to participate at the various levels. Northern Cape and Western Cape residents seemed to be the least interested in participating. Participation in KwaZulu-Natal was relatively low as well, but this only pertained to provincial and national levels. The intention to join at local level was relatively high among the respondents in KwaZulu-Natal (Table 11.7).

The intention to participate at local and provincial level was higher among black[6] respondents than among coloured and Asian respondents. White respondents showed the least willingness to participate. The differences between black, coloured and Asian respondents were insignificant regarding participation in national bodies. White respondents, however,

Table 11.7: Intention to participate in policy making in each province through public hearings*

Province	Local council	Provincial legislature	National parliament	Government department
			Percentage	
Eastern Cape	74	50	58	55
Mpumalanga	74	58	36	36
Gauteng	70	49	38	30
KwaZulu-Natal	76	32	22	23
Free State	65	45	31	28
Northern Province	62	49	32	30
North West	58	43	32	40
Western Cape	53	38	35	34
Northern Cape	48	29	19	24
Total	67	44	35	35

* The percentages reflect the proportions of respondents who said they would participate.

also showed the lowest interest in participation at this level (see Appendix A of this chapter).

It should be noted that racial differences were smaller than the disparities between the provinces. Differences in the intention to participate between racial groups within provinces were more significant than between the racial groups at national level.

In the question, *"How often would you say you (personally) participate?"*, respondents were asked about various aspects of civil participation. Four aspects of participation were distinguished:

- opinions in local councils;
- statements at public hearings;
- participation in organisations active in neighbourhood affairs; and
- enquiries at parliamentary constituency offices.

In terms of reported activity or participation in the nine provinces, the following was found: Reported participation was relatively high among respondents from the Eastern Cape and Northern Province. The Free State, Northern Cape and Western Cape samples shared relatively low levels of participation (Table 11.8).

Table 11.8: Reported participation per province*

Province	Local council	Public hearing	Activity – organisa- tion	Enquiries at parliamentary constituency offices
			Percentage	
Eastern Cape	31	32	67	21
Northern Province	26	28	42	12
KwaZulu-Natal	22	19	36	9
Gauteng	20	23	43	8
Mpumalanga	18	15	28	3
North West	13	15	28	5
Northern Cape	7	8	39	2
Free State	9	9	28	2
Western Cape	9	6	20	8
Average	19	19	38	9

* The percentages reflect the proportions of people who said they participated often or continuously.

Participation, Standard of Living and Trust in Government

Participation in policy-making processes can be assumed to be generally more likely among South Africans who trust the government than among citizens who do not feel they can trust the government. This assumption was confirmed by this study. As is shown in the following two tables, the higher the level of trust,[7] the more frequently respondents expressed the intention to join and the more often they reported to have participated in various activities.

Political participation seemed to be far from an élitist endeavour. A rough categorisation into lower, middle and higher standards of living reveals that those worse off tended to participate more often than those who had a higher standard of living, as shown in Table 11.9.[8] The intention to participate did not differ between the groups, which suggests that class was not such an important factor in participation.

Table 11.9: Participation and levels of trust in government*

Trust in government	Intention to participate in			
	Local council	Public hearing	Provincial legislature	Government department
	Percentage			
Low (never/seldom)	61	35	27	28
Middle (sometimes)	69	48	38	27
High (mostly/always)	76	53	43	43

* The percentages reflect the proportions of respondents who intended to participate.

Table 11.10: Reported participation and levels of trust in government*

Trust	Local council	Public hearing	Activity—organisation
		Percentage	
Low	15%	15%	26%
Middle	23%	24%	43%
High	23%	22%	52%

* The percentages reflect the proportions of respondents who said they participated often or continuously.

Table 11.11: Reported participation based on living standard measure (LSM)*

LSM	Local council	Public hearing	Activity—organisation	Enquiries at constituency offices
			Percentage	
Low	23	22	46	8
Middle	19	23	44	10
High	18	15	30	10

* The percentages reflect the proportions of respondents who said they participated often or continuously.

Participation and Knowledge

Knowledge about the four stages of policy formulation was related to willingness to attend public hearings at the provincial and national level, and to the intention to participate in the policy formulation processes of a government department: The greater the knowledge, the more willing respondents were to participate. Attending public hearings of local councils was more likely among respondents who had a better understanding of the functioning of local councils. Respondents who felt well informed about the political decisions made in parliament were more willing to participate in all four types of policy-making processes.

Respondents who reported higher levels of participation in their local council and in public hearings displayed a better understanding of local councils and felt better informed about parliamentary decisions. Participation in activities of community organisations seemed to have a positive effect on understanding, feeling informed and knowledge of policy making.

It should be noted that the correlation between participation and knowledge is to be understood in two ways: Knowledge helps and motivates people to participate, and participation adds to people's knowledge of policy-making processes and institutions.

Political Preferences

Respondents who confessed allegiance to the ANC were somewhat more likely to be involved in public processes. At the same time, however, participation among respondents belonging to other political parties varied by province and political party.[9] Further analysis revealed that belonging to a specific party did make a difference, but could not explain why provinces and rural/urban areas differed from each other.

Issues

At a national level, the three most often reported issues that respondents would raise at a public hearing were services, the economy, and safety and security.

In answer to an open question, *"What are the most important issues in your community that you would raise at a public hearing?"*, more than one-quarter of the respondents indicated that services had the greatest priority, followed by economic issues and then by safety and security, with about one-fifth of the respondents saying that they would raise these issues (see Table 11.12).

Table 11.12:   Issues raise at public hearing

Services	28%
Economy	20%
Safety	18%
Education	6%
Health care	3%
Politics	3%

*   As percentages were rounded off and some respondents did not give a definite answer to all questions, the totals reflected in some cases do not add up to 100%.

The priority order above differed from what South Africans generally saw as the most pertinent issues in the country according to the SABC/Idasa/Markinor Opinion '99 surveys, as well as HSRC surveys conducted between October 1998 and March 1999. These surveys suggested that South Africans saw job creation, safety and housing as the three most pertinent issues in the country. Services in terms of water, electricity, roads and so on were less often mentioned when respondents were asked what (national) government should do (Opinion '99, SABC/Idasa/Markinor). This was in line with the issues that South Africans seemed to be the most willing to protest against (HSRC social movement study, March 1999).

The fact that respondents in this survey most frequently mentioned services when asked about issues to be raised at public hearings indicates a concern over the responsibility of local and provincial government to provide, sustain and enhance basic services in the community.

Prioritisation of issues that respondents would put forward at public hearings varied from province to province. The three most reported issues at a provincial level are listed in Table 11.13.

Table 11.13: Issues at provincial level per province

Province	Services	Economy	Safety
		Percentage	
Northern Province	53	24	4
North West	46	21	8
Eastern Cape	37	21	14
Mpumalanga	32	24	11
Free State	28	21	8
Gauteng	27	17	27
Northern Cape	21	22	13
KwaZulu-Natal	16	21	21
Western Cape	6	22	33

* As percentages were rounded off and some respondents did not give a definite answer to all questions, the totals reflected in some cases do not add up to 100%.

In KwaZulu-Natal and the Western Cape, safety and security and economic issues were more often mentioned than community problems related to absent or inappropriate services. Gauteng, another province characterised by extensive levels of crime, also scored high on safety and security issues (GIS Centre, HSRC, forthcoming crime report).

Although some differences in percentages were evident, the three most topical issues in all the provinces remained services (service provision and delivery) at local level, the economy, and issues related to safety and security.

Information

As knowledge and participation seemed to be linked, the survey attempted to establish how respondents and thus presumably the citizenry in South Africa obtained most of their information.

Respondents were asked, *"Where do you get most of your informa-tion on political decisions that affect your community?"* More than half of the respondents (58%) mentioned the media (radio 20%; television 18%; newspapers 85%; other media 16%) as their primary source of information about political affairs affecting them. One-quarter (25%) said that the community was their main source. A further 7% mentioned political parties and 4% local government.

The community played a more important information role in the Northern Province, the Free State and Mpumalanga than elsewhere. Respondents in the Eastern Cape and KwaZulu-Natal, on the other hand, were more likely to mention the media as their most important source of information (see Table 11.14).

For those who believe that South Africa is well on its way to have an informed citizenry as a result of Internet access and the "information revolution", the results of the survey are disconcerting to some extent.

The percentage of respondents relying on or receiving information through the Internet was insignificant: less than 0,5%. Posters and billboards were only mentioned by 1% of the respondents.

Table 11.14:   Two main sources of information in provinces

Province	Media	Community
	Percentage	
Eastern Cape	77	12
KwaZulu-Natal	62	21
Western Cape	59	28
Gauteng	57	24
North West	51	25
Northern Province	49	39
Free State	47	36
Mpumalanga	47	34
Northern Cape	34	29

*   As percentages were rounded off and some respondents did not give a definite answer to all questions, the totals reflected in some cases do not add up to 100%.

The survey also attempted to establish *"the most important organisa-tion/institution in the view of respondents"* to address problems in the community. From the results it transpires that the community played a very important role in assisting people with problems in their immediate surroundings (30%). Local government came second with 24% (see Table 11.15).

Table 11.15: Appropriate organisation to address problems (%)

Community	30
Local government	24
Political organisation	12
National government	11
Provincial government	4
Business/labour	2

* As percentages were rounded off and some respondents did not give a definite answer to all questions, the totals reflected in some cases do not add up to 100%.

Interestingly, respondents did not differentiate much between certain community organisations. By far the majority just said that the "community block" (living area) or the community in general was the most appropriate body to address their problems. Respondents were not questioned about the role of community leaders and street leaders, in particular, but they seemed to be implied in the reported "community" category. Almost one-third of those who mentioned the community referred to "leaders".

Further analyses revealed an interesting relation between the issues respondents would raise and the most appropriate organisations to address these issues in the community. Generally, the street leaders seemed to perform an important role. Regarding safety and security, however, friends were mentioned relatively frequently. Civics were most often mentioned by respondents who would raise problems like access to water, electricity, roads and other services.

Focus on Gender

In the course of the struggle for liberation in South Africa, the exiled ANC stressed the attainment of a non-racial and non-sexist South Africa (Moosa · in Corder, 1989, pp. 90, 92; Adam & Moodley, 1986, pp. 95-96, 99, 102, 213ff). However, even before going into exile the ANC together with other organisations resolved at the "Congress of the People" (resulting in the *Freedom Charter*) that their aim was to establish a state with political rights for all "regardless of race, colour or sex". Moreover, equality for all national groups, a fairer distribution of wealth, social security, the right to education and co-operation with others within the international community were stressed (Pampallis, 1991, p. 200). The simple point of departure at the time was that harmony was to be achieved through "equal rights and opportunities" and that "only a democratic state based on the will of the people, can secure to all their birthright without distinction of colour, sex or belief" (Farouk Meer in Polley, 1988, pp. 30, 31). During the 1980s mass resistance against apartheid (and its modernisation in the form of the tricameral parliament) escalated. The internal democratic protagonists such as the United Democratic Front (UDF) were outspoken about their non-racial and non-sexist approach in activist and militant politics (see Gottschalk in Liebenberg et al., 1994, pp. 192ff).[10]

The ANC's guidelines for a democratic South Africa issued in 1989 (the Harare Declaration) stressed equality on gender and racial basis and re-affirmed the ANC's commitment to non-racialism (Liebenberg, 1990). While women were central to the struggle for liberation, liberation organisations did not always live up to the ideal of non-sexism (Gouws & Kadalie, 1994, pp. 20ff). Rantete (1998, p. 45) is perhaps more explicit: "In the end, while the [ANC's women's] league made significant strides advancing the rights of women [within the ANC] this continued to be counterbalanced by serious weaknesses." Hence, for theorists like Gouws, Kadalie and Rantete, major challenges had to be met after 1994, and presumably also after the adoption of South Africa's first democratic constitution. In this regard the reader is referred to the Constitution as well as to the Bill of Rights.

Women's issues (violence against women and rape in particular) enjoy a higher profile than ever before on the political agenda of the incumbent government. In order to assess gender-related differences in knowledge about policy-making processes and participation in political decision making, separate analyses were performed for testing the influence of gender on the indicators of public participation discussed in the preceding sections.

The results are based on univariate and multivariate analyses of variance that tested for provincial, educational and gender main effects as well as interaction effects between the independent variables. The provincial and educational analysis discussed in the preceding sections did not take cognisance of gender. Therefore this section focuses on the main and interaction effects of gender only.

Knowledge, Understanding and Being Informed

Generally, satisfaction with level of knowledge, understanding and in-formedness seemed to be more likely among men than among women. Male respondents reported somewhat more, just significant, satisfaction with knowledge about the stages of policy-making processes, under-standing of the local town council and informedness about decisions made in parliament.

Hassim and Gouws (1998, p. 69) argue that:

the development of institutions inside and outside government for the purpose of making and influencing social policy from a gendered perspective has shifted the terrain of politics more closely into and around the state, rather than around society.

Thus the extent to which women and men differ in their knowledge/ participation will be described in order to assess women's readiness to get involved in political decision-making processes at an individual level.

However, men and women in the lowest and highest educational groups reported the same level of knowledge of white and green papers, acts and bills. No correlation was found between educational level and understanding of the local town council and feelings of being informed about parliamentary decisions.

Table 11.16 (a) (b) and (c): Knowledge/Understanding

"Do you feel that you have enough knowledge about a white paper, green paper, act, and bill?"

(a) Knowledge of policy making	Male respondents	Female respondents
	Percentage	
None	68	76
One/two	22	18
Three/four	10	6

"What would you say about your understanding of what goes on in your local council?"

(b) Understanding of local council	Male respondents	Female respondents
	Percentage	
Little (no/a bit understanding)	77	84
More (understand/ understand completely)	24	16

Agreement with *"I am well-informed about the political decisions in parliament that affect my community"*.

(c) Informed about parliament	Male respondents	Female respondents
	Percentage	
Do not agree (disagree completely/disagree)	69	75
Do agree (agree/totally agree)	31	25

* As percentages were rounded off and some respondents did not give a definite answer to all questions, the totals reflected in some cases do not add up to 100%.

Furthermore, it should be noted that differences between male and female respondents were not influenced by province. Gender differences were found in all nine provinces.

Participation

Interestingly, gender-related disparities regarding participation seemed to be extremely marginal. Regarding willingness to join in decision making at the various levels of policy making, men seemed to be more likely than women to attend hearings in parliament. The intention to attend local and provincial public hearings, as well as the intention to join in governmental department policy processes were the same for men and women as shown in Table 11.17. These findings were not moderated by province or by level of education.

Table 11.17:   Intention to participate

Participation intention	Male respondents	Female respondents
	Percentage	
Join public hearing in local council		
No	32	33
Yes	68	67
Join public hearing in provincial government		
No	55	57
Yes	45	43
Join public hearing in national parliament		
No	62	67
Yes	38	33
Join governmental department policy processes if invited to do so		
No	64	66
Yes	36	34

*   As percentages were rounded off and some respondents did not give a definite answer to all questions, the totals reflected in some cases do not add up to 100%.

Contrary to what the above results on knowledge suggest, women were as likely as men to join in policy making at the local, provincial and national levels of government—reported participation did not seem to be gender related. Moreover, in all provinces and at all levels of education, gender differences were insignificant in respect of reported participation (see Table 11.18).

According to Hassim and Gouws (1998, p. 68):

> the challenge for women's movements now appears to be centred more directly on the ways in which institutional gains can be used to address different women's needs".

Little is known, however, about how female citizens act or intend to act upon grievances typically associated with gender inequality, such as poverty and violence, which are often associated with the motherhood role of the majority of women. Hence the extent to which political participation of women is linked to gender and to motherhood will now be analysed.

Women seemed to be more likely than men to raise services and health-related issues at public hearings, respectively 30% (versus 26%) and 4% (versus 2%).

Table 11.18:   Reported participation

Actual participation	Male respondents	Female respondents
	Percentage	
Speak to councillor	21%	19%
Make a statement in public hearing	22%	18%
Active in community activities	42%	37%
Make enquiries at constituency office	10%	9%

*   As percentages were rounded off and some respondents did not give a definite answer to all questions, the totals reflected in some cases do not add up to 100%.

The data do not suggest that certain issues enjoyed more priority among women with children (the motherhood hypothesis) than among women without children. The only statistically significant difference that was found, pointed to the opposite: Women with children were less likely than childless women to mention health-related issues (3% versus 5%). This can be partly explained by the fact that older women—for whom the motherhood role perhaps decreased in relevance or for whom health might have become a personal issue—more frequently mentioned this issue.

In short, while understanding, knowledge and the intention to join in policy-making processes at national level seemed to be higher among men than women, actual or reported participation was not related to gender. The survey results suggest that gender-related differences marginally contributed to disparities in public participation.

The implications of these findings for the policy maker and agents active in civil society are that provincial/regional differences are more salient and perhaps therefore in need of more attention. More specifically, provincial differences stemming from socio-historical dynamics and fiscal disparity seem to have more impact on public participation than gender-related differences.

This is not meant to demean the gender initiatives taken by policy makers and/or civil society, which should be continued. However, the research in this study points towards other areas that are of equal—if not greater—relevance in terms of public participation. (See also Roefs & Liebenberg, 1999; Rule, 1999.) These areas will be discussed in more detail below.

Discussion

The following recommendations fall within the broad ambit of policy. The recommendations are based on the assumption that, in addition to regular elections, democracy entails continuous public participation. In other words, although regular elections are the minimum requirement for a democracy, they do not suffice to sustain democracy (KID press release, 8 June 1999).

> *"We need first to embrace participatory democracy, transparency and accountability—then one can implement a good programme of public participation ..."* (KID Conference on Public Participation and Governance in South Africa, 22-23 October 1998, Cape Town).

> *"When we struggled for freedom in South Africa, we also struggled for access to information. While services are essential, so is information. Let us not alienate people from information that can empower"* (KID Conference on Public

Participation and Governance in South Africa, 22-23 October 1998, Cape Town).

Factors emerging from the survey results which require the attention of policy makers and other role players are discussed below.

Access to Proposed Legislation

The public should be provided with executive summaries of each bill and policy paper in an easily accessible and crisp format to enable them to grasp the contents and practical implications of the proposed legislation. The findings of this survey suggest that such information should be communicated primarily through the radio (local, provincial and national), followed by television (preferably national television), and newspapers. The findings of the study suggest that these media are far more effective than posters and websites.

Posters and websites/the Internet seem to be unattractive options for respondents. The multitude of posters that still adorn South Africa's streets, often illegible and poorly designed, may cause information overload and reader aversion. Moreover, whereas state officials and academics may have access to the Internet and websites, few citizens have access to them.[11]

The survey also suggests that provincial differences in knowledge and information sources need to be taken into account. This implies that provinces and provincial stakeholders should adapt their communication and information (education) strategies to the citizenry in their particular region.

Formal Education

Various theorists and observers regard education for the citizenry on the functioning of the state and state processes, inclusive of public institutions, as very important. Education increases awareness and understanding of state structures, institutions and processes. It is suggested here that education around the composition and functions of such structures should be included in secondary school curricula. Citizen education, if formalised within the educational system, is likely to advance understanding as well as knowledge, and will foster the will to participate in state functions, which may ultimately manifest in active participation in and the sustainment and deepening of democracy in South Africa.

Involvement of Civil Society

Civilian organisations should be drawn into the law-making process at national, provincial and local level at an early stage so that their inputs have a bearing right from the start. *Early and timely invitations to participate are crucial.*

Responses to Submissions

Previous reports suggested that protocols be established to guide national and provincial legislatures in responding to submissions from the public. This study showed that there was a strong overall intention to participate in policy processes among the respondents, regardless of the political parties to which they belonged. This strong interest should be translated into active involvement to add value to public participation in democracy in South Africa. Apart from giving written feedback to organisations, groups, civic structures or institutions on whether their submissions have made an impact upon the legislation (and to what extent), broader feedback should be given to the public in general by means of the radio, the print media and television. Talk shows and phone-in programmes on radio and television could be used to good effect in addition to more formal feedback via news and/or actuality programmes.

National, provincial and local authorities (elected representatives) should also ensure that communication is thorough and effective by evaluating their feedback to their constituencies.

Focus on Issues

The survey showed that an issue-based approach was effective in attracting people's interest and involvement in the law-making process. Respondents provided information about the issues uppermost in the public's mind. It follows that they would rather participate in activities that address and resolve such issues, than in those that they do not consider important. Therefore legislatures at various levels should be aware of the concerns of their constituencies when providing feedback and/or inviting participation.

Constituency Offices

The role of constituency offices is to inform the citizenry about political parties and law-making processes. The opinions and "street wisdom" of elected representatives to national and provincial parliaments suggested that parliamentary constituency offices were important. However, only 9% of the respondents in this survey indicated that they made use of constituency offices.

Parliamentary constituency offices should therefore be redefined as vehicles for improving public participation in governance. This would include setting standards for the training of staff, defining the functions of constituency offices, and getting clarity about who is served by these offices. It may be best to centralise the development and management of such offices as well as the training of staff. Constituency offices need to provide links with the communities in their particular areas. They need to be seen as forums where the public can articulate local interests, and where the general public is being exposed to information about legislation and government policy at national, provincial and local levels.

To fulfil their purpose, constituency offices should embark on effective communication on their role and how this role relates to the needs of their constituencies. This should be done through the relevant media. According to the KID report on public participation (October 1998),

> [t]he media, especially the radio, should be used more effectively in public participation programmes, e.g. the broadcasting of parliamentary deliberations, and phone-in radio programmes. Newspapers could have dedicated columns to inform and educate the public about new legislation and the process of participating in policy formulation and the legislative process.

Moreover, regular feedback is essential.

Constituency offices can be a useful information and communication tool. However, this study seems to indicate a need to popularise constituency offices and enhance their efficiency through benchmarking and performance evaluation, although the approach may have to be adapted to the particular province.

It is perhaps also appropriate to consider the regulation of consti-tuency offices through legislation. Their exact roles need to be defined to ensure that they serve their constituency as a whole and that the resources are optimally utilised. Training programmes and refresher courses for staff in such offices should become an entrenched practice.

Disadvantaged Groups

The recommendations so far can primarily be realised among so-called "literate" people, i.e. people able to read, and people who have access to the radio and television. Other people should however not be excluded from public participation, the more so as this study found that the intent to participate in political processes was overall high, thus including the "poor" and rural dwellers, those sectors who are most likely to be illiterate and without access to radio and television.

Other means of communication should therefore be employed to reach these people, for example audio-visual media, theatre and creative workshops. More resources should be allocated to the arts, for example street theatre, to overcome language and literacy barriers in communica-tion between communities and government. The popular media can assist in highlighting, explaining and debating complex issues around govern-ance. "Road-shows" by government departments, political parties and other stakeholders may also enhance communication—especially in rural areas or smaller towns.

Conclusion

Perhaps the most promising finding in this chapter is people's willingness to join in public hearings. The information and opinion exchange that occurs here is crucial for a successful democracy. The study found that, at the end of Nelson Mandela's presidency in 1999, the majority of South Africans seemed to be quite willing to engage in local policy making, which augurs well for the country's democratic political institutions.

However, the study also found that the public was poorly informed: Less than one in ten respondents indicated that they felt adequately equipped with knowledge about the various stages in the legislative process (green and white papers, bills and acts). Moreover, two-thirds felt ill informed about parliament and indicated that they had little understanding of their own local councils.

It should be noted that the functioning of a democracy is not necessarily related to public knowledge about the legislative process. It is also impossible to determine the optimal level of understanding required to ensuring the proper working of democratic political institutions. However, cognisance should be taken of the perceptions and opinions of the South African public. The study asked respondents what they thought of their own knowledge about the various stages of policy making. Those respondents who indicated that they did not have enough knowledge and understanding, presumably felt a need for being better informed.

In short, the respondents were generally willing to participate in legislative processes. However, they also felt that they did not understand the workings of political institutions. Education might contribute to overcoming obstacles (lack of knowledge and understanding) to realising the intention to participate in governance. However, the weak relation between understanding and education evidenced by the results as well as that between understanding and class-related factors suggest that education would have little effect on a better understanding of the legislative process. What would have a much better effect on understanding of the legislative process are information provided by community leaders and relatively accessible media, such as radio and television. Active use of these media and alternative interactive and local educational and informative initiatives are recommendable.

South Africa harbours various population groups—segmented by race, language, class, area, age and political affiliation—of which some might explain disparities in engagement in legislative processes. Province emerged as a very strong explanatory variable in this study. Generally, respondents living in the Northern Province, Western Cape and North West felt less well informed than respondents from the other provinces. It was also in these provinces where people reported lower levels of participation in public hearings. Since other demographic characteristics proved less relevant, the findings suggest that interventions aimed at promoting public participation should address local disparities in knowledge and understanding while focusing on proper means of informing the public.

Notes

[1] The survey on which this chapter reports, was initiated and sponsored by the Khululekani Institute for Democracy (KID). The former executive director of KID, Campbell Lyons, and staff members Vusi Sibiya and Thabo Liphoko constructed the questionnaire and executed the survey.

[2] In this regard see Milbrath (1965). Populist societies—even if termed "undemocratic" (by, for example, Dahl, 1977)—also stress the need for public or citizen participation. Examples include populist regimes (such as Burkina Faso under Thomas Sankara), young democracies in the aftermath of authoritarianism (such as Italy after 1945) and popular autocracies (such as Libya under Ghadaffi or the United Arab Emirates). Diamond, 1993.

[3] See Jabu Sindane in the Centre for Policy Studies report on democratic consolidation cited above.

[4] The percentages do not all add to 100%, due to missing data.

[5] Note that the responses reflected the respondents' own knowledge and perceptions of the process/institutions.

[6] KID prefers to refer to "black" rather than "African" respondents. The authors followed KID guidelines in this regard.

[7] Respondents were asked, *"How often do you feel you can trust the government to do what is right for people like you?"* The options were: never, seldom, sometimes, mostly and always.

[8] The living standard measure (LSM) was calculated for each respondent according to his/her access to a range of household appliances, municipal services, shops and financial services. The LSM is a standardised measure for living circumstances in South Africa. The low, middle and high categories each constituted one-third of the people interviewed.

[9] Appendix B contains data referring to national levels of participation among members of the ANC, NNP, DP, UDM, IFP and other voters. Provincial data are presented for the two biggest parties in each province.

[10] This in itself did not provide the ANC with a "moral superior status". Robert Sobukwe of the Pan-Africanist Congress made it clear at the time that the distinctive quality for citizenship was not colour but whether a person as an African was in favour of a polity ruled by Africans for Africans to the benefit of Africans. Various sources point out that nepotism and corruption existed on various levels within the ANC during the "struggle" years. (See, for example, Johannes Rantete, 1998, pp. 55, 59ff; Sechaba & Ellis, 1990.)

[11] More cynically put: They are the "hype" of corporate executives and young bureaucrats.

References

Adam, H. & Moodley, K. (1986), *South Africa without Apartheid: Dismantling Racial Domination*, Maskew Miller Longman, Cape Town.

Corder, H. (ed.) (1989), *Democracy and the Judiciary*, Idasa, Mowbray.

Dahl, R. (1977), *What after the Revolution?* Massachusetts University Press, Massachusetts.

Diamond, Larry (1993), *Political Culture and Democracy in Developing Countries*, Lynne Rienner, Boulder.

Gouws, A. & Kadalie, R. (1994), "Women in the Struggle: The Past and the Future", in Liebenberg, I., Lortan, F., Nel, B. & Van der Westhuizen, G. (eds), *The Long March: The Story of the Struggle for Liberation in South Africa*, Kagiso-Haum, Pretoria.

Gottschalk, K. (1994), "The United Democratic Front, 1983-1991: Rise, Impact and Consequences, in Liebenberg, I., Lortan, F., Nel, B. & Van der Westhuizen, G. (eds), *The Long March: The Story of the Struggle for Liberation in South Africa*, Kagiso-Haum, Pretoria.

Hassim, S. & Gouws, A. (1998), "Redefining the Public Space: Women's Organisations, Gender Consciousness and Civil Society in South Africa", *Politikon*, vol. 25, no. 2, pp. 53-76.

Liebenberg, I. (1990), *Ideologie in Konflik,* Taurus, Emmerentia.

Liebenberg, I., Lortan, F., Nel, B. & Van der Westhuizen, G. (eds) (1994), *The Long March: The Story of the Struggle for Liberation in South Africa*, Kagiso-Haum, Pretoria.

Lijphart, A. (1996), *Unequal Participation: Democracy's Unresolved Dilemma*, Presidential Address, American Political Science Association, University of California, San Diego.

Meer, F. (1988), "The Freedom Charter and the Future: The Position of the Natal Indian Congress", pp. 26-37, in Polley, J. (ed.), *The Freedom Charter and the Future*, Idasa, Mowbray.

Milbrath, L.W. (1965), *Political Participation: How and Why do People Get Involved in Politics?*, Chicago, Illinois, Rand McNally College Publishing.

Moosa, E. (1989), "The Role of Lawyers in a Future Democratic South Africa", in Corder, H. (ed.), *Democracy and the Judiciary*, Idasa, Mowbray.

Pampallis, J. (1991), *Foundations of the New South Africa*, Maskew Miller Longman, Cape Town.

Polley, J. (ed.) (1988), *The Freedom Charter and the Future*, Idasa, Mowbray.

Rantete, J.M. (1998), *The African National Congress and the Negotiated Settlement in South Africa*, J.L. van Schaik, Pretoria.

Roefs, M. & Liebenberg, I. (1999), *Non-Racialism on the Eve of 2000*, paper presented at the Bi-annual Congress of the Political Science Association (SAPSA), Military Academy, Saldanha, 29 June to 2 July.

Rule, S. (1999), *Public Opinion and National Priority Issues*, Human Sciences Research Council, Pretoria.

Sechaba, T. & Ellis, S. (1990), *Comrades against Apartheid: The ANC and the SACP in Exile*, Indiana University Press, London.

Appendix A

Intention to Participate

Intention to participate in local council by race and province*				
Province	African	Coloured	Asian	White
		Percentage		
Western Cape	89	47	–	34
Northern Cape	41	52	–	48
Eastern Cape	73	88	–	77
Free State	25	–	–	86
KwaZulu-Natal	82	–	60	43
Mpumalanga	74	–	–	80
Northern Province	67	–	–	59
Gauteng	85	94	–	27
North West	60	–	–	40
Average	75	56	54	37

* Empty cells contained less than 10 respondents.

Intention to participate in provincial legislature by race and province*				
Province	African	Coloured	Asian	White
		Percentage		
Western Cape	45	38	–	32
Northern Cape	20	33	–	32
Eastern Cape	50	48	–	55
Free State	52	–	–	5
KwaZulu-Natal	34	–	34	11
Mpumalanga	55	–	–	78
Northern Province	49	–	–	42
Gauteng	63	60	–	10
North West	46	–	–	8
Average	49	40	35	22

* Empty cells contained less than 10 respondents.

Intention to participate in national parliament by race and province*				
Province	African	Coloured	Asian	White
		Percentage		
Western Cape	48	34	–	25
Northern Cape	11	25	–	14
Eastern Cape	58	54	–	68
Free State	37	–	–	0
KwaZulu-Natal	21	–	39	11
Mpumalanga	35	–	–	37
Northern Province	32	–	–	39
Gauteng	45	35	–	16
North West	34	–	–	8
Average	37	35	42	20

* Empty cells contained less than 10 respondents.

Intention to participate in government department by race and province*				
Province	African	Coloured	Asian	White
		Percentage		
Western Cape	48	32	–	28
Northern Cape	13	29	–	27
Eastern Cape	54	63	–	73
Free State	31	–	–	41
KwaZulu-Natal	23	–	34	11
Mpumalanga	35	–	–	37
Northern Province	30	–	–	39
Gauteng	45	53	–	22
North West	31	–	–	14
Average	36	36	38	25

* Empty cells contained less than 10 respondents.

Appendix B

Levels of Participation

Party	Local council	Provincial legislature	National parliament	Government department
Intention to participate by political preference at national level				
			Percentage	
ANC	74	51	41	39
NNP	46	33	32	34
DP	54	30	26	28
IFP	73	38	24	35
UDM	73	39	41	36
Other	50	30	31	29

Province	Party	Local council	Provincial legislature	National parliament	Government department
Intention to participate by political preference at provincial level					
			Percentage		
Western Cape	ANC	70	40	45	42
	NNP	45	41	36	35
Northern Cape	ANC	44	27	12	20
	NNP	80	46	38	42
Eastern Cape	ANC	74	52	61	56
	UDM	79	46	49	48
Free State	ANC	74	49	37	29
	NNP	14	–	–	3
KwaZulu-Natal	ANC	86	34	25	23
	IFP	76	37	24	35
Mpumalanga	ANC	77	58	34	35
	NNP	51	23	3	3
Northern Province	ANC	60	46	31	28
	NNP	67	67	37	37
Gauteng	ANC	89	66	46	48
	DP	41	25	38	36
North West	ANC	64	50	33	31
	Other	62	23	18	7

Reported participation by political preference at national level*			
Party	Contact with councillor	Statement at public hearing	Participation in community organisation
		Percentage	
ANC	24	24	46
NNP	7	9	18
DP	8	7	31
IFP	34	33	46
UDM	18	22	43
Other	21	14	34

* The findings related to making enquiries at parliamentary constituency offices were not broken down due to the small number of respondents who engaged in this activity.

Reported participation by political preference at provincial level

Province	Party	Contact with councillor	Statement at public hearing	Participation in community organisation
			Percentage	
Western Cape	ANC	22	18	37
	NNP	1	–	5
Northern Cape	ANC	7	12	40
	NNP	7	2	36
Eastern Cape	ANC	33	30	70
	UDM	24	30	51
Free State	ANC	9	10	29
	NNP	–	–	23
KwaZulu-Natal	ANC	29	26	45
	IFP	34	35	49
Mpumalanga	ANC	14	17	31
	NNP	–	0	3
Northern Province	ANC	26	25	41
	NNP	45	42	59
Gauteng	ANC	28	33	52
	DP	4	3	25
North West	ANC	14	16	27
	Other	7	–	23

Chapter 12

Profiles of Party Political Support

Stephen Rule

Introduction

Since the establishment of South Africa as a national entity in 1910, incumbent governments have been defeated in parliamentary elections only on four occasions.[1] This is attributable to uniformity in the historical voting behaviour of ethnic electoral blocs, both before and after the implementation of a universal franchise democracy in 1994. As the new democracy matures it is therefore of particular interest to determine the potential for the emergence of political alignments capable of bridging or cross-cutting strategic ethnic and racial cleavages. Most other African democracies have similarly been characterised by political stasis as a consequence of repeated ethnic voting patterns. Exceptions have included Benin and Zambia in 1991 where incumbent leaders were outvoted in national elections (Esterhuysen, 1992; IDEA, 1997). During 2000, Senegal's Diouf lost the election to Wade and Zimbabwe's ruling ZANU (PF) narrowly retained its parliamentary majority when the traditionally monolithic Chishona-speaking section of the electorate split along an urban-rural cleavage.

Most contemporary South African political parties go to great lengths to portray themselves as multi-ethnic non-racial organisations. Individuals from groups not historically associated with the party are propelled into positions of prominence as a means of attracting the support of those groups. This chapter explores the extent to which party support profiles continue to reflect traditional historical cleavages, using the results of a national survey of public opinion conducted during November 1999. Responses to three of the survey questions are analysed to determine feelings of closeness to each political party, intention to vote for that party and reasons for voting for that party in the June 1999 election.

Voter Identification with a Political Party

In a nationally representative survey of public opinion conducted by the Human Sciences Research Council (HSRC) during November 1999 (Rule, 2000a), the electorate was questioned about its party political loyalties. Fieldworkers made the following statement to each respondent.[2] "I would like to ask how close or distant you feel towards various political parties and organisations. If you feel close to a party you would support it. If you feel distant you would oppose it." The responses to this statement were particularly interesting in the light of the shifts in political allegiance that occurred in the June 1999 election, five months before the survey. Table 12.1 lists the percentages of respondents who indicated closeness, neutrality, distance or uncertainty in respect of each of 15 political parties.

An expressed feeling of closeness to a political party did not necessarily imply a real commitment to the party. However, the distribution of respondents who indicated that they felt "very close" to each political party reflected the same broad pattern of support received by each party that contested the June 1999 election. Almost half (46%) of the respondents indicated that they felt "very close" to the African National Congress (ANC). Much smaller proportions of respondents stated the same about the other parties, even the main opposition parties, namely the Democratic Party (DP) (3%), Inkatha Freedom Party (IFP) (2%) and New National Party (NNP) (3%). If those who felt "close" to each party are added to those who felt "very close", the ANC came out on top at 65%, followed by the DP (13%), NNP (10%) and IFP (6%). Given the election results, it is apparent that feeling "very close" or "close" to the ANC translated more easily into voting for the ANC than was the case with opposition parties (Table 12.1).

Table 12.1: Feelings of closeness, neutrality or distance from each political party, November 1999

Political party	Very close	Close	Neutral	Distant	Very distant	Uncertain/ Don't know
				Percentage		
ACDP	0,8	3,9	10,4	12,6	46,2	26,0
ANC	46,4	18,7	7,9	5,5	16,0	5,5
AEB	0,2	0,6	5,8	12,3	52,4	28,7
AZAPO	0,5	3,1	9,7	12,5	52,4	21,8
CP	0,1	1,7	6,7	14,5	54,5	22,3
DP	3,4	9,7	9,5	12,9	46,9	17,7
FA	0,3	1,1	6,0	13,6	53,1	25,9
FF	0,7	1,8	6,3	13,5	54,3	23,3
IFP	2,1	3,5	7,7	13,6	57,3	15,8
MF	0,3	0,9	5,1	11,4	55,8	26,4
NNP	2,5	7,9	9,3	13,9	51,3	15,2
PAC	0,9	5,9	10,8	13,2	51,6	17,8
SACP	1,7	4,9	8,2	12,6	50,4	22,1
UCDP	0,5	2,4	8,7	13,3	50,5	24,7
UDM	1,3	4,2	9,6	13,7	51,2	20,1

The proportions of respondents who indicated closeness to the DP (13%) and NNP (10%) were slightly more than those who actually supported them in the election (10% and 7% respectively). The IFP was an exception to this trend, however. In all previous HSRC surveys, the proportions of respondents who indicated closeness to the IFP were lower by as much as half the actual proportion that voted for the IFP in June 1999. Whereas 6% indicated that they felt "very close" or "close" to the IFP, more than 8% voted for the IFP in June 1999 (Table 12.2). This was attributable to fear among respondents of revealing their support in a continuously volatile political environment. In successive opinion surveys, residents of KwaZulu-Natal, the provincial stronghold of the IFP, were those most likely not to reveal political preferences.

Of utility to analysts and political party organisers are the demographic characteristics of political support bases. Table 12.2 indicates the proportions of each population group who felt "very close" or "close" to each political party in November 1999.

Table 12.2: Feelings of closeness to each party by population group, November 1999

Political party	Blacks	Whites	Coloureds	Indians	Total
			Percentage very close or close		
ACDP	4	8	8	6	5
ANC	80	7	42	21	65
AEB	0	4	0	1	1
AZAPO	5	0	1	0	4
CP	1	9	2	1	2
DP	4	54	22	35	13
FA	1	6	0	2	1
FF	1	16	1	0	3
IFP	6	7	1	2	6
MF	1	1	1	12	1
NNP	5	23	33	25	10
PAC	9	0	3	0	7
SACP	9	0	2	0	7
UCDP	2	4	5	1	3
UDM	5	8	7	2	6

The distribution of "closeness" to each political party by population group suggests a fairly high degree of racial polarisation in the South African electorate. This was most evident among the black respondents, four-fifths (80%) of whom indicated that they felt "very close" or "close" to the ANC. This was not surprising given the history of that party under Nelson Mandela both before and after the liberatory election of April 1994 and under his successor, Thabo Mbeki since 1999.[3] In contrast to blacks, only 7% of white respondents felt "close" or "very close" to the ANC. "Close" and "very close" levels were significantly higher among coloureds (42%) than among Indians (21%) (Table 12.2). The latter two groups were also politically oppressed under the apartheid system and would understandably have been more supportive of the ANC than would whites.

Although closeness to the DP was highest among whites (54%), closeness to the DP was much lower than closeness to the ANC. A greater divergence of opinion existed among whites, who also exhibited a degree of apathy and cynicism that clearly impacted on commitment to a particular political party. Only 4% of black respondents felt close to the DP, many of the others having been alienated by a DP election campaign that was perceived to imply resistance to the ANC's social development policies. Intermediate were the other two groups, with 22% of coloureds and 35% of Indians indicating closeness to the DP. Its major competitor, the NNP, on the other hand, elicited feelings of closeness from one-third (33%) of coloureds, and one-quarter of Indians (25%) and whites (23%) (Table 12.2). Fierce contestation for political turf by the DP and NNP resulted in victory for the DP among whites and equal DP and NNP support among coloured and Indian respondents. The termination of FW de Klerk's leadership of the NNP, his successor's (Marthinus van Schalkwyk's) lower public profile and a distaste for perceived NNP collaboration with the ANC were reasons for the dramatic decline in support for the NNP since 1998.

Only 6% of black respondents admitted to feelings of closeness to the IFP, as did 7% of whites. Sentiments portraying a more conservative approach to economic policy and trade unionism had been clearly articulated by IFP leader Dr Mangosuthu Buthelezi, in spite of his position as Minister of Home Affairs in the ANC government. A surprising phenomenon was the lack of closeness among respondents to the ANC's partner in the liberation movement, the Pan-Africanist Congress (PAC). In spite of its parallel efforts in the struggle for political freedom, it managed only to elicit feelings of closeness of 7% of the respondents (9% of blacks and 3% of coloureds), most of whom clearly did not translate their sentiments into votes. This was attributable to the failure of the PAC to capture the imagination of the electorate and its inability under Clarence Makwetu and Stanley Mokgoba to match the vision and charisma exuded by Nelson Mandela. Seven per cent (7%) of the respondents indicated that they felt close to the South African Communist Party (SACP), a member of the tripartite ruling alliance (ANC, SACP and COSATU) (Table 12.2). This closeness figure echoed the SACP's electoral contribution to the alliance, although the party contributed proportionally more to the policy directions of the alliance's dominant partner, the ANC.

Six per cent (6%) felt close to the United Democratic Movement (UDM) of General Bantu Holomisa and his co-leader at the time, Roelf Meyer. The UDM appeared to draw similar levels of support from whites, blacks and coloureds, but less support from Indians. Five per cent (5%) felt close to the African Christian Democratic Party (ACDP), demonstrating the appeal of a Christian fundamentalist approach to politics, in this case at levels ranging from 4% to 8% across all four population groups (Table 12.2). Opposition to the permissive policies of the ANC with regard to abortion, gambling and capital punishment was clearly enunciated by ACDP leader Reverend Kenneth Meshoe before the June 1999 election.

Voting Intention

Intention to vote for a party was gauged by a separate question that enquired more directly, "Which party would you support if an election were held tomorrow?" Fifty-six per cent (56%) indicated support for the ANC. The DP and NNP followed with 6% and 4% respectively and the IFP with 3% (again, clearly an underestimate given its 8% of votes in June 1999) (Table 12.3). The UDM would have received the vote of 2% and the ACDP 1% of the votes. The proportions of respondents who indicated that they would not vote (6%) or did not know for which parties they would vote (12%) were higher than those in the pre-election survey of March 1999 (Rule, 1999a). A similar proportion of respondents refused to divulge their intentions in both March and November 1999 (8%) (Table 12.3).

Table 12.3: Voting preferences for each party "if an election were held tomorrow", 1996-1999

Party	Feb. 96	Feb. 97	Feb. 98	Dec. 98	Mar. 99	Nov. 99
			Percentage			
ANC	55,3	52,8	44,5	48,8	56,2	56,1
DP	1,0	1,5	2,5	6,7	5,8	6,4
NNP	13,4	11,7	10,9	10,5	8,5	4,4
IFP	6,3	4,3	3,1	4,4	4,4	2,8
UDM	-0	-	5,9	5,4	3,2	1,5
ACDP	0,4	0,4	1,1	1,1	1,1	1,2
FF	2,0	1,3	2,3	1,8	1,3	0,6
FA	-	-	-	0,4	0,4	0,3
PAC	0,8	1,8	2,1	1,1	0,9	0,2
CP	1,1	0,4	0,4	1,0	0,3	0,1
AZAPO	0,2	0,4	0,2	0,3	0,2	0,1
SACP	0,1	0,6	0,6	0,0	0,0	0,0
Other	0,5	3,5	0,6	0,6	1,1	0,6
Would not vote	6,0*	10,2*	11,0*	10,8	3,6	5,8
Don't know	12,9	11,1	14,8	3,8	5,3	12,2
Refused				3,4	8,3	7,5

* "Would not vote" and "Refused" were combined in these surveys.

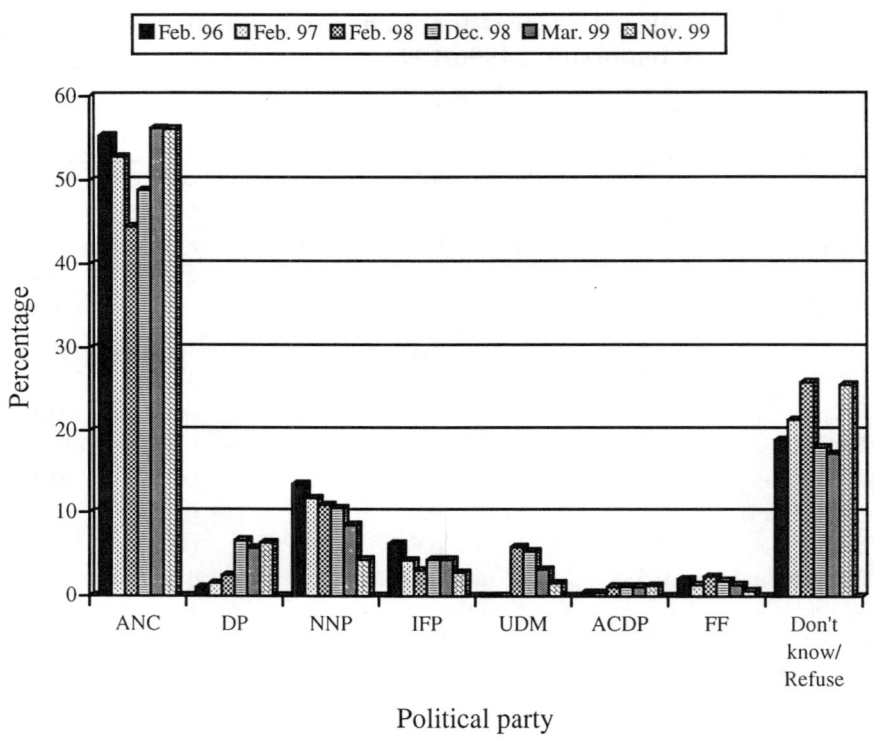

Figure 12.1: Voting preferences for each party "if an election were held tomorrow", 1996-1999

In order to estimate the likely distribution of votes had an election been held in November 1999, certain adjustments to the survey statistics were required. First, those who indicated that they would not vote were removed from the equation. Second, the feelings of closeness to any party that were expressed by those who were "uncertain", indicated that they "don't know" or refused to divulge their voting preference were taken into account where applicable. Third, the IFP proportion was adjusted upwards by the extent to which the March 1999 survey under-predicted the June 1999 election results (i.e. half).

The results of the hypothetical November 1999 election did not differ significantly from those of the June 1999 election. The ANC would once again have achieved almost two-thirds of the votes, followed by the DP with just short on one-tenth. The IFP would have followed with just over 8% and the NNP would have lost more ground by achieving only 6% of the votes. The UDM's total would have declined marginally to 2,4% and the ACDP's would have increased to 1,8%. Seven smaller parties would have obtained results similar to those of the June 1999 election. Interestingly, even though the CP had not participated in the June 1999 election, a small proportion of the respondents nevertheless indicated that they would have voted for the CP.

Table 12.4: Distribution of votes had an election been held in November 1999

Party	% of votes: committed + balance	Party	% of votes: committed + balance
ANC	56,3+10,0=66,3	FF	0,6+0,6=1,2
DP	6,4+3,2=9,6	UCDP	0,3+0,6=0,9
IFP	(2,9+1,3)*1,95=8,1	FA	0,3+0,3=0,6
NNP	4,4+1,8=6,2	AEB	0,1+0,4=0,5
UDM	1,6+0,8=2,4	AZAPO	0,1+0,3=0,4
ACDP	1,2+0,6=1,8	CP	0,1+0,3=0,4
PAC	0,2+0,9=1,2	MF	0,1+0,1=0,2

The November 1999 survey facilitated a breakdown of the ethno-linguistic characteristics of potential voters for each party. Clearly, ANC support was very solid among blacks. Even amongst isiZulu speakers, almost one in two was a potential ANC voter. Support was also strong among the coloureds, where almost one in three indicated that they would have voted for the ANC. The DP drew most of its support from white respondents. Afrikaans-speaking whites had a slightly weaker tendency than other whites to support the DP (Table 12.5).

Table 12.5: Party support by ethno-linguistic grouping, November 1999

Party	Black Zulu	Black other	White Afrikaans	White other	Coloured	Indian	Total
				Percentage			
ANC	46,9	79,8	0,8	4,6	30,7	8,0	56,1
DP		0,5	29,5	46,8	6,6	26,4	6,4
IFP	11,6	0,3	2,3		0,5	0,8	2,8
NNP		0,7	15,8	4,7	19,2	21,3	4,4
UDM	0,1	2,1	1,9	1,5	1,5	0,2	1,5
ACDP	0,6	1,0	0,9	2,9	2,2	4,0	1,2
FF			6,1	1,8	0,4		0,6
PAC	0,1	0,4					0,2
CP			0,7	0,6			0,1
FA		0,1	2,6	1,2		0,5	0,3
AZAPO		0,2			0,1		0,1
SACP					0,1		0,0
UCDP		0,5		0,9			0,3
Other		0,3		0,5	0,7		0,6
Won't vote	7,0	5,0	4,8	3,2	7,9	12,0	5,8
Don't know	5,7	4,1	10,9	6,1	12,1	8,2	6,0
Uncertain	8,5	2,4	13,1	17,6	11,3	5,8	6,2
Refused	19,4	2,6	10,6	7,7	6,6	10,2	7,6
Total	20,6	53,7	7,8	4,9	9,7	0,7	

However, twice as many Afrikaans-speaking whites felt close to the DP than to the NNP, and the DP:NNP ratio for "other" whites was 10:1. These figures represent a dramatic shift away from the NNP. Its predecessor, the (old) National Party, commanded a majority or at least significant support among white Afrikaans speakers (Rule, 1989) throughout the apartheid era and until as recently as 1997. Among coloureds, the NNP:ANC ratio was 2:3. Indians were divided in their loyalties between the DP, the NNP and the ANC.

The average supporter of the ANC was thus black and a speaker of one of the five most common African languages in the country (isiXhosa, isiZulu, Sepedi, Sesotho or Setswana). In terms of other variables, he/she was likely to have an educational qualification of lower than Standard 8 and, in only two out of five cases, some form of employment. Although he/she was not satisfied with his/her household financial situation or with the general economic situation in South Africa, the typical ANC supporter thought that things would improve during the next 12 months. Most ANC supporters lived in Gauteng, the Eastern Cape or the Northern Province. Three church groupings were most highly represented amongst ANC supporters, namely the Zionist Christian, Roman Catholic and Methodist churches (see Rule, 1999b).

On the other hand, supporters of the DP were most likely to be white and English or Afrikaans speaking. More than one-third had a post-matric education and 57% had jobs (many of the balance being students, pensioners or full-time housewives). The majority held pessimistic views about the economy and about their own financial situations. DP supporters were most likely to live in Gauteng, KwaZulu-Natal or the Western Cape. The two largest church denominations among them were the Nederduitse Gereformeerde Kerk (NGK) and the Methodist Church. Supporters of the NNP were mainly coloured or white speakers of Afrikaans or English. About half had passed Standard 8 or 9 or matric and half were employed in full-time or part-time jobs, indicative of a standard of living higher than that of their ANC and lower than that of their DP counterparts. Most felt negative about the economy and its prospects for the next year. The majority of NNP supporters were residents of the Western Cape, Gauteng and KwaZulu-Natal. The largest religious groups among the NNP supporters were the NGK, the Roman Catholic and the Anglican Church.

Speakers of isiZulu who live in KwaZulu-Natal are likely to vote for the IFP. Half had an education of below Standard 8 level and only two in five were employed. Although not positive about the national or their personal economic circumstances, those who expected an improvement during the next year were more than those who did not. The largest church membership groups amongst IFP supporters were the Zionist Christian and Roman Catholic churches.

UDM supporters were more likely to be female than male and predominantly speakers of isiXhosa or isiZulu. Most lived in the Eastern Cape or KwaZulu-Natal and just over half had an education of at least Standard 8. A sizeable proportion of UDM supporters was Methodists and generally they were dissatisfied with both their household financial situations and the economic situation in South Africa as a whole. Two in five anticipated an improvement in their circumstances during the next 12 months.

Reasons for Voting Preferences

It should not be presumed that voters automatically vote for parties that are perceived to represent their particular population, ethnic or linguistic group. The November 1999 survey indicated that motivations for voting for a particular party were not overtly related to population group or ethnicity. Respondents were asked, "If you did vote in the 1999 election, for what reason did you choose the party that you did?"

One-third (36%) of the responses were related to a specific policy of the party concerned (Table 12.6). Most frequently mentioned were jobs, followed by housing and crime or security issues. Other responses contained generalisations such as "good promises", "good economic policy" or the "vision" of the party concerned. A further one-third (34%) of responses referred to an improved quality of life in the country, including "for a better life in South Africa", "for improvement", "to make things right" or "for stability". The first of these statements resonated with a catchy ANC campaign slogan that promoted electoral support for the ANC. Less tangible reasons (e.g. "trust or belief in the party", "like for the party", "a good opposition") were offered by 22% of the respondents. Significantly, and as was the case in a Namibian election survey (Keulder, 1998), only 4% suggested overt racial identity as their motivation for supporting a particular party. Nevertheless, given the apartheid history, race/population group probably determined for which parties most South Africans voted, even if this merely assumed a subliminal role (Table 12.6).

Table 12.6: Reasons for party selection by population group, 1999 election

Reason	Black	White	Coloured	Indian	Total
			Percentage		
Improved life quality	34,2	21,0	42,3	47,7	33,7
Specific party policy	37,5	26,2	29,9	10,0	35,7
Identification with specific party	18,0	48,3	22,2	36,9	22,2
Racial identity of party	4,4	3,4	1,8	1,5	4,0
Other reasons	1,7	0,0	1,2	0,7	1,6
Did not vote	0,4	1,2	1,8	2,5	0,7

The November 1999 survey revealed that seven provinces would again have been won by the ANC with large majorities; two, the Western Cape and KwaZulu-Natal, would have been narrowly lost to opposition parties. The latter provinces were localities of the most dissatisfied sectors of the electorate. New opposition parties, namely the UDM and UCDP, would have retained the support of significant numbers of voters in ANC strongholds, that is, the Eastern Cape and North West, respectively. Both were led by former homeland leaders, namely Bantu Holomisa and Lucas Mangope. Lodge (1999a, p. 85) observed that these trends pointed "to a future in which the ANC's predominance within the borders of former non-Zulu homelands is no longer guaranteed".

The massive shift in voting allegiance that occurred among whites (from the NNP to the DP) appeared to have stabilised. The DP's share of the vote had risen from 1% to almost 10% between 1994 and 1999. Although the policies of the DP did not change (Welsh, 1999), the image and presentation thereof had become more robust, appealing to whites who felt that the NNP was not opposing the ANC effectively. The trend began during the inter-election period with the DP's increasing ability to win by-elections at local government level in Afrikaner-dominated municipalities such as Witbank and Boksburg. This culminated in the DP displacing the NNP as the second largest party in parliament and major opposition to the ANC in June 1999.[4] Remaining votes for the NNP appeared mainly to come from the coloured electorate of the Western and Northern Cape.

Even in this sector, however, both the DP and ANC made significant gains. In the case of the ANC, the shift in allegiance resulted in the Northern Cape becoming an ANC-dominated province in 1999. In 1994 it was marginally held by the ANC with the support of the single DP member of the provincial legislature.

A new phenomenon in South African politics was the dramatic increase in support for the ACDP. Although starting from a small base, the ACDP more than doubled its absolute share of the votes in comparison with 1994, in spite of the significantly lower poll. Lodge (1999b, p. 193) observed that although the support base of the ACDP was predominantly white, the "sociology is likely to alter as the suburban evangelical congregations increasingly represent a 'rainbow' middle class".

Estimates of the proportion of support for each party from each population group (Reynolds, 1999) in the June 1999 election appear to be borne out by the November public opinion trends. In the latter survey, the ANC received most of its support from blacks (90%) and the DP most of its support from whites (77%). The IFP's support base remained almost exclusively speakers of isiZulu in rural KwaZulu-Natal. Almost half (44%) of the NNP's support came from coloureds, with relatively high white (31%) and black (18%) components. These patterns also correlate strongly with the profiles of party support extracted from the March 1999 survey (Rule, 1999a).

The June 1999 election illustrated that the individual voting stations at which the major parties achieved their highest proportions of votes were their regional strongholds (Rule, 2000b). Thus, the ANC did best in a rural locality in a former Ciskei homeland area of the Eastern Cape and the DP in a former white (now racially mixed) urban residential suburb of Durban, KwaZulu-Natal. The IFP achieved its best result in rural northern KwaZulu-Natal and the NNP in a rural coloured Afrikaans-speaking locality in the Western Cape. The UDM did best at a location near Richmond, KwaZulu-Natal, where its provincial leader was killed a few months before the election. However, the core of its support came from disenchanted chiefs and public servants in the Umtata region of the former

Transkei (Maseko, 1999). The ACDP achieved its best result in Butterworth, Eastern Cape, with other concentrations of support in the suburbs of metropolitan Cape Town, especially Fish Hoek.

Table 12.7: Best performing voting district per party, June 1999 election

Party	Locality	District	Province
ANC	Zozo Public School	East London Rural TLC	EC
DP	Forest View Primary School	Durban Outer West MLC	KZN
IFP	Landulwazi School	Zululand Regional Council	KZN
NNP	Kruidfontein Stoor	Prince Albert TRC	WC
UDM	Magoda School	Richmond TLC	KZN
ACDP	Bava Junior Sec. School	Butterworth-Gowa TRC	EC

Conclusion

The political landscape as determined by the first democratic election of April 1994 appears to have stabilised. The 1999 election and a subsequent poll of public opinion indicate a slight strengthening of the ANC's dominance among the black electorate and a significant strengthening among the coloured electorate. With most white Afrikaans speakers as well as significant numbers of Indian and coloured voters having shifted allegiance to the DP, as well as its alliance agreement with the NNP in June 2000, that party has consolidated its position as the country's major opposition party. The IFP retains its power base in rural northern KwaZulu-Natal, almost exclusively amongst isiZulu-speaking voters. The NNP's remaining power bases in the Western and Northern Cape largely mirror the distribution of the coloured population. The local government elections scheduled for 2000 will reveal the extent to which the opposition Democratic Alliance retains traditional NNP support. The growth of the UDM appears to have been stalled and that of the next largest party, the ACDP, to be expanding amongst all sectors of the electorate, although at a slow rate.

Notes

[1] In 1924 the National Party (NP) unseated the South African Party government; in 1938 the United Party defeated the NP; in 1948 the NP returned to power and in 1994 the African National Congress (ANC) assumed control.

[2] The realised sample totalled 2 678 respondents in all nine provinces.

[3] For more than eight decades the ANC fought and negotiated for the transformation of the racially exclusivist hegemony under FW de Klerk and his predecessors so as to institute universal franchise and a multi-party democracy.

[4] The shift in voter allegiance later precipitated a political alliance between the two parties in order to consolidate opposition support in the local government elections scheduled for late 2000.

References

Esterhuysen, P. (ed.) (1992), *Africa at a Glance*, Africa Institute of South Africa, Pretoria.

Institute for Democracy and Electoral Assistance (IDEA) (1997), *Voter Turnout from 1945 to 1997: A Global Report on Political Participation*, IDEA, Stockholm.

Keulder, C. (1998), *Voting Behaviour in Namibia: Local Authority Elections 1998*, United States Agency for International Development and Friedrich-Ebert Stiftung, Windhoek.

Lodge, T. (1999a), "The African National Congress", in Reynolds, A. (ed.), *Election '99 South Africa: From Mandela to Mbeki*, David Philip, Cape Town, Chapter 4, pp. 64-87.

Lodge, T. (1999b), *Consolidating Democracy: South Africa's Second Popular Election,* Witwatersrand University Press, Johannesburg.

Maseko, S. (1999), "The PAC, Azapo and the UDM", in Reynolds, A. (ed.), *Election '99 South Africa: From Mandela to Mbeki*, David Philip, Cape Town, Chapter 8, pp. 125-132.

Reynolds, A. (1999), "The Results", in Reynolds, A. (ed.), *Election '99 South Africa: From Mandela to Mbeki,* David Philip, Cape Town, Chapter 12, pp. 173-209.

Rule, S.P. (1989), "Language, Occupation and Regionalism as Determinants of White Political Allegiances in South Africa", *South African Geographical Journal*, vol. 71, no. 2, pp. 94-101.

Rule, S. (ed.) (1999a), *Democracy SA: Public Opinion on National Priority Issues, Election '99*, Human Sciences Research Council, Pretoria.

Rule, S. (1999b), "Outcome of the Election", in Muthien, Y. (ed.), *Democracy South Africa: Evaluating the 1999 Election*, Human Sciences Research Council, Pretoria.

Rule, S. (ed.) (2000a), *Democracy SA: Public Opinion on National Priority Issues, March 2000*, Human Sciences Research Council, Pretoria.

Rule, S.P. (2000b), *Electoral Territoriality in Southern Africa*, Ashgate, Aldershot.

Welsh, D. (1999), "The Democratic Party", in Reynolds, A. (ed.), *Election '99 South Africa: From Mandela to Mbeki,* David Philip, Cape Town, Chapter 5, pp. 88-100.

Chapter 13

Decoding South Africa's 1999 Electoral Geography

Stephen Rule

Introduction

Variations in the support given to the African National Congress (ANC) and its political opponents in the June 1999 election are attributable to several factors. This chapter examines the election results in relation to regional differences in public opinion about government priorities and economic performance during the months prior to the election. The extent to which political contestation occurred in each province is shown to be a function of the levels of satisfaction with and trust in the government. Also of importance is the distribution of the racial and ethnic diversities of the population, a dimension that has marked effects on electoral outcomes elsewhere in southern Africa. Data used in this chapter were generated by the Human Sciences Research Council's (HSRC) national sample survey in March 1999, which was conducted to test the pre-election mood of potential voters.

Although it is difficult to determine the causes of individual voting behaviour, studies of election results have demonstrated that political allegiances are related to a variety of factors. Prominent among these are the socio-economic characteristics of an electorate and the spatial context within which their political socialisation has occurred.

The second round of fully democratic national election in South Africa was held on 2 June 1999. The ANC government was returned to office with just less than two-thirds (266) of the 400 seats in the National Assembly. Since the April 1994 election, substantial progress has been made in the transformation of the former apartheid state into a non-racial democracy. The extent to which this has been perceived to benefit different sectors of the population in different parts of the country varies in relation to historical perceptions of relative material or other deprivation.

The intention of this chapter is to examine voting behaviour in relation to regional differences in public opinion about government performance, the economic and crime situations and race relations. The relationship between political contestation in each province and public opinion about levels of satisfaction with and trust in the government is explored. The extent to which regionalism impacts on public opinion and voting behaviour, independent of the racial and ethnic diversities of the population in each province, is also investigated.

Determinants of Voting Behaviour

The academic study of elections from a geographical perspective has focused primarily on long-standing western democracies. The electoral cleavage model developed by Lipset and Rokkan (1967) has informed much of this work. They postulated that electorates are sub-divided along cleavages based on social class differences. In economic terms, these could be portrayed as representing the respective views of labour and capital or producers and consumers. Less prominent cleavages between groups of voters were also identified in the model, namely urban and rural localities, economic core and peripheral regions, and religious and secular interests.

Both social class and regional cleavages occur in the United Kingdom. The industrial north of the country, with a dominant working-class population, has traditionally been a Labour Party stronghold. In contrast, the Conservative Party has dominated the wealthier region of southern England (Johnston, Pattie & Allsopp, 1988). In the United States, political cultures pertaining to three regions, namely the East, South and West, are seen to represent the dominant electoral cleavages (Archer & Shelley, 1986). Place and locality sectionalism have been shown to be more influential than class in determining voting behaviour in that country. Public opinion about social issues such as capital punishment, homosexuality, abortion, racial segregation and women in politics has shown consistent regional differences in the United States, although these differences have declined in recent decades. More liberal views predominate in the New England and Pacific coastline regions, whereas conservative views predominate in the southern states. These views usually translate into electoral support for the Democratic and Republican parties respectively, although the regional origin of the candidate concerned also plays a role (Weakliem & Biggert, 1999).

In the newer democracies of the developing world, electoral cleavages in several countries have been shown to follow both ethnic and socioeconomic lines. During the initial years of independence, Zimbabwean voters were split along a regional and ethnic cleavage. Matabele speakers in the southwest supported the Zimbabwe African People's Union (PF-ZAPU), while the Chishona-speaking community in the rest of the country voted for the Zimbabwe African National Union (ZANU). After the merging of the two parties in 1987, voter participation among the Matabeles decreased significantly and politics has since been dominated by Robert Mugabe's ZANU-PF. Cracks in this dominance showed up in the 1995 election when one independent candidate was elected from within a Shona-dominated Harare constituency. Additionally, during 1999 workers began to mobilise against the Mugabe regime, presenting further evidence of the emergence of new non-ethnic electoral cleavages (Bond, 1999). Namibian voters still largely vote along ethnic lines, with support bases for SWAPO and the DTA existing among the Ovambo and Okavango/Herero/white/coloured/Nama groupings respectively. In Botswana, the BDP has won every election since 1965 on the basis of strong support from most of the numerically dominant Setswana-speaking groups, especially the Bangwato, Bakwena, Bakgatla and Batlokwa. The opposition BNF has, however, garnered growing support amongst urbanised voters of all groups and obtained almost two-fifths of votes cast in the election of 1994 (Rule, 1995).

In the watershed 1991 election in Zambia, Kaunda's United National Independence Party (UNIP) was routed by the trade union-based Movement for Multiparty Democracy (MMD) under Chiluba. The exception was Kaunda's home province (Eastern Province), where UNIP maintained majority support on the basis of its historical clientelist relationship with the former president. The spectre of political sectionalism in the west, a remnant of the old Barotseland polity, re-emerged in 1993 when the National Party (NP) was formed by several MPs in the Western Province (Rule, 1996).

Nairn (1977) asserts that socio-cultural differences between voters are secondary to the material economic factors of uneven development. Politicians mobilise voters by encapsulating their material interests in broader ethnic, cultural or nationalistic visions. He ascribed the rise of Scottish nationalism to a growing awareness of the wealth of the North Sea oil-fields from which Britain as a whole has derived substantial economic benefit. In Sri Lanka, Hennayake (1992) held that a nation is nothing more than an ethnic group which happens to be in control of the state apparatus. She explains Tamil minority activism as a counter-hegemonic force in the face of Sinhalese domination of the polity. While the basis of the coherence of "ethnic" groups is tenuous, the power of regional ethnic sentiment in mobilising political support is manifest in southern Africa. The hegemonies of the Ovambo, Shona and Tswana-dominated regimes are arguably portrayed and propagated as broadly representative "nationalisms" in Namibia, Zimbabwe and Botswana respectively. The case of Tanzania differs somewhat in that the cross-cutting factors of ethnic territoriality, urbanisation and religious differences tend to blur any monolithic party support blocs among specific cultural groupings (Myers, 1998). Nevertheless, opposition to the dominant Chama cha Mapinduzi (CCM) government originates mainly from two regions with particular social characteristics. The first is the predominantly Muslim electorate of the Zanzibar island of Pemba represented by the Civic United Front (CUF), which won 28 seats in the Tanzanian parliament of 269 seats in the 1995 election. The second is the Chagga linguistic community of the Kilimanjaro region in the south, where the National Convention for Constitutional Reform (NCCR) won 19 parliamentary seats.

In Ghana, Dunn (1980) concluded, the electorate tended to vote for the parties that their "sense of social identity suggested that it would be appropriate for them to vote". Popular obligation towards a party was not a deep existential commitment but an ideological category manipulated for individual advantage. In states that are economically peripheral in the world economy, insufficient resources prevent the government from any widespread and meaningful distribution wealth in terms of the expectations of a social democracy. Elections thus constitute a means whereby the local elite legitimises its control of the state apparatus (Taylor, 1991). Decalo (1992) expresses the view that multi-party democracy is an inappropriate form of government in developing countries, a sentiment echoed by President Museveni of Uganda earlier this decade (Kahl, 1993). Decalo (1992) maintains that

> competitive politics is an imported luxury neither needed nor affordable in developing countries, that can in any case devise other equally democratic structures (notably one-party democracy) more suitable to their unique circumstances. A multiplicity of political parties mainly mirrors, even politicises, existing social cleavages (ethnic, clan, regional, religious).

Given the lengthy history of segregation and apartheid, it is inevitable that race and ethnicity will play a prominent role in electoral politics in South Africa. In order to achieve success, the nation-building project of the present government will have to overcome decades of perpetuated social consciousness among the different groups of the country. It should therefore not be surprising that contemporary electoral cleavages identified in this study are closely associated with the social geography of the apartheid state. Of greater pertinence is an exploration of the dimensions of public opinion underlying the contemporary racial polarisation of the South African electorate.

Research Methodology

The data used in this chapter were generated by a national sample survey of 2 207 households throughout South Africa conducted during March 1999. The sample comprised randomly selected clusters of eight households each, stratified by nine types of enumerator areas (EAs) (Table 13.1) identified in the national census of 1996. The data were then weighted in accordance with the numbers of households in the EA concerned. The resultant weighted data set was adjusted marginally to replicate the national distribution of population by race and province.

Statistical correlations between the responses to questions about several issues were calculated, and aggregated indices of satisfaction were determined for the respondents in each province by a living standard measure (LSM) and by racial category. These were then compared with actual election results in each province.

Table 13.1: March 1999 survey sample stratification

Enumerator area type	Number of households
Rural former homelands	655
Urban informal settlements	136
Hostels and hotels	160
Urban former coloured areas	184
Urban former Indian areas	48
Urban former black townships	481
Non-metropolitan urban former white areas	105
Metropolitan former white areas	208
Rural areas excluding former homelands	230
Total	2 207

Political Parties in South Africa

Political parties endeavour, using politically "correct" terminology, to encapsulate the needs and priorities of the segments of the electorate that they perceive to be their constituencies. The major parties in South Africa made concerted efforts to attract votes from beyond the bounds of their historical race or ethnic support bases. Thus the African National Congress (ANC) emphasised non-racialism in order to attract whites and the Democratic Party (DP) stressed the importance of merit-based good quality governance without regard to race. Similarly the New National Party (NNP) made frequent reference to the racial diversity of its support base, as did the Inkatha Freedom Party (IFP) and the United Democratic Movement (UDM) to inter-ethnic co-operation. The African Christian

Democratic Party (ACDP) stressed the importance of morality and Christian family values irrespective of race.

Not surprisingly, the election manifestos of the major political parties reflected a broad consensus about the importance of building a strong and united nation. Policies that favoured the poor and disadvantaged components of the population dominated the goals of most parties. Only after careful study is the reader able to discern policy differences in relation to tackling the national priority issues of job creation and crime prevention. The average voter would be hard-pressed to differentiate between parties committed to large-scale national public works employment creation programmes, the stimulation of entrepreneurship, the privatisation of state assets or a system of monetary vouchers exchangeable for vocational training. In terms of the fight against crime, nuances of approach relative to the control of the security sector, the treatment of sentenced criminals and the effective operationalisation of the justice system are similarly absent from the popular consciousness. It is likely that policy awareness is dictated by media sound bites and electioneering slogans. Most voters would conceptualise the parties in terms of simplistic phrases such as "Working together for change" (ANC), "Fight back against corruption" (DP), "Partnership is the only option" (UDM), "Make South Africa governable" (IFP), "Hang rapists and murderers" (NNP) and "Restoring order to the nation" (ACDP).

South African Public Opinion

Pre-election public opinion throughout South Africa reflected a range of apparently contradictory opinions about various national issues. Only one-quarter of the electorate was satisfied with the economic situation and only one in ten thought that the government had the crime situation under control. Not surprisingly therefore, 41% felt that the creation of employment should be the government's top priority and 32% felt that fighting crime should have number one priority status (Table 13.2).

Nevertheless, more than half said that they were satisfied with the way the country was being governed and that race relations had improved in South Africa since the April 1994 election. Most encouraging to the government was that two-thirds of the adult population expressed trust or strong trust in it.

The Economy

Opinions about the national economy varied substantially from province to province. The March 1999 survey showed that satisfaction with the general economic situation in South Africa ranged from only 11% in KwaZulu-Natal to 40% in Mpumalanga. Satisfaction levels (with the general economic situation in South Africa) in the three provinces with large metropolitan populations (KwaZulu-Natal, the Western Cape and Gauteng) were all lower than the national average of 23% (Table 13.2). The electorates of the economic core areas of the country were thus more dissatisfied with the state of the economy than were those of the economically peripheral regions.

A slightly higher proportion (28%) (Table 13.2) indicated satisfaction with the financial situations of their own households. Again, however, KwaZulu-Natal and the Western Cape registered below average levels of satisfaction, in this case together with the population of the Free State. Gauteng respondents were, on the other hand, slightly more satisfied than average in respect of their household finances. This was not surprising, given the province's below average rate of unemployment in relation to other provinces.[1]

Nearly one in five adults felt that government policies during the preceding twelve months had been beneficial to the economy of the country. This proportion was as low as one in ten in KwaZulu-Natal, with similarly low approval of the impact of economic policies in the Northern Cape, Northern Province and Western Cape.

Lower than average proportions living in the Western Cape and Gauteng felt that employment creation should be prioritised by the government. This is probably attributable to the relatively low levels of unemployment in those two provinces. In contrast, more than two-thirds of people in the (relatively poor) Northern Province mentioned job creation as top priority (Table 13.2).

Table 13.2: Public opinion on key issues in SA by province, March 1999

	Opinion	EC	FS	GT	KZN	MP	NC	NP	NW	WC	Total
Economy	Satisfied with general economic situation in SA*	32	18	20	11	40	30	33	29	16	23
Economy	Satisfied with financial situation: own household*	31	20	31	20	37	41	32	32	26	28
Economy	Government policies in last 12 months have had a good effect on the SA economy*	32	21	23	10	26	11	12	22	14	19
Jobs	Job creation should be the top national priority	38	36	30	42	52	39	68	50	28	41
Crime	Government is in full control of crime situation*	25	3	4	7	12	4	13	6	3	9
Crime	Fighting crime should be the top national priority	40	32	44	28	23	26	13	21	41	32
Gover-nance	Satisfied with the way the country is being governed*	71	63	46	32	80	58	76	69	26	53
Gover-nance	Trust or strong trust in the national government*	84	72	59	50	83	76	88	84	46	66
Race	Race relations improved since April 1994*	55	49	50	49	83	42	85	64	31	55
Race	Racial tensions against people like me decreased since April 1994*	50	52	47	41	82	34	84	69	26	52
	Satisfaction Index*	47	37	35	27	55	37	53	47	23	38
	Satisfaction ranking	3	6	7	8	1	5	2	4	9	-

* Average percentage of the eight satisfaction levels asterisked in the table.

The Crime Situation

A small minority (less than one in ten people) was of the view that the government was in full control of the crime situation. Lowest levels of confidence occurred in the Western Cape, Northern Cape, Gauteng and Free State, where 4% or less felt the government had full control over crime (Table 13.2). Inexplicably, the Eastern Cape was an exception, where 25% of the population felt that the government was in full control of the crime situation.

Overall, one-third (32%) of the population felt that fighting crime should be accorded top priority by the government. However, in three provinces the proportion was substantially higher. In Gauteng, the Western Cape and Eastern Cape, larger proportions prioritised the crime situation over job creation as the government's number one priority.

Governance

In spite of the aforementioned concerns about the economy and the crime situation, more than half (53%) of the population expressed satisfaction with the manner in which the country was being governed (March 1999). However, provincial variations were marked, with only one-quarter of those in the Western Cape and one-third in KwaZulu-Natal expressing satisfaction. A slightly lower than average proportion (46%) of satisfied citizens was also to be found in Gauteng. In contrast, more than three-quarters of the population of Mpumalanga and the Northern Province were either satisfied or very satisfied with national governance.

A similarly surprising finding of the survey was that two-thirds of the population had either strong trust or trust in the national government. In the Northern Province this proportion was a massive 88%, with the Eastern Cape and North West close behind at the 84% level. Once again, residents of the metropolitan provinces, namely the Western Cape, KwaZulu-Natal and to a lesser extent Gauteng, were less likely to be satisfied with national governance (Table 13.2).

A previous HSRC survey (November 1998) found that two-thirds of South African adults agreed with the statement that "democracy is always preferable to any other system of government". The attitudinal differences between the races were less significant than the differences between those respondents with higher versus lower levels of education. Among both blacks and whites, more education correlated positively with support for democracy (Alence, 1998). In conjunction with the high levels of satisfaction with and trust in the government, this sentiment bodes well for the country's new democratic system.

Race Relations

Respondents were asked whether they thought that relations between the different races of South Africa had improved since the first democratic election of April 1994. More than half (55%) replied in the affirmative and more than eight in ten in Mpumalanga and the Northern Province felt that this was the case. However, only three in ten in the Western Cape thought that race relations had improved. This may be attributable to relatively minor improvements in race relations in the traditionally more liberal politics of the Western Cape, compared with other provinces. A similar pattern emerged when respondents were asked more specifically whether they thought that racial tensions "against people like you" had decreased since April 1994. Just over half (52%) said that there had been an improvement, with much higher proportions holding this view in the Northern Province (84%) and Mpumalanga (82%). Again, only 26% of the Western Cape population felt this way (Table 13.2).

Overall Satisfaction

Different overall levels of satisfaction emerged in each province. Satisfaction ranged from a level of 55% in Mpumalanga to only 23% in the Western Cape. Ironically three of the top provinces (Mpumalanga, Northern Province and Eastern Cape) constitute the poorest in the country, whereas the bottom three (Western Cape, KwaZulu-Natal and Gauteng) have the highest levels of economic activity and wealth (Figure 13.1). This suggests that the ANC government's deliberate targeting of the poor in its economic policies since 1994 has met with success in the perception of the electorate. At another level, however, the distribution of levels of satisfaction was largely a reflection of the racial distribution of the South African population. Satisfaction levels were generally highest in provinces with the greatest proportion of black residents and lowest where other races comprised larger proportions of the population. The only exception to this pattern was KwaZulu-Natal, where isiZulu speakers comprise the vast majority of the population. Nationally, the correlation between ranked satisfaction indices and ranked percentage black population in a province was strongly positive (0,8). Conversely, non-black population and satisfaction index by provincial ranking correlated strongly negatively (-0,7).

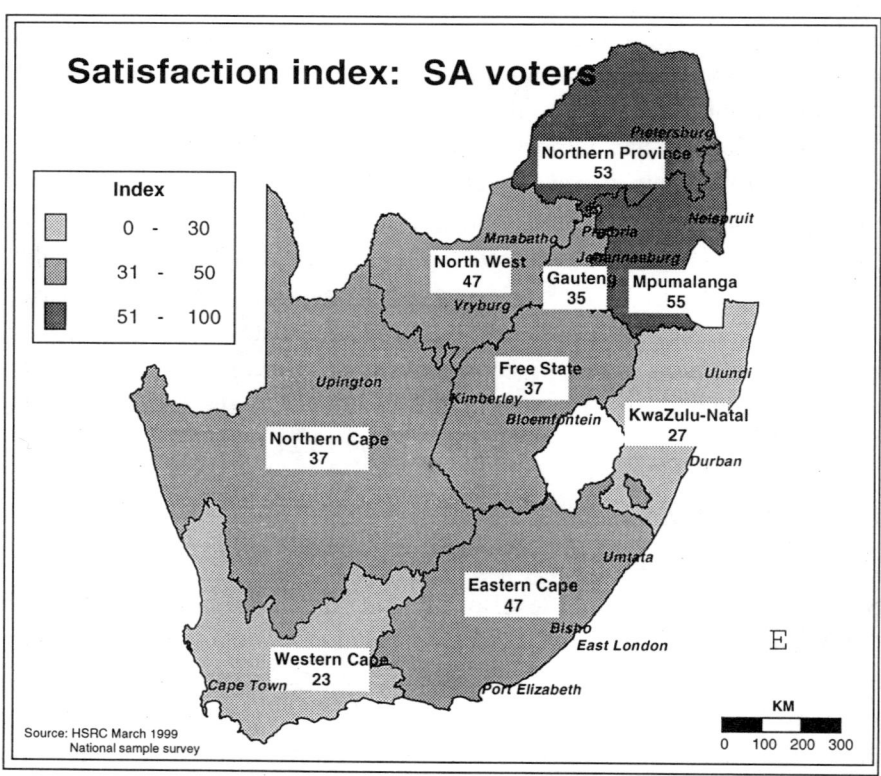

Figure 13.1: Satisfaction index: SA voters

The Effect of Race and Standard of Living

Given the apartheid history of South Africa, political opinion and voting behaviour could be expected to reflect the cleavages not only of race and ethnicity but also of living standard. Regional patterns in levels of satisfaction could thus be expected to be mirrors of socio-economic differences.

In order to test the hypothesis that regional differences are only significant because of the geographical distribution of races in the country, the satisfaction indices for each race group were calculated using the same methodology as in the previous section of this chapter. Among the black population, the national satisfaction index was 45, much higher than that for the other three races. This nevertheless represents a decline since the euphoric months shortly after the 1994 election when Møller (1994) found that 80% of blacks expressed satisfaction about their lives (albeit using different questions). Similarly, 86% indicated that they were happy in 1994.

The relatively high level of satisfaction among blacks in March 1999 was not uniform across all nine provinces, however. Mpumalanga (60) and the Northern Province (54) scored highest and KwaZulu-Natal (28) was at the bottom end of the satisfaction scale. This is indicative of the relevance of regional politics in accounting for variations in public opinion, regardless of race (Table 13.3).

White satisfaction was highest in the Eastern Cape (36), significantly more so than the national average index of only 15. This constitutes a drastic decline since 1988 and 1994, when 82% and 78% respectively said that they were satisfied with their lives (Møller, 1994). In 1999, white satisfaction was lowest in the Northern Province, where black satisfaction was highest. Whites in that peripheral region of the country are historically the most politically conservative and have arguably experienced the greatest paradigm shift since the inception of the new democratically elected government in 1994.[2] That component of the white electorate was the only one where the majority even voted against the initial liberalisation of the constitution in 1983. However, the rank correlation between white and black satisfaction levels was only weakly negative overall (rS= 0,207).

347

Table 13.3: Satisfaction level by race and province

Satisfaction level by race		EC	FS	GT	KN	MP	NC	NP	NW	WC	Total
Black	Satisfaction index	49	42	46	28	60	53	54	50	49	45
	Provincial rank	5	8	7	9	1	3	2	3	6	–
White	Satisfaction index	36	5	14	22	13	12	4	14	11	15
	Provincial rank	1	8	4	2	5	6	9	3	7	–
Coloured	Satisfaction index	40	–	29	–	–	35	–	–	20	25
	Provincial rank	1	–	3	–	–	2	–	–	4	–
Indian	Satisfaction index	–	–	16	–	–	–	–	–	–	14
	Provincial rank	1	–	2	1	–	–	–	–	–	–
Total population	Satisfaction index	47	37	35	27	55	37	53	47	23	38
	Provincial rank	3	6	7	8	1	5	2	4	9	–

Blacks were thus not necessarily most satisfied where whites were least satisfied, and vice versa.

Like whites, coloured people were most satisfied in the Eastern Cape (40). Coloureds were least satisfied where the largest proportion of this group is domiciled, namely the Western Cape (20). In the case of the small Indian population, those in KwaZulu-Natal (16) were more satisfied than those in Gauteng (4) (Table 13.3). These are the only two provinces where South African Indians live in significant numbers. These intraracial differences between provinces further illustrate that region is a determinant of public opinion, acting independently of race.

If race is replaced with a different social indicator, namely standard of living, a broader picture emerges. A living standard measure (LSM) was derived from a set of 19 questions asked in March 1999 in respect of lifestyle (Table 13.4). For the high LSM group, the national average satisfaction index was 31. The Northern Province population in this group was most satisfied (50) and the Western Cape (24) least satisfied. Overall, the medium-level LSM group was generally more satisfied (44) than the high-level group. Mpumalanga residents in this category indicated the highest level (66) of satisfaction and, again, those in the Western Cape the lowest level (22) (Table 13.5). Living standard group categories were high, medium and low. These comprised of 24%, 38% and 38% of the population respectively (Table 13.5).

Among the low-LSM group, average satisfaction was marginally lower (40) than the medium LSM group (44). The satisfaction indices (in the low LSM group) ranged from 51 in the Northern Province to only 20 in KwaZulu-Natal, with the Western Cape only marginally more satisfied, at 21 (Table 13.5) (in the low LSM group).

Thus, controlling for the effects of living standard, the broad pattern of satisfaction across the country remained the same. The residents of Mpumalanga and the Northern Province across all living standard groups were generally more satisfied than those living elsewhere in the country, especially those in the Western Cape and KwaZulu-Natal.

Table 13.4: Indicators used to determine value of Living Standard Measure (LSM)

Household possession of appliances:	Respondent personally:
• fridge or freezer • polisher or vacuum cleaner • hi-fi or music centre • television • microwave oven • washing machine	• does household shopping at supermarkets • shops at supermarkets
Household has:	**Respondent personally:** • has insurance policy/ies • has a bank account, ATM card or credit card
• electricity • hot running water • a domestic servant • at least one car • a flush toilet • buys dishwashing liquid	• has account or credit card at retail store **Household lives:** • in a hut • in a rural area

The Resultant Electoral Geography

The foregoing detail points to a particular national distribution of public satisfaction levels. Residents of Mpumalanga and the Northern Province were consistently the most satisfied and those living in the Western Cape and KwaZulu-Natal were the least satisfied. It is therefore no surprise that the distribution of support for the different political parties in the 1999 election mirrored this pattern of public opinion. The pattern was also predicted by the high correlation between satisfaction and the expressed intention to vote for the ANC.

The March 1999 survey data revealed a correlation of 0,463 between the overall satisfaction index and the intention to vote for the ruling ANC. In contrast, there were negative correlations between satisfaction index and the intention to support an opposition party. The correlations were more strongly negative for the NNP (-0,212) and the DP (-0,195) than for the IFP (-0,123), UDM (-0,042) and ACDP (-0,064), however

Table 13.5: Satisfaction level by LSM and province

Satisfaction level by standard of living		EC	FS	GT	KN	MP	NC	NP	NW	WC	Total
HIGH 24% 99% electricity 94% refrigerator 58% insurance	Satisfaction index	44	30	31	29	39	27	50	40	24	31
	Provincial rank	2	6	5	7	4	8	1	3	9	–
MEDIUM 38% 80% electricity 52% refrigerator 13% insurance	Satisfaction index	51	43	42	29	66	46	55	55	22	44
	Provincial rank	4	6	7	8	1	5	3	2	9	–
LOW 38% 19% electricity 9% refrigerator 1% insurance	Satisfaction index	44	37	36	20	50	31	51	42	21	40
	Provincial rank	3	5	6	9	2	7	1	4	8	–
Total population	Satisfaction index	47	37	35	27	55	37	53	47	23	38
	Provincial rank	3	6	7	8	1	5	2	4	9	–

(Table 13.6). This is indicative of a higher absence of satisfaction amongst NNP and DP supporters than among those of other opposition parties. This was corroborated by another survey in March 1999. Conducted by MarkData (Johnson, 1999), the survey found that whereas only 27% of ANC supporters felt that the government had run the country well, this was as low as only 5% among supporters of the IFP.

Table 13.6 shows that indicators of support for the ANC were satisfaction with the national economy and the government's economic policy, trust in the national government, positive views about race relations and racial tension and satisfaction with the way the country was being governed. In contrast, there were much lower levels of correlation between ANC support and satisfaction with household financial situations and views about the crime situation. ANC supporters also demonstrated a much stronger interest in the prioritisation of employment creation (48%) than in fighting against crime (26%). The implication here is that although supporters of the ANC were generally unhappy about crime and unemployment, they trusted the government, were satisfied with the way the country was being governed and felt that race relations were improving.

The intention to vote for the DP, IFP, NNP, UDM or ACDP correlated negatively with satisfaction with the economy, trust in the national government, the crime situation and national governance. Supporters of the DP and NNP tended to favour the prioritisation of the fight against crime (67% and 40% respectively) above employment creation (14% and 30%). The other three parties were more in favour of employment creation as a top national priority than fighting crime.

Thus, in spite of the high levels of dissatisfaction with the national economy and with the crime situation, the majority of those surveyed in March 1999 said that they would have voted for the ruling party had the election been held at that time. Whereas more than three-fifths of South African adults were dissatisfied or very dissatisfied with the economic situation in the country and with their own household financial situation, 56% said that they would have voted for the ANC in March 1999. The survey revealed that even amongst ANC supporters, 58% and 61% respec-

Table 13.6: Correlation between intention to vote for a party and opinion about each issue*

Party	Satisfied with general economic situation in South Africa at present	Satisfied with financial situation of household at present	Government policies have had a good effect on general economic situation in past year	Trust or strong trust in the national government	Government is in full control of the crime situation	Race relations have improved in South Africa since April 1994	Racial tension against people like me has diminished since April 1994	Satisfied with the way South Africa is being governed at present	Overall satisfaction index
ANC	,218	,088	,235	,420	,108	,273	,317	,426	,463
DP	-,096	,024	-,075	-,214	-,027	-,111	-,170	-,197	-,195
IFP	-,062	-,074	-,057	-,076	-,033	-,080	-,083	-,086	-,123
NNP	-,071	,023	-,129	-,181	-,040	-,149	-,159	-,224	-,212
UDM	-,019	-,039	-,023	-,008	,000	-,024	-,033	-,034	-,042
ACDP	-,023	,037	-,046	-,024	-,027	-,085	-,066	-,064	-,064

* Pearson's correlation coefficients, all significant at the 0,01 level (two-tailed).

tively were dissatisfied or very dissatisfied with the economic situation of the country and with their own household financial situation. Clearly, views about the economy and its impact at the national or household level did not affect political allegiance to the ANC in March 1999.

Distribution of actual votes cast in favour of each of the parties on 2 June 1999 largely reflected the range of public opinion as determined in the March 1999 survey. Seven provinces were won by the ANC with large majorities and two were only narrowly lost to opposition parties. The latter were the localities of the most dissatisfied sectors of the electorate, namely the Western Cape and KwaZulu-Natal.

The province that expressed the highest average level of satisfaction, the Northern Province, rewarded the ANC with the highest proportion of votes cast (89%) (Table 13.7). This was closely followed by the second most satisfied province, namely Mpumalanga, with an 85% level of support for the ruling party. In the Western Cape and KwaZulu-Natal, the proportions of votes cast for the ANC were only 43% and 40% respectively (Table 13.7). A strong positive correlation (rS=0,82) between support for the ANC and the satisfaction index was thus evident.

An alternative methodology of depicting the relative electoral successes of the different political parties is the application of the location quotient (LQ). This indicates the degree to which support for a party in each of the nine provinces exceeds or is less than the national average. Relative provincial strongholds for each party are thereby easily identifiable.

The ANC achieved LQs of well in excess of one, in five of the nine provinces. The exceptions were Gauteng, the Northern Cape, Western Cape and KwaZulu-Natal. The latter all recorded lower than average levels of satisfaction (Table 13.8). The DP's relative strongholds were the metropolitan provinces of Gauteng and the Western Cape. The IFP's support was highly concentrated only in KwaZulu-Natal, where it achieved more votes than predicted by pre-election polls (Johnson, 1999) in spite of lower than average levels of voter registration (Alence & O'Donovan, 1999). The very low satisfaction index for the province accounts for this large vote against the ANC. For the NNP, the Western

Table 13.7: Proportion of votes cast for each party (national ballot) by province, June 1999

Party	EC	FS	GT	KN	MP	NC	NP	NW	WC	Total
ACDP	1,11	0,92	1,17	1,82	1,10	1,61	1,09	0,90	3,11	1,43
ANC	73,91	81,03	68,16	39,77	85,26	64,40	89,30	80,53	42,62	66,35
AEB	0,18	0,39	0,29	0,20	0,38	0,51	0,37	0,47	0,19	0,29
AZAPO	0,13	0,18	0,14	0,15	0,09	0,38	0,49	0,11	0,06	0,17
DP	6,38	5,87	17,69	9,76	4,97	5,78	1,69	3,72	14,18	9,56
FA	0,19	0,83	0,85	0,30	0,75	0,70	0,37	0,56	0,55	0,54
IFP	0,30	0,45	3,54	40,45	1,41	0,44	0,32	0,45	0,20	8,58
MF	0,03	0,03	0,03	1,45	0,04	0,06	0,04	0,03	0,08	0,30
NNP	3,32	5,00	3,85	3,96	2,37	22,49	1,72	2,38	34,38	6,87
PAC	1,00	1,03	0,69	0,28	0,61	0,64	1,21	0,68	0,50	0,71
GPGP	0,03	0,03	0,06	0,07	0,02	0,03	0,03	0,02	0,18	0,06
SOPA	0,03	0,08	0,05	0,09	0,05	0,05	0,08	0,06	0,02	0,06
UCDP	0,12	0,73	0,21	0,09	0,21	0,25	0,10	7,48	0,11	0,78
UDM	12,88	1,65	2,15	1,29	1,40	0,94	2,57	1,42	3,07	3,42
VF/FF	0,31	1,75	1,10	0,20	1,30	1,59	0,53	1,16	0,66	0,80
AITUP	0,08	0,04	0,03	0,11	0,04	0,12	0,08	0,04	0,09	0,07
Total	100,00	100,00	100,00	100,00	100,00	100,00	100,00	100,00	100,00	100,00

Table 13.8: Location quotient of each political party by province, June 1999

Party	EC	FS	GT	KN	MP	NC	NP	NW	WC
ACDP	0,78	0,64	0,82	1,27	0,77	1,13	0,76	0,63	2,17
ANC	1,11	1,22	1,03	0,60	1,28	0,97	1,35	1,21	0,64
AEB	0,63	1,33	1,02	0,69	1,30	1,77	1,35	1,62	0,67
AZAPO	0,73	1,03	0,84	0,90	0,55	2,21	2,87	0,64	0,34
DP	0,67	0,61	1,85	1,02	0,52	0,60	0,18	0,39	1,48
FA	0,35	1,52	1,56	0,56	1,38	1,29	0,69	1,04	1,02
IFP	0,03	0,05	0,41	4,71	0,16	0,05	0,04	0,05	0,02
MF	0,11	0,11	0,11	4,81	0,12	0,18	0,13	0,09	0,26
NNP	0,48	0,73	0,56	0,58	0,35	3,27	0,25	0,35	5,00
PAC	1,42	1,46	0,97	0,40	0,87	0,90	1,71	0,96	0,71
GPGP	0,55	0,45	1,02	1,15	0,38	0,52	0,60	0,43	3,09
SOPA	0,60	1,35	0,82	1,58	0,81	0,90	1,36	1,01	0,43
UCDP	0,15	0,93	0,26	0,12	0,27	0,32	0,13	9,53	0,14
UDM	3,76	0,48	0,63	0,38	0,41	0,28	0,75	0,42	0,90
VF/FF	0,39	2,20	1,38	0,26	1,63	2,00	0,67	1,45	0,82
AITUP	1,20	0,58	0,47	1,63	0,58	1,78	1,16	0,60	1,38

Cape and the Northern Cape were the two strongest provinces, and for the UDM, only the Eastern Cape yielded an LQ of more than one. The ACDP achieved above average proportions of the total vote in the Western Cape, KwaZulu-Natal and the Northern Cape (Table 13.8).

Conclusion

At one level, provincial variations in the degree of support for each political party in South Africa's June 1999 election were largely but not exclusively attributable to the spatial distribution of the black and white sectors of the electorate. However, this chapter has shown that black voters were not necessarily most satisfied about the economic and crime situation in provinces where white voters were least satisfied, and vice versa. Similarly, when sub-divided into three standard of living categories, there was no clear correlation between voter satisfaction with the government and standard of living across the provinces. To portray the election results only as a racial or ethnic census is therefore reductionist, owing to the obfuscatory effects of standard of living cleavages that cut across racial divides.

What emerges most clearly from this chapter is the regional differentiation in levels of voter trust in and satisfaction with the national government and the resultant variations in support given to the ANC in the June 1999 election. The electorates of the provinces of Mpumalanga, the Northern Province and North West were in most respects more satisfied with the government than those of the other provinces. Likewise, voters in KwaZulu-Natal and the Western Cape expressed consistently lower levels of satisfaction than the rest of the country. The correlation of the ranked aggregated satisfaction index for each province with the proportion of votes won by the ANC in June 1999 was, unsurprisingly, strongly positive. The high level of voter dissatisfaction in the Western Cape correlates with a population composition unlike any of the other provinces, namely a majority of coloured and white voters. In KwaZulu-Natal, on the other hand, most voters are black speakers of isiZulu. In both cases, surveys found repeatedly that the voting behaviour of most members of these groupings could be expected to constitute opposition to the ANC.

Broadly, support for the ruling ANC in South Africa has been shown to be unrelated to perceptions about its degree of control over the crime situation in the country or to satisfaction with the economic situation at either the national or the household level. Although job creation and fighting crime were mentioned most frequently as top national priorities, concerns about high rates of unemployment and crime appear to have been sublimated in the minds of most voters when casting their votes in the election. Rather, a wide-spread sense of trust or strong trust in the government, satisfaction with the way it has governed the country and a perception that race relations have improved since April 1994 account for the high proportion of votes cast in its favour on 2 June 1999.

Notes

[1] The unemployment rate in Gauteng was only 17% in comparison with a national average of 29% (Central Statistical Service, 1996).

[2] Bornman (1999) found that white Afrikaners were the South African ethnic group most likely to say that they belonged to a unique cultural community (89%). Most whites (92%) in the Northern Province are Afrikaans speaking.

References

Alence, R. (1998), *Race, Class and Democratic Consolidation in South Africa: A Preliminary Analysis of Attitudinal Data*, HSRC paper read at the South African Sociological Association congress, Rand Afrikaans University, Johannesburg, 30 June-1 July.

Alence, R. & O'Donovan, M. (1999), *If South Africa's Second Democratic Election had been Held in March 1999: A Simulation of Participation and Party Support Patterns*, Human Sciences Research Council, Pretoria.

Archer, J.C. & Shelley, F.M. (1986), *American Electoral Mosaics*, American Association of Geographers, Washington D.C.

Bond, P. (1999), "Zimbabwe: Another Liberation?", *Indicator South Africa*, vol. 16, no. 1, pp. 95-103.

Bornman, E. (1999), *Groepsidentifisering in 'n Post-Apartheid Suid-Afrika*, Human Sciences Research Council, Pretoria.

Central Statistical Service (1996), *Living in South Africa: Selected Findings of the 1995 October Household Survey*, Pretoria.

Decalo, S. (1992), "The Process, Prospects and Constraints of Democratization in Africa", *African Affairs*, vol. 91, pp. 7-35.

Dunn, J. (1980), *Political Obligation in its Historical Context: Essays in Political Theory*, Cambridge University Press, Cambridge.

Hennayake, S.K. (1992), "Interactive Ethnonationalism: An Alternative Explanation of Minority Ethnonationalism", *Political Geography*, vol. 11, pp. 526-549.

Johnson, R.W. (1999), "Gains and Losses at the Grassroots", *Briefing*, vol. 15, pp. 2-7.

Johnston, R.J., Pattie, C.J. & Allsopp, J.G. (1988), *A Nation Dividing? The Electoral Map of Great Britain 1979-1987*, Longman, London.

Kahl, H. (1993), "Dilemma Over Democracy", *The Star*, November, Johannesburg.

Lipset, S.M. & Rokkan, S. (1967), *Party Systems and Voter Alignments: Cross-National Perspectives*, Free Press, New York.

Møller, V. (1994), "Post-election Euphoria", *Indicator South Africa*, vol. 12, no. 1, pp. 27-32.

Myers, G.A. (1998), *Introductory Human Geography, Democratization and Regionalism in Tanzania*, Unpublished monograph, University of Kansas.

Nairn, T. (1977), *The Break-up of Britain: Crisis and Neo-nationalism*, NLB, London.

Rule, S.P. (1995), "Electoral Trends in Botswana: A Geographical Perspective", *Africa Insight*, vol. 25, no. 1, pp. 21-30.

Rule, S.P. (1996), "Zambian Politics and Eastern Sectionalism", *Africa Insight*, vol. 26, no. 4, pp. 363-374.

Taylor, P.J. (1991), "Extending Electoral Geography", Ch. 17, in Johnston, R.J., Shelley F.M. & Taylor, P. *Developments in Electoral Geography*, pp. 257-271, Routledge, London.

Weakliem, D.L. & Biggert, R. (1999), "Regional and Political Opinion in the Contemporary United States", *Social Forces*, vol. 77, no. 3, pp. 863-886.

Appendix 13.1:   South Africa's 1999 national election results

Voting totals per party per province (national assembly)

Party	EC	FS	GT	KN	MP	NC	NP	NW	WC	TOTAL
ACDP	24 344	10 031	43 359	53 799	12 415	5 295	18 151	11 774	49 807	228 975
ANC	1 617 329	887 091	2 527 676	1 176 926	962 260	211 206	1 483 199	1 052 895	682 748	10 601 330
AEB	3 996	4 228	10 922	5 878	4 256	1 686	6 095	6 130	3 101	46 292
AZAPO	2 743	1 919	5 293	4 525	1 059	1 237	8 121	1 426	934	27 257
DP	139 520	64 262	655 883	288 738	56 114	18 952	28 116	48 665	227 087	1 527 337
FA	4 097	9 041	31 386	8 984	8 481	2 292	6 198	7 376	8 849	86 704
IFP	6 511	4 938	131 296	1 196 955	15 868	1 448	5 389	5 929	3 143	1 371 477
MF	750	351	1 271	43 026	401	182	653	362	1 281	48 277
NNP	72 639	54 769	142 749	117 107	26 779	73 766	28 559	31 072	550 775	1 098 215
PAC	21 978	11 300	25 412	8 414	6 929	2 083	20 070	8 878	8 061	113 125
GPGP	693	285	2 179	1 952	246	98	570	320	2 850	9 193
SOPA	741	838	1 718	2 658	516	167	1 285	750	389	9 062
UCDP	2 528	8 019	7 619	2 671	2 393	830	1 684	97 755	1 781	125 280
UDM	281 748	18 073	79 627	38 080	15 807	3 092	42 643	18 574	49 146	546 790
VF/FF	6 822	19 210	40 782	6 044	14 687	5 229	8 835	15 106	10 502	127 217
AITUP	1 745	421	1 146	3 206	437	387	1 281	520	1 468	10 611
Total	2 188 184	1 094 776	3 708 318	2 958 963	1 128 648	327 950	1 660 849	1 307 532	1 601 922	15 977 142

Chapter 14

Democracy and Governance in Transition

Yvonne Muthien, Meshack Khosa and Bernard Magubane

Introduction

The first term of ANC-led government witnessed dramatic changes in the transition from apartheid to post-apartheid society. This transition, which brought back the country from the brink of civil war through mature and courageous leadership, provides an insightful case study of political transformation. The end of the first year of office (June 2000) of the second democratically elected government provides a fine opportunity to assess the state of democratic consolidation and democratic governance in South Africa as well as examine the subtle shifts between the Mandela and Mbeki reigns.

Institutionalisation of Democracy

Political exclusion, social discrimination and lack of respect for human dignity and individual civil liberties, all based on racial prejudice, characterised the authoritarian institutional and political culture of apartheid society. The sustainability of democracy in the wake of such a culture depends on the ability and willingness of citizens to "trust" democracy and its institutions and political leaders to adopt democratic behaviour, a process often referred to as "habituation" to democracy. What is South Africa's status in respect of such habituation?

The results of the March 1999 Democracy and Governance Survey of the Human Sciences Research Council (HSRC) indicate that 74% of the respondents supported democracy, while only 7% supported authoritarianism. The respondents were also largely positive about the use of institutional means to express dissatisfaction. In fact, 48% indicated that they would vote differently if they were dissatisfied with their current situation and 28% indicated that they would petition the relevant authorities, while 10% indicated that they would resort to violent means (Muthien, 1999a). (Elsewhere in this publication Khosa (Chapter 10) provides evidence of democratic consolidation and the increasing legitimacy of governance in the eyes of the public.)

International Comparison

In a comparative study of support for democracy in middle-income countries with similar political transitions, especially since the 1980s, South Africa ranked the third highest with 74% support for democracy (Muthien, 1999a). Only Uruguay rated significantly higher with 86% support for democracy. Brazil, with a similar socio-economic profile as South Africa, showed 50% support for democracy, while Poland, a more recently established democracy, showed a low 31% support in 1992 (Muthien, 1999a).

Expectations of Economic Democracy

The degree to which democratic states improve the material well being of their citizens plays a key role in the consolidation of democracy. Hence the main challenge for the new South African government is to substantially improve the material well being of the impoverished majority. The results of surveys of public expectations of economic prospects in South Africa reveal interesting patterns. Public optimism by income group indicates that the richest 20% are pessimistic, while the middle and poor income groups are optimistic. Although the poorest and second poorest groups fall below the poverty line, they nevertheless remain optimistic. The second poorest group shows the highest level of optimism (43%). This group is most likely to be the beneficiaries of improved service delivery through the Reconstruction and Development Programme (Khosa, 2000).

The continued inequality and material deprivation in South Africa prompt us to revisit current debates on state-civil society relations, in particular in relation to debates on economic democracy. These debates seem to highlight that development in highly unequal societies demands a democratic state that is strong and extended, and committed to a clear developmental trajectory, a notion which rests somewhat uncomfortably with the values of liberal democracy (Glassman & Samatar, 1999; White, 1995).

Race and Democracy

South Africa has emerged from the extremities of a history in which access to material wealth, basic opportunities and services, and degrees of human dignity were defined by one's racial classification. The legacy of this history continues to be reflected in public attitudes to key national issues. According to various surveys, whites are much less satisfied with government performance than Africans. Trust in government reveals similar racial divisions. Whites are less inclined to trust government, whereas government enjoys the trust of 60% of Africans. Khosa (Chapter 10) elsewhere in this book provided a comprehensive assessment of changing perceptions within the context of democratic consolidation in South Africa.

The support bases of several political parties also reveal historical racial patterns. For instance, African National Congress support is overwhelmingly black, while that of the Democratic Party is largely white. However, some interesting shifts have occurred since 1994. In the case of the New National Party, whose support base was largely white and Afrikaner before 1994, coloured support eclipsed white support in the 1994 election, and Indian support eclipsed coloured support during the 1999 election. In the 1999 election coloured support was roughly equally divided between the African National Congress and the New National Party. Thus the traditional racial support bases of political parties have begun to shift (see Chapter 12 in this book by Stephen Rule).

The social identity and social movement studies conducted by the HSRC reveal that class factors or socio-economic status is an increasingly important determinant of satisfaction with living standards, employment, housing, citizen safety, health care delivery and government performance. On a composite score of satisfaction levels, the trends indicate that as living standards increase, levels of dissatisfaction decline, irrespective of race.

According to Habermas (in Benhabib, 1996) democracy requires the co-ordination of divergent interests in society and the creation of solidarity among citizens. Although all societies are complex, multiple and hetero-geneous by nature, historical patterns of polarisation around race, language, etc. can solidify group identities within a particular society. Democratic politics thus need to recognise and accommodate difference. *Respect for diversity and racial tolerance should be a test of the maturity of a democracy.*

However, democratic politics in South Africa also need to attend to continued poverty among the majority of the population, as this constitutes the single greatest threat to South Africa's democracy. This realisation calls for the deracialisation of our society in material terms, a change in the traditional patterns of racial identification and the creation of a society where merit, human capacity and equality of opportunity, rather than skin colour, determine the dignity of the individual. *For as long as race coincides with inequality, democracy cannot flourish.*

Gender and Democracy

A vast body of feminist literature (Benhabib, 1996; Shanley & Narayan, 1997; Yuval-Davis, 1997) has examined the naturalised (socially con-structed) roles of women in the biological, cultural and civil sphere. Based on the naturalisation of their roles, they often have lesser access than men do to power, material well being, resources and public institutions. Gender equality is therefore a central challenge in creating a mature democracy.

Because women constituted the majority of the registered voting population in South Africa, their votes were clearly sought after in the 1999 election. But did political parties know what women wanted? According to the results of the Democracy and Governance opinion poll, women's priorities in order of preference were equal decision making, family well being, education, women's rights, job opportunities and personal safety. This prioritisation clearly has implications for policy institutions and government decision making.

The new democracy has made great strides in levelling the playing field: women have achieved formal constitutional rights to gender equality and gender advocacy institutions have been established, such as the Commission for Gender Equality, the Office for the Status of Women in the President's Office and the parliamentary Joint Monitoring Committee on Improvement of Quality of Life and Status of Women. Furthermore, since 1994 the African National Congress has pursued a quota policy of 30% representation of women in Parliament, although opposition parties have not followed suit. However, much remains to be done in respect of gender equality in the sphere of state-market-family relations, access to employment and service/benefit opportunities (Muthien, 1999b).

Elections and Democracy

The success of the 1999 election augurs well for democratic consolidation and electoral administration (Muthien, 1999b). There were, however, a number of potential threats to the second democratic election. These included racial politicking, reproducing racial stereotypes, fanning racial hatred, fear and intolerance, especially through subliminal advertising; reproducing the deep divisions of the past through violence and intimidation; and irregularities at the ballot box. The indicators that augured well for the election included the existence of a robust civil society; high levels of participation in the electoral process through high levels of voter registration and voter turnout; greater realism about the pace of delivery and change; and confidence in the electoral machinery to deliver free and fair elections.

Pulling off the first democratic election in 1994, given the scale of the operations, the tight time frames and lack of experience, remains an extraordinary feat of human resolve, dedication and bold spirit borne out of the passion to deliver freedom, justice and democracy to the entire nation. The second democratic election took place after five years of momentous changes, bold experimentation in transformation and sincere reconciliation through dealing with the atrocities of the past, all in the hope of accelerating the restoration of human dignity, respect for human rights and tolerance of diversity.

Creating a Culture of Democratic Governance

The South African constitutions of 1993 and 1996 provided for a complex set of mechanisms to institute a new state form and public institutions that portray democratic values and structures. Most of these institutions have overlapping mandates and some are underfunded. The constitutional drafters had no idea of the cost of establishing multiple levels of government, new statutory commissions and other institutions for participatory democracy.

Institutions Buttressing Democracy

The 1996 South African Constitution enshrines an elaborate array of institutions supporting constitutional democracy by serving as a check on political and administrative authority. These include the Public Protector, the Auditor-General, the Public Service Commission, the Human Rights Commission, the Commission for Gender Equality, the Independent Electoral Commission and the Commission for the Promotion and Protection of the Rights of Cultural, Religious and Linguistic Communities. Nevertheless, exercising scrutiny and setting limits on government's political power produce major strains. Indeed, the ability of these institutions to set limits on the arbitrary exercise of power is dependent on:

- their location, standing and status within the system of governance,
- the standing of their champion/guardian/protector within government, i.e. minister or president,
- the unqualified support of the legislature in the exercise of their functions,
- their level of resourcing and ability to fulfil their constitutional mandates.

Public Accountability

In a parliamentary democracy, the legislature constitutes the supreme authority as the elected representatives of "the people". The executive derives its authority from the legislature and is accountable to the legislature for its actions. As the law-making authority, the legislature assumes the role of final arbiter of government policy and has the task of balancing the diverse interests of the broader society. The effectiveness of the legislature to hold government accountable depends on the quality of the elected representatives in terms of professional expertise and direct accountability to constituencies. Both of these conditions have somewhat been compromised in South Africa with the exodus of skilled professionals from Parliament and the party electoral system. The degree of democratic accountability is further compromised by

- the complexity of modern public administration which requires technical expertise that is not always available among the lay representatives in the legislature,
- the volume, complexity and time constraints in enacting legislation, and
- the fact that legislation originates in the executive and is seldom initiated by the legislature, thereby ceding control to the executive in respect of legislation.

Specialised committees and the holding of public hearings and opening proceedings of parliamentary committees to the public, as well as the provision of research support, enhance the capacity of the legislature to scrutinise government accountability. However, the interests of governance have to be balanced with the interests of the public. Hence a robust though small and representative opposition is the best option for public scrutiny.

Public Service Accountability

The issue of public service accountability raises the perennial question: How can the public service, removed from the people through its profession and career-based structure, technocratic approach and command over resources, and hence the innate ability to dispense patronage, be made to function in a manner compatible with democracy? The history of centralised state agencies demonstrates that excessive control of public institutions does not guarantee increased effectiveness. Quite the contrary, excessive control can constrain efficient administration (Laver, 1999;

Philip, 1999). Furthermore, the creation of multiple accountability mechanisms and institutions does not in itself increase accountability.

South Africa's public administration after 1994 has evolved by condensing the following four contradictory models of state administrators: agency specialists and technocrats, civil service mandarins, political appointees and corporate managers.

Undoubtedly, a professional civil service, insulated from political power, serves democracy best. Furthermore, its distance from direct democracy in itself may strengthen accountability and limit political influence. However, the inherent problem of democratising the modern administrative state is vested in reconciling the political imperatives of public accountability with the managerial imperatives of administrative flexibility and responsiveness (Balfour, 1997; Ruscio, 1997).

The provisions of the Access to Information Act, which safeguards whistle-blowing and independent access to public information, bode well for accountability. Other central agencies of democratic accountability are the judiciary, especially the Constitutional Court, independent commissions of inquiry and an independent press. The government's discomfort with press scrutiny has been expressed in various attacks on the press, but it challenges the press in terms of fair and accurate reporting rather than challenging or threatening its right to independent inquiry. Clearly, the most demonstrable commitment to democratic accountability is vested in the subordination of political rule to constitutionality through the operation of the Constitutional Court as the ultimate safeguard and recourse of citizens when they wish to protect their individual civil rights and liberties.

Instituting Good Governance and Development

Good governance and development are based on sound policy. Hence we now take a look at the way in which policy is currently made in South Africa, the impact of the macro-economic policy and the need for the further development of the state.

The New Policy-Making Culture

A significant feature of the new culture of governance in South Africa is the proliferation of public policy-making processes and institutions. Examples of these at the local level include local development forums, local water committees, and community police forums. What these demonstrate is the replacement of top-down decision making with bottom-up decision making. However, the proliferation of consultative forums gave rise to two contradictory consequences for civil society organisations. On the one hand, because consultative bodies and other forums draw members from particular interest groups, some organisations have grown markedly. The Women's National Coalition, for example, consists of 90 organisations and 13 regional coalitions. On the other hand, consultative and policy-making institutions have lost their most competent leaders to the government, which has led to their demobilisation. The South African National Civic Organisation (SANCO), for example, only registered 5 000 members in 1997, compared to its vast membership before 1990.

Macro-Economic Policy Making

The poor record of the Growth, Employment and Redistribution (GEAR) policy to deliver on economic growth, job creation and social upliftment has led to conflict between the majority party (ANC) and its alliance partners, the Congress of South African Trade Unions (COSATU) and the South African Communist Party (SACP). GEAR implies a commitment to market-orientated economic reforms in line with what has been termed the "Washington consensus", that is, economic measures demanded by the World Bank and the International Monetary Fund. These reforms include fiscal discipline and a reduction of the budget deficit; the reallocation of state expenditure to health, education and infrastructure; tax base broadening and a reduction in marginal tax rates; the abolition of the dual exchange rate and the phasing out of exchange controls; the securement of property rights; increased deregulation, trade liberalisation and privatisation; the removal of barriers to direct foreign investment; and financial liberalisation. In short, it appears that the government has restricted its role to setting the framework for a free market economy. By the end of 1998 the ANC was forced to concede that GEAR failed to live up to its promise and the RDP was re-centred as the government's primary development agenda. This raises critical questions around the South African state's mandate to foster development. To what extent has it had an impact upon the level and distribution of resources within civil society? Although the answer is inconclusive, the outcome does not look good. The ANC government seems to have subjected itself to a global, neo-liberal orthodoxy that constrains its transformative agenda. The resultant weakened redistributive economic policy is likely to bear fruit at a slow rate if at all.

The Need for a Developmental State

The deterministic literature on path dependency (Putnam, 1993) has focused amongst others on impediments to development. These include low levels of economic growth, high levels of poverty and inequality, poor infrastructure and inequality in the global system of development. This focus has foreclosed careful scrutiny of the potential for a mutually beneficial state-civil society relationship and an activist role for the state in development. This potential has however been explored in recent debates on the developmental state, which debates highlight civil society as agents of delivery and development in public-private sector partnerships. Effective public-private sector partnerships and robust institutions of civil society are shown to be able to contribute to good governance and economic growth.

The social constructionist literature has established a relation between conditions of rapid economic growth and industrialisation on the one hand, and sound state-civil society relations on the other hand. This relation creates enabling conditions for private and community capital accumu-lation (see Evans, 1995; Samatar, 1999). Unlike the earlier state interven-tionist theories, which posited a strong, highly interventionist role for the state in the economy, the social constructionist view has centred the role of the state, but asks not only about the nature of the state but also about class, development and the societal context, as well as the fabric of civic culture and state-civil society relations.

In successful public-private co-operative ventures, state and community leaders forge equitable relations in infrastructure development and other production ventures, which relations transcend ordinary relations of subsidisation or clientelism. Thus a synergy as well as a division of labour are forged between state and civil society agents around common projects and common goals, with equal shares of responsibility and gain apportioned to the partners (see Tendler, 1997).

Although the South African state is committed to delivering development to the majority of the population, it still lacks a coherent implementable development strategy. The transitional government (1994-1999) was overwhelmed by the task of transforming state and society; hence the defining ethos of the Mandela reign was reconciliation and transformation. The Mbeki reign has introduced the ethos of the African Renaissance. Both governments have been weak on mobilising civil society behind a coherent, integrated development programme despite the rhetoric slogans. The Reconstruction and Development Programme has been left to line-function government agencies to implement. The clustering of cabinet portfolios into larger co-ordinated portfolios (committees) goes some way towards forging greater co-operation between line-function ministries in terms of service delivery and policy making. Although this has revived the prospects for efficient service delivery, it is still too early to make a judgement.

Conclusion

There is no short cut to the sustainment of democratisation (Liddle, 1999; Törnnquist, 2000). Nevertheless, South Africa has made significant strides towards the establishment and consolidation of democracy. Within the space of five years the political landscape changed for the better amid the creation of new institutions to promote and protect democracy. However, the new democratic state faces a number of other challenges:

- The need to institutionalise transformation and reform. A plethora of new policy statements in the form of White Papers and Green Papers have been issued, but in many instances the institutional infrastructure needs to be aligned with the new policy objectives. Budgetary measures also need to be introduced to finance the new programmes.

- Economic empowerment has been limited to a few beneficiaries of the transition, the so-called "transitory bourgeoisie". Hence the base of economic empowerment needs to be widened.

- Reconciliation without social justice, which includes redress and improving the material well being of the majority, holds great potential for instability. Whilst the country is well endowed in terms of democratic institutions and infrastructure, the lack of delivery on economic democracy could well jeopardise the newly founded democracy.

The sustainability of democracy and the rule of law requires that political authority and public officials accept limits to their authority, as well as subject themselves to public scrutiny, either through incentive or sanction (Weingast, 1997). Effective public scrutiny of public figures requires an informed citizenry who does not accept habitual corruption. This in turn requires a commitment to the democratic value of clean government. If the political economy of corruption becomes embedded in the social fabric of communities or localities and particular citizens become the beneficiaries of corruption, the sustainability of democracy is fundamentally compromised. Hence public education must forge a commitment to democracy and clean government as ends in themselves.

The greatest challenge for democracy in South Africa in the 21st century remains the sharp divide between rich and poor. Our democracy can only survive if this divide is minimised, and the state implements ameliorative policies to empower those who are still disadvantaged. Otherwise the growing anger of this sector of the population might very well erupt into social conflict.

References

Balfour, D. (1997), "Reforming the Public Service: The Search for a New Tradition", *Public Administration Review*, vol. 57, no. 5, Sept./Oct.

Benhabib, S. (1996), *Democracy and Difference: Contesting the Boundaries of the Political*, Princeton, Princeton University Press.

Brandy, H.E. (1999), "Contributions of Survey Research to Political Science", *Political Science and Politics*, vol. XXXIII, no. 1, pp. 47-57.

Carroll, B.W. & Carroll, T. (1999), "The Consolidation of Democracy in Mauritius", *Democratisation*, vol. 6, pp. 179-197.

Evans, P. (1995), *Embedded Autonomy: States & Industrial Transformation*, Princeton, Princeton University Press.

Glassman, J. & Samatar, A. (1999), "Development Geography and the Third World State", *Progress in Human Geography*, vol. 21, no. 2.

Habermas, J. (1996), in Benhabib, S. *Democracy and Difference: Contesting the Boundaries of the Political*, Princeton, Princeton University Press.

Human Sciences Research Council (HSRC) (1999), *Public Opinion on National Priority Issues*, Pretoria, HSRC.

Khosa, M. (ed.) (2000), *Empowerment through Service Delivery*, Pretoria, Human Sciences Research Council.

Laver, M. (1999), "Government Formation and Public Policy", *Political Science and Politics*, vol. XXXIII, no. 1, pp. 21-23.

Liddle, R.W. (1999), "Indonesia's Democratic Opening", *Government and Opposition*, vol. 34, no.1, pp. 95-116.

McHenry, D.R. Jr (2000), "Quantitative Measures of Democracy in Africa: An Assessment", *Democratisation*, vol. 7, no. 2, pp. 168-185.

Muthien, Y. (ed.) (1999a), *Democracy South Africa: Evaluating the 1999 Election*, Pretoria, Human Sciences Research Council.

Muthien, Y. (1999b), "Addressing Race and Gender Inequalities in Public Administration", in Wessels, J. & Pauw, J. *Reflective Public Administration*, Cape Town, Oxford University Press.

Philip, G. (1999), "The Dilemmas of Good Governance: A Latin American Perspective", *Government and Opposition*, vol. 34, no. 2, pp. 227-242.

Putnam, R. (1993), *Making Democracy: Civic Traditions in Modern Italy*, Princeton, Princeton University Press.

Ruscio, K. (1997), "Trust in the Administrative State", *Public Administration Review*, vol. 57, no. 5, Sept./Oct.

Samatar, A. (1999), *An African Miracle: State and Class Leadership and Colonial legacy in Botswana Development*, Portsmouth, Heinemann.

Shanley, M. & Narayan, U. (1997), *Restructuring Political Theory: Feminist Perspectives*, Oxford, Polity Press.

Tendler, J. (1997), *Good Government in the Tropics*, Baltimore, John Hopkins University Press.

Törnnquist, O. (2000), "Dynamics of Indonesian Democratisation", *Third World Quarterly*, vol. 21, no. 3, pp. 383-428.

Weingast, B. (1997), "The Political Foundations of Democracy and the Rule of Law", *American Political Science Review*, vol. 91, no. 2, June.

White, G. (1995), "Towards a Democratic Development State", *IDS Bulletin*, vol. 26, no. 2.

Yuval-Davis, N. (1997), *Gender & Nation*, London, Sage.

Index

254, 259, 282, 286, 289, 290, 291, 295, 296, 312, 313, 314, 315, 329, 331, 342, 344, 354, 357

Northern Cape Local Government Association (NOCLOGA) 137, 140, 141, 142, 143, 144, 148, 150

Northern Province 92, 97, 98, 185, 244, 249, 254, 282, 286, 290, 291, 295, 296, 309, 312, 313, 314, 315, 327, 342, 344, 345, 347, 349, 350, 354, 357, 358

Ntsika Enterprise Promotion Agency 56

Office for the Status of Women 365
Omar, Dullah 41

Pan Africanist Congress (PAC) 23, 109, 161, 319, 320, 321, 323, 325, 326, 332

Pan South African Language Board (PanSALB) 205, 207, 210, 219, 221, 222

People Against Gangsterism and Drugs (PAGAD) 184
Policy making 52
Portfolio Committee 47, 139
Presidential Review Commission (PRC) 48, 49, 50, 62, 66, 85, 88, 98, 104
Provinces 44, 95, 101, 104, 105, 114, 280, 285
Public accountability 10, 46, 69
Public administration 81
Public hearing 291, 292
Public Service Act 75, 136
Public Service Commission (PSC) 48, 50, 51, 63, 73, 74, 76, 77, 78, 80, 81, 82, 83, 84, 85, 87

Reconciliation 31, 64, 172, 192, 195, 372
Reconstruction and Development Programme (RDP) 6, 9, 15, 42, 54, 55, 57, 65, 123, 130, 175, 183, 188, 195, 362, 370, 371
Relly, Gavin 21
Residential segregation 159
Resistencia Nacional Mozambicana (RENAMO) 23
Roefs, Marlene 5, 15, 194, 311
Rule, Stephen 303, 311, 318, 322, 326, 327, 330, 332, 333, 337, 338, 359